Mark Thomas is a practising barrister on the North Eastern Circuit. Mark practising solely in criminal law and has experience prosecuting and defending cases in both the Crown Court and magistrates' courts. He regularly prosecutes and defends in Probation breaches and applications, and regularly advises the Probation Service on the relevant legal principles relating to Probation matters.

Prior to his time as a barrister, Mark taught law at an undergraduate and postgraduate level. Mark has published widely in the field of criminal law and evidence, and holds a key role in the development of a series of texts designed for those embarking on a career as a solicitor.

A Practical Guide to Probation Breaches and Other Applications

FOREWORD

Sentencing is now much more difficult than ever it was when I started at the Bar in 1980. The advent of the Sentencing Act 2020 has assisted judges and practitioners, as the law is now all in one place. One area of the law about sentencing, which is often overlooked, is when an order fails and an offender is alleged to be in breach of the original order.

One of the purposes of sentencing is to rehabilitate an offender if that is feasible and proper. That is usually undertaken by way of a Community Order or as a component of a Suspended Sentence Order. Regrettably, there are occasions when an offender fails to engage at all or does not comply with the terms of the order. When that happens breach proceedings are instituted. It all sounds engagingly straightforward, and yet it is an area of law which can be complicated because of highly technical provisions. Sometimes it is difficult to discern the will of Parliament.

This practical guide to breach proceedings shines a torchlight into a very important corner of the law and illuminates it extremely well. It should be the manual to which judges and practitioners go when there is a technical problem involving an alleged breach of an order made in a criminal court. The technical provisions can be abstruse and sometimes counter-intuitive. There is usually a reason why they are drafted in a particular way, but the navigation of these technical provisions is often littered with difficulty. This book will unquestionably assist practitioners with navigation in this technical area of law.

I wish to congratulate Mark Thomas for writing a very readable and clearly set out professional manual on this important topic. It covers all angles of the process from the initiation of proceedings, to when and how orders need amendment or modification, as well as a helpful guide to breach proceedings from beginning to end.

This is a "must have" book for any criminal practitioner, judge, or magistrate who has to deal with any breach proceedings.

As a judge I have been asked to adjudicate upon difficult issues in breach proceedings in the Crown Court. This book would have been invaluable, had it then existed. It now does; and these problems will be able to be determined much better, and more speedily, than was the case.

I commend this book to all criminal practitioners.

THE RECORDER OF SHEFFIELD
His Honour Judge Jeremy Richardson KC
August 2024

PREFACE

A Practical Guide to Probation Breaches and Other Applications began life as a checklist of matters to be aware of when conducting Probation cases. This included the likes of the powers of the court on breach of orders, and the tests to be applied when amending/ revoking court orders.

As I undertook more Probation work as an early part of my career at the Bar, I soon realised that there was very little written on the law relating to Probation matters. Whilst the primary practitioner texts included some discussion on some of the key principles, it was evident that there was no specialist text guiding practitioners through the quagmire that is often Probation cases. This was, and remains, somewhat surprising to me given that Probation cases are a daily and regular feature of both a magistrates' court and the Crown Court.

A *Practical Guide to Probation Breaches and other Applications* is therefore designed to fill that void and provide what is hoped to be a one-stop-shop for all matters relating to cases involving the Probation Service.

Structure of Text

The text is broken down into three parts, and is structured in this manner to assist practitioners at all stages of the process.

- Part I provides the reader with an introduction to community-based court orders and the involvement of the Probation Service. Readers wishing to understand the numerous requirements that may be imposed as part of these court orders, and the responsibility of an offender and the Probation Service during this time will benefit from these chapters.

- Part II reflects the bulk of this text and its desired readership: Breaches of orders. This Part will guide readers through the entire process of Probation breaches from getting the offender to court, the procedure at court, contested hearings, and the powers of the court following a proven breach.

- Part III deals with the ancillary applications that may be made in respect of existing court orders, including revocation and amendment of such orders.

Throughout this text, readers will benefit from a full raft of case and statutory authorities to support propositions, with key quotations provided where appropriate. Academic commentary is avoided where possible to focus the reader on the practical workings of Probation cases.

Future of Probation Cases

At the time of writing, a general election has been held on 4 July 2024 which resulted in a new Government being formed. The Labour Manifesto pledged to "Take back our streets". As part of this Pledge, the Manifesto cites a focus on reducing reoffending, which will inevitably require a consideration of the present community-based court orders and the support within the prison regime.

The Manifesto also recalled that the Probation Service struggles to keep the public safe as a result of a lack of co-ordination between prisons, probation and other local services. Such lack of co-ordination, according to the Manifesto, has the result that offenders who leave the prison setting do not receive the right support, raising the risk that they revolve back into crime and the prison environment. The Labour Manifesto promised to conduct a strategic review of probation governance, including considering the benefits of devolved models. The Manifesto gives the example of Greater Manchester, where probation is linked up with housing and health services. Finally, the Manifesto cites that parts of the Sentencing Act 2020 are outdated and require reform.

One of the first steps taken by the Labour Government was to propose the reduction of the standard determinate sentence faced by offenders; the intention being that offenders will be released from custody having served 40% of their sentence. The impact that this will have on the supervision of offenders on licence is yet to be seen, nor is the inevitable knock-on effect on the supervision of offenders subject to court-based community orders.

At this stage, it is unknown what else the new Labour Government has in store for the criminal justice system, and the effects such new governance will have on the contents of this text.

Acknowledgements

I am delighted that the text has already received positive feedback from members of the Judiciary and colleagues at the Bar. I am honoured that The Recorder of Sheffield, His Honour Judge Jeremy Richardson KC, has provided a foreword for this text to reflect the important of such guidance to practitioners and judges at all stages of their practice. My thanks to HHJ Richardson KC for his continued support of the Bar generally, and for his personal support to this text.

I would also like to take the opportunity to thank a number of colleagues at the Bar who have assisted with this publication in one way or another. My thanks to Rebecca Tanner whom I regularly face in court in Probation matters for her insight into a defence-focused Probation practice, and for reviewing many of these chapters. My thanks also go to Sam Magee for his assistance in providing "real-world" examples for this text, and his motivation in the production of this work. I also want to take the opportunity to thank the entire Probation Service team at Sheffield Crown Court, of which there are so many to thank, for their unwavering assistance throughout this process, for their practical insight into the Probation Service, and for always being on hand to assist me with my regular Probation-related case work. Lastly, my thanks go to Tim Kevan and Garry Wright at Law Brief Publishing Ltd for taking on this project and for their enthusiasm with the importance of this text to practitioners across the country.

Conclusion

It is my hope that *A Practical Guide to Probation Breaches and Other Applications* acts as a reliable companion to all practitioners, and may find a home on many court benches throughout England and Wales.

Any mistakes are my own and feedback, suggestions and recommendations for new additions are always welcome. The law is stated as of 9th August 2024.

Mark Thomas
August 2024

CONTENTS

PART ONE

THE PROBATION SERVICE AND COURT ORDERS

CHAPTER ONE

AN INTRODUCTION TO PROBATION BREACHES AND OTHER APPLICATIONS

Introduction

Welcome to *A Practical Guide to Probation Breaches and other Applications.*

This book is designed to provide a practical and pragmatic manual to guide readers through the often-complex provisions relating to court orders in the community, the involvement of the Probation Service and subsequent proceedings relating to those orders.

Focus of this book

This book, as the name suggests, is concerned with Probation breaches and other Probation applications. "Probation breaches" is not a legal term, per se. It is used in this text, primarily, as a helpful shorthand to describe the circumstances where an offender is before the court in respect of a court order previously made because the offender has failed to comply with the court order or has committed further offences during the order.

A phrase that will be used repeatedly throughout this text is "community-based court orders". Once more, this is not a legal term of art, but does neatly describe the practical realities of both community orders and suspended sentence orders. Both orders permit the person convicted of an offence and subject to the order (referred to as "the offender" throughout this text) to reside in the community with the court order hanging over their head and, in general, with requirements to complete in the community.

This book is specifically concerned with community orders and suspended sentence orders on the basis that these account for the majority of Probation breaches. As a result, this book does not consider post-sentence supervision, licence, or orders relating to youths.

Structure of this book

The book is broken down into three parts, namely:

- *Part I: The Probation Service and Court Orders:* These Chapters will introduce readers to community-based court orders and the interaction of the Probation Service with those orders.

- *Part II: Probation Breaches*: These Chapters will take readers through the full process of breach of orders, including getting the offender to court, preparing for the breach, contested breach proceedings, and powers of the court following breach.

- *Part III: Probation Applications:* These Chapters will provide readers with a full appreciation of the various ancillary applications that can be made in respect of court orders, including amendment and revocation.

The chapters are divided in this manner to assist practitioners in every stage of the proceedings, in both a magistrates' court and the Crown Court, involving orders subject to Probation supervision; they are designed to focus the mind of readers on the topic in question.

The book also features an appendix that is designed as a quick reference tool for practitioners, and details some of the common mistakes/ errors made in respect of Probation cases.

Probation Breaches and other applications

It will first be necessary to identify what we mean by Probation breaches, and the relevance of that discussion of practice.

What amounts to a Probation breach?

For the purposes of this text, a "Probation breach" includes a failure to comply with the requirements of a court order, and the conviction of a further offence during the order. There are varying degrees of breach which focus on the offender's compliance with the order – a breach may be particularly serious because the court considers the offender's lack of compliance to be "wilful and persistent", or minor where the court considers the compliance to be "high", for example.

As will be discussed in subsequent chapters, however, whilst "breach" is a useful shorthand, it is not entirely accurate in law. For example, the conviction of a further offence during the currency of a community order is *not* a breach the community order. Only a failure to comply with the community order requirements amounts to a "breach" in the eyes of the law.[1] This is unlike suspended sentence orders where the court regards both a failure to comply with community requirements, and commission of further offences during the operational period of the order, to be breaches.[2]

Are probation breaches criminal offences?

Perhaps one of the key questions that has to be asked in a book of this nature is whether the breach of a community order or a suspended sentence order amounts to a criminal offence in its own right (and thus meaning one can be convicted of such an offence). The short answer is "no". Breaches of suspended sentence orders and community orders *are*

---

1 The distinction is explained in Chapter 6.

2 See Chapter 7.

not criminal offences; breaches do not result in a *conviction.* Whilst not the focus of the case, Haddon-Cave J did make this point very clear in *R v Maunder*[3] where his Lordship, when referring to failures to comply with the requirements of an order, stated that "there is no such offence in law".[4] It will be worthwhile to briefly develop the point from Haddon-Cave J.

The use of the word "breach" is intentional in the legislation; it is used to reflect the fact that an offender's conduct during the currency of a court order renders them liable for a penalty in respect of that original court order. In fact, an analogy can be drawn with breach of bail conditions which are also not criminal offences.[5] Where an individual is said to have breached their bail conditions, they may be subject to arrest and may be remanded in custody in respect of the offence that they are charged. However, they are not convicted of a separate offence of breach of bail conditions.[6]

There are a number of key differences between an offence, and a breach. The first is the charge; a defendant is *charged* with a criminal offence. However, an offender is not charged with breach of an order. There is no charge sheet or Indictment to reflect the alleged breach.

The second relates to the plea that is entered in respect of breaches. A defendant to a criminal charge must enter a plea of "guilty" or "not guilty". On the other hand, an offender will be asked to "admit" or "deny" a breach of order. This approach is similar to that in breach of bail conditions cases (which are also not criminal offences).

---

3 [2015] EWCA Crim 778, [2015] 2 Cr. App. R. (S.) 26.

4 ibid, [10] (Haddon-Cave J). *Maunder* is discussed in greater detail in Chapter 7.

5 See *R v Rowland* (CA, 14 February 1991), cited in *R v Ashley* [2003] EWCA Crim 2571, [2004] 1 Cr. App. R. 23.

6 Unlike failing to surrender whilst on bail which is a criminal offence (see Chapter 4).

The third relates to the punishment for breaches. An offender who admits or is found to have breached their order is not "sentenced" for it. Rather, the court exercises its powers against the offender.[7] It is often said that an offender is "dealt with" for the breach, as opposed to being "sentenced" for it. Whilst it is correct that an offender can be penalised for a breach (e.g. by the issuance of a fine), the powers of the court generally relate to the court order that the offender is subject to. Unlike most statutory offences, the legislation does not proffer a maximum sentence for breach of court order when dealt with summarily or on indictment.

In totality, therefore, whilst an offender's breach will be present on their antecedent record (see Chapter 5), it does not result in a separate criminal conviction.

The relevance of this to practitioners is that a failure to comply with a community order or suspended sentence order cannot be used to argue that there has been a conviction for a further offence during the currency of an order.[8]

What of Probation applications?

In addition to Probation breaches, this book would be lacking if it did not deal with the various applications that can be made in respect of court orders. These applications may range from minor amendments to the orders to entire revocation of orders. Such applications may be made by both the offender and the Probation Service. It is important that any practitioner is aware of the court's powers to amend/ revoke orders and this is discussed in Part III of the book.

---

7 See Criminal Procedure Rules (CrimPR) 2020, r.32.4(a)(iii).

8 See chapters 6 and 7 where this is discussed with examples.

Parties to a Probation Breach

In any case where an offender is allegedly in breach of a court order, or has been convicted of further offences during a court order, there will be a number of parties involved. This section will briefly discuss the various parties of relevance in proceedings.

The Probation Service

The reference to "Probation", of course, reflects the fact that breach proceedings are brought by the National Probation Service, as opposed to the Crown Prosecution Service or some other prosecuting authority.

The Probation Service is responsible for the assessment, sentence implementation, and management of offenders. It does so by working with offenders and other organisations to ensure the effective supervision of offenders who are "known" and "current" to the Probation Service.

The Responsible Officer

Where the court imposes a court order and the offender is subject to the supervision of the Probation Service, the offender will be allocated a "responsible officer". The responsible officer is a member of the Probation Service, either a Probation Services Officer (PSO) or Probation Officer (PO) dependent on the Risk of Serious Harm an offender presents with and the nature of their offence(s). The duties of the responsible officer are discussed in Chapter 3; in short, the responsible officer must make any arrangements that are necessary in connection with the requirements imposed by the order, and promote the offender's compliance with those requirements.[9]

As will be discussed in Chapter 11, the responsible officer has the power to amend certain parts of the offender's order, including (in certain

[9] Sentencing Act 2020, ss.214(2) and 300(2).

cases), the offender's place of residence and their curfew requirement. Where the responsible officer's powers do not extend to a particular amendment, the matter must be determined by the relevant court.

Enforcement officer

The enforcement officer is an officer of the Probation Service and works within the Enforcement Hub of the Probation Service. Amongst other things, an enforcement officer is responsible for ensuring that breach proceedings and applications are fully prepared to the required standard, and ready to proceed before a court. Enforcement officers will quality-check breach information, and will usually be responsible for laying the breach information and applying for a summons/ warrant in the first instance.

Organisations worked with

The Probation Service does not work alone in the management of offenders; many of the services offered are provided through third parties, including treatment requirements and unpaid work requirements. These organisations are separate to the Probation Service; it is important, therefore, to be aware that if an update is required from one of these services, it must be made in good time given the separation from the Probation Service itself.

Advocate for the Probation Service

The responsibility of prosecuting breaches, and making/responding to applications, lies with the Probation Service (either in-house or by instructing counsel to appear on their behalf). In the magistrates' court, all uncontested breaches are prosecuted by Probation Service Officers (PSOs) whilst contested breaches are generally prosecuted by instructed counsel. However, there is a movement in the Probation Service towards training PSOs to prosecute such contested hearings. In the Crown Court, all breaches and applications (contested or otherwise) are prosecuted by instructed counsel.

The offender

The "offender" is the terminology used in the Sentencing Act 2020 to describe the individual subject to the community-based court order. They are a person who has already been convicted of an offence (and thus "offender" properly reflects that fact). The term "defendant" is not used at all in the Sentencing Act 2020 to describe an individual subject to a court-order or breach proceedings. This is on account that they have already been found guilty of the offence relevant to the court. This text shall use the term "offender" throughout, unless it is necessary to use alternate terminology.

The responsibilities of the offender are discussed in Chapter 3; in short, the offender must comply with any requirement of an order. The Sentencing Act 2020 makes provision that certain obligations, including the need to obtain permission before changing residence, are to be treated in law as a requirement.[10]

The Crown Prosecution Service

The Crown Prosecution Service (CPS) will generally not have involvement in Probation breaches. The CPS will only take over proceedings in circumstances where an offender is convicted of a further offence and falls to be sentenced for that new offence.

The court

Probation matters occur in both the magistrates' court and the Crown Court. In the magistrates' court, determination of breaches and

[10] Sentencing Act 2020, ss.215(3) and 302(3).

applications can be made by either a lay bench of magistrates[11] or a District (and Deputy District) Judge.[12] Generally, court centres will list Probation cases on a particular day of the week, in a particular court (colloquially referred to as "Breach Court").

In the Crown Court, breach proceedings and applications are determined by a Crown Court Judge (which includes Recorders).[13] Any question whether the offender has breached a requirement of an order, and any question whether the offender has been convicted during the operational period of the suspended sentence, is to be determined by the court and not by the verdict of a jury.[14]

Future of Offender Supervision

In this section, we shall briefly discuss recent developments in the supervision of offenders by the Probation Service in light of workload demands, prison overcrowding, and the impact of legislative amendments. We shall also discuss court-focused initiatives which may impact on the nature of an offender's supervision.

Early release of prisoners

On 12 July 2024, the Lord Chancellor and Secretary of State for Justice, Shabana Mahmood MP, announced plans that from 10 September 2024, offenders serving a determinate sentence will be released from custody having served 40% of their sentence, as opposed to the present one-half

---

[11] Addressed as "Sir" or "Madam" (singular), or "Your Worships" (collectively).

[12] Addressed as "Judge".

[13] Addressed as "Your Honour", unless they are a Presiding Judge or High Court Judge, in which case "My Lord/Lady".

[14] Sentencing Act 2020, Schedule 10, para 11(8); Schedule 16, para 12(4).

(or 50%).[15] Any offenders who have reached the 40% threshold by this date must be released on licence.

Applicability

This new scheme will not apply to all offenders; certain sexual, violent and domestic abuse related offences will be excluded. Eligibility for release will be based on the offence-type rather than the offender. Therefore, there is no scope to exclude an offender based upon the individual judgement of the Probation Service on the offender's risk, MAPPA level, security categorisation, or past offences or behaviour.

Termination of End of Custody Supervised Licence Scheme

At present, offenders were being released from prison up to 70 days prior to their conditional release date. This was called the End of Custody Supervised Licence Scheme (ECSL). This scheme was introduced on 16 October 2023 and permitted certain offenders to be released a maximum of 18 days prior to their conditional release date. This was increased to a maximum of 35 days on 8 March 2024, and a maximum of 70 days on 23 May 2024. The Government has announced that when the law changes to reduce the release date to 40%, ESCL will cease to be in effect.

Relevance to this text

The relevance of the early release provisions are limited in respect of this text given its focus on community-based court orders, as opposed to offenders who are released on licence following a term of imprisonment. However, this change in the law will be of great relevance for the Probation Service which will be faced with a wave of offenders being released from the custodial setting and requiring management in the community. It is questionable what impact this will have on the present

[15] Criminal Justice Act 2003, s.244.

supervision of offender's subject to court-based community orders, and whether the Probation Reset (discussed immediately below) will continue to apply, or may even be extended.

Probation Reset

The landscape of Probation Supervision was changed with the introduction of "Probation Reset". On 11 March 2024, a Written Ministerial Statement to Parliament was laid by the then Lord Chancellor, Alex Chalk MP. In this Ministerial Statement, the Lord Chancellor explained that the reset would ensure intervention and engagement is prioritised towards the first two-thirds of the sentence, on account that experience shows that this most effectively rehabilitates offenders.

Purpose of Probation Reset

It cannot be denied that the Probation Service is stretched to beyond capacity. In addition to the need to alleviate the workload demands of Probation staff, the Probation Reset has been informed by:

- The fact that attention needs to be placed where it will have the greatest impact (i.e. in the early stages of any requirement).
- Measures to handle prison capacity, including the extension to the End of Custody Supervised Licence Scheme (ECSL) to allow certain offenders to be released from custody up to 70 days before the end of their sentence,[16] and the increased use of Fixed Term Recalls for offenders under 12-months imprisonment.
- The anticipated impact of the Sentencing Bill 2023-24 which includes proposals for changes to the use of short custodial

[16] Though as noted above, ECSL will cease when the new law relating to release of prisoners at the 40% mark comes into force.

sentences and the extension of Home Detention Curfew to offenders sentenced to over four years' imprisonment.

It is questionable whether Probation Reset will continue to be a policy adopted by the new Labour Government.

What does Probation Reset involve?

Probation Reset impacts on offenders subject to post-sentence supervision, licence, and offenders subject to community orders and suspended sentence orders. It is, of course, the latter that we are concerned with.

For offenders subject to a community order or suspended sentence order, Probation supervision will not continue in the final third of the offender's sentence. For example, an offender subject to a two-year suspended sentence order will be subject to Probation Reset where they have completed two-thirds of the supervision period of the suspended sentence order.

This means that the offender will not be required to attend appointments with their Responsible Officer.[17] Furthermore, all rehabilitation activity requirement (RAR) appointments and activity days will stop after the offender has served two-thirds of their order. The Reset is mandated across all Probation Areas and applies to both existing and new cases.

The Reset does not impact on non-RAR requirements in a community order or suspended sentence order, including programme requirements, unpaid work requirements, drug rehabilitation requirements (DRR) or requirements involving electronic monitoring.

---

[17] Thus meaning they will not be required to Keep In Touch as obligated by ss.215 and 301 of the Sentencing Act 2020.

Offenders on a court order can still be breached in the normal way, particularly if further offences are committed. These changes do not affect other interventions that offenders may be subject to.

Who is eligible for Probation Reset?

Probation Reset applies to all offenders subject to a community order or suspended sentence order, with the following exemptions:

- Multi-agency public protection arrangements (MAPPA) cases (all categories and levels),
- All cases directly managed by the National Security Division (NSD),
- All cases where the offender's risk is assessed as "Very High Risk of Serious Harm",
- Cases with current active Child Protection Plan procedures in place,[18]
- Offenders subject to an Intensive Supervision Court Pilot (ISC).[19]

These exemptions can apply at any time during the court order (i.e. an offender who is subject to Probation Reset is capable of having contact with the Probation Service reinstated) if circumstances change which means that the case meets the exemption criteria.

---

18 This exemption does not include N-Delius register for Child Concern nor cases involving children assessed as being a Child in Need.

19 Until such time as the evaluation is completed.

Building Choices

At the time of writing, HMPPS are currently preparing to roll out the "Next Generation of Accredited Programmes" which are scheduled for national rollout in 2025. This is a single programme titled 'Building Choices' which has been developed and is currently being tested in three prisons and two probation regions. The ambition of HMPPS is that this programme will provide a streamlined, more coherent, and person-centred approach. It will remove the various accredited programmes under a programme requirement and replace them with the single Building Choices requirement.

Building Choices will be a 26-session programme, with a post-programme module (Moving Forward) to be delivered via a five-day rehabilitation activity requirement (RAR). This means that any offender who is on the waiting list for the Thinking Skills Programme will be transferred to Building Choices.

Reducing the Crown Court Backlog

It is common knowledge that the criminal courts are presently facing a monumental backlog in the case load presenting itself. This is evident across both the magistrates' courts and in the Crown Court. Different court centres are adopting various initiatives to seek to reduce that backlog, including the listing of Pre-Trial Reviews (PTRs) in the hope of resolving cases without the need for a trial.

A particular initiative of note at this stage is that undertaken by Preston Crown Court. His Honour Judge Altham, Resident Judge for Lancashire and Recorder of Preston, announced on 25 July 2024 that judges at Preston Crown Court, when imposing a court-based community order (i.e. community order or suspended sentence order) will give "particular consideration" to whether such orders should include a direction that they be subject to magistrates' court supervision.[20] His Honour noted the large number of breach cases listed in the Crown Court daily, and the increasingly large number of offences that are committed for sentence simply because the defendant is also subject to a Crown Court order. The power to direct magistrates' court supervision will be used where appropriate. This means, as his Honour indicates clearly, that the Crown Court will deal only with cases in which the powers of the magistrates' court are clearly insufficient/ inadequate.

It will be interesting to see whether other court centres adopted the same or similar approach moving forward in an attempt to assist with the ever-increasing Crown Court backlog.

Summary

This Chapter has covered a general introduction to the Probation Service and probation breaches. In this Chapter, we have discussed:

- The focus of this text on court-based community orders, specifically community orders and suspended sentence orders.
- Probation breaches are not criminal offences and do not result in convictions.
- The parties to a probation breach, including their role and responsibilities.
- The development and future of supervision by the Probation Service and the courts.

---

[20] Sentencing Act 2020, ss.211 (community orders) and 297 (suspended sentence orders).

CHAPTER TWO

COMMUNITY-BASED COURT ORDERS: AN INTRODUCTION

Introduction

In this Chapter, we introduce readers to community-based court orders and the requirements that may be imposed as part of those orders. References to "community-based court orders" is intentional; our focus will be on the primary community-based disposals – namely community orders and suspended sentence orders. This text does not consider orders in respect of youths, for example Youth Referral Orders, Youth Rehabilitation Orders, or Detention and Training Orders. This text is also not concerned with offenders subject to post-sentence supervision or licence.[1]

This Chapter provides readers with a full discussion on the imposition of community orders and suspended sentence orders, and their requirements. It is hoped that by taking readers through the process of imposing such orders, the reader will also be better prepared for any breach proceedings or applications to revoke/amend that may follow.

1 Should, of course, there be a call for such inclusion, subsequent editions of this text can accommodate that request.

Key provisions

The relevant provisions are provided in the Sentencing Act 2020, as such:

- Community orders: Chapter 2
- Suspended sentence orders: Chapter 5
- Requirements of community orders and suspended sentence orders: Schedule 9.

This Chapter shall be broken down into three parts:

- Community orders
- Suspended sentence orders
- Requirements under both orders.

Before we turn to those specific discussions, let us first consider the purposes of sentences.

Principles and purposes of sentencing

As a starting point, it is worth emphasising the purposes of sentencing. When determining the appropriateness or suitability of requirements of an order, the court must have regard to the respective purposes or objectives of sentencing. When dealing with an offender aged 18 or over, the court must have regard to the following purposes of sentence:

- the punishment of offenders,
- the reduction of crime (including its reduction by deterrence),

- the reform and rehabilitation of offenders,
- the protection of the public, and
- the making of reparation by offenders to persons affected by their offences.[2]

Advocates are encouraged to seek out a specialist practitioner text which has a focus on sentencing specifically. The purposes of sentencing are relevant throughout the period of the court order; i.e. from the imposition of the order, to the consideration of action taken on breach of such an order.

Community-based court orders

As discussed in Chapter 1, this textbook is primarily concerned with orders featuring the involvement of the Probation Service. For our purposes, we can refer to them as "community-based court orders". The primary orders of relevance, therefore, are community orders and suspended sentence orders.

Whilst the Probation Service will be involved with an offender who has been released on licence as part of post-sentence supervision, this text will focus on community orders and suspended sentence orders. Given the presence and focal nature of the Probation Service, it is for that reason that we use the term "probation breaches" to describe the lack of compliance by an offender with the imposed court order.

---

2 Sentencing Act 2020, s.57(2).

Community orders

A "community order" means an order imposing one or more community order requirements.[3]

Availability

A community order is available to a court when sentencing an offender where the offender is aged 18 or over, and the offence is punishable with imprisonment.[4] Where an offender cannot be sentenced to the possibility of imprisonment, a community order is not available. A community order is not available where the offence features a mandatory sentence requirement.[5]

Combining a community order with other orders

Importantly, when sentencing an offender, a court cannot make both a community order and a suspended sentence order at the same time.[6] For example, a court dealing with offences A and B cannot impose a community order for offence A, but a suspended sentence order for offence B.[7]

This does not, however, prevent the offender, presently serving a suspended sentence order or a community order, from being further sentenced to a community order or suspended sentence order. In fact, this is a common state of affairs in both the magistrates' court and Crown Court. Where a court does impose a further suspended sentence or

---

3 ibid, s.200(1).

4 ibid, s.202(1).

5 ibid, s.202(3). See also s.399 Sentencing Act 2020.

6 ibid, s.203.

7 See *R v Robinson* [2013] EWCA Crim 199 under the former law under the Criminal Justice Act 2003.

community order, it may direct that the orders run concurrently or consecutively.[8] Suppose, for example, an offender is sentenced to a community order, with 100 hours of unpaid work, and then sentenced at a later date to a suspended sentence order with 80 hours of unpaid work. If the court allows the community order to continue, the court may order them to run concurrently or consecutively. The effect of that decision is as such:

- If ordered to run concurrently, the offender will be required to complete a total of 100 hours.

- If ordered to run consecutively, the offender will be required to complete a total of 180 hours.

Whilst the number of hours in total differ dependent on how the orders are to run, the completion of those orders does not change. In the example above, it is not the case, for example, that where an offender only performs 14 hours of unpaid work he is only in breach of the first order as he had never begun the second. This was the judgment of the Court of Appeal in *R v Meredith*[9] where it was stated that:

> If that is right, it leads to the remarkable result that he would never be in breach of the second order as long as he remained in breach of the first, because the time would never arrive for him to start performing the second order. That cannot be right.

In the absence of a specific direction that the orders should be consecutive orders, the orders were running alongside each other.

The practical consequence of multiple orders was explained in *Meredith* as such:

---

8 *R v Evans* [1976] 64 Cr. App. R. 127 (CA).

9 [1994] 15 Cr. App. R. (S.) 528 (CA) 529 (Staughton LJ).

> The truth of the matter is that once two community service orders are made they are, for all practical purposes, one order and he was in breach of them both.[10]

Furthermore, in *R v Butt,*[11] Globe J would explain that the effect of two orders running concurrently or consecutively is therefore that a failure to comply with a shared requirement (i.e. one in both orders), such as an unpaid work requirement will produce a breach of both orders.[12] In practice, this means that Probation Service records will show a deduction of hours against each order when the work had been done.

Key point

The key takeaway from the above discussion is that whilst the court cannot impose both a suspended sentence order and a community order at the same time, the court can impose a community order or suspended sentence order on an offender already subject to a court order. This means that an offender may be subject to two or more community orders, suspended sentence orders, or a mixture of the two.

In practice, a direction that the orders run concurrently or consecutively will not impact on the court's ability to take action on either order. Rather, it will simply impact on the total amount of time expected under each order.

Test to be applied

By s.204(2) of the Sentencing Act 2020, a court is not permitted to make a community order, unless it is of the opinion that the offence (or combination of offences) was serious enough to warrant the making of

10 ibid. *Meredith* was cited and approved by the Court of Appeal in *R v Butt* [2012] EWCA Crim 462.

11 [2012] EWCA Crim 462.

12 ibid, [18] (Globe J).

such an order.[13] In considering whether the community order threshold has been crossed, the court is obligated take into account all the information that is available to it about the circumstances of the offence, or of it and the associated offence or offences, including any aggravating or mitigating factors[14] and may be assisted by a pre-sentence report.[15] Importantly, the simple fact that the community order threshold has been passed, does not mean that the court is obligated to make a community order.[16]

Length of order

A community order must specify a date (known as "the end date") by which all the requirements in it must have been complied with.[17] The end date cannot be more than three years after the date of the order (quite simply, a community order may last no longer than three years).[18] There is, however, no minimum period by which the end date must be set (though it cannot be so short as to set the offender up to fail).

In *R v Khan,*[19] the Court of Appeal emphasised that the end date of a community order cannot be longer than any of the requirements imposed as part of that order. Mrs Justice McGowan explained that a community order itself "cannot exist other than as a vehicle through which a particular requirement is performed."[20] Her Ladyship concluded:

---

13 Sentencing Act 2020, s.204(2). Known as the "community order threshold".

14 ibid, s.204(3).

15 ibid, s.204(4).

16 ibid, s.204(5).

17 ibid, s.209(1).

18 ibid, s.209(2).

19 [2015] EWCA Crim 835, [2015] 2 Cr. App. R. (S.) 39.

20 ibid, [8] (McGowan J).

> A community order is one which enables an offender to be punished and/or receive therapeutic treatment whilst remaining in the community. The order exists to provide the mechanism through which either the punitive and/or the therapeutic element can be completed. It cannot be an empty order; it must contain and enforce one or more of the requirements.[21]

To assist with understanding this quotation, consider the following examples:

- The court imposes an 18-month community order with a rehabilitation activity requirement (RAR), and directs that the RAR is to be completed in a shorter period (e.g. 12 months).
- The court imposes a 12-month community order with an alcohol abstinence and monitoring requirement (AAMR), and an RAR.
- The court imposes a two-year community order with a single requirement of unpaid work.

In the first example, there is nothing to attach the community order to for the second year of that order. In short, the end date of the order must be the same as the end date of the single requirement. In a similar vein, should the court impose a community order with a single requirement of a six-month curfew, the order could not last beyond six months.

Where the court imposes multiple requirements, it may specify different dates for each of those requirements (though the last of which must be the end date).[22] This leads to our second example: As will be discussed below, the maximum period for an AAMR is 120 days. The court must therefore specify the "end date" of that requirement. Given that the order

---

21 ibid, [13] (McGowan J).

22 Sentencing Act 2020, s.209(3).

also contains a second requirement (namely an RAR), the end date of the community order must be the same as the end date of the RAR.

In the final example, the community order is unlawful because an unpaid work requirement must be completed within 12 months from the making of the order.[23] Whilst the court has the power to extend the unpaid work requirement,[24] the requirement must, *at first*, be completed within 12 months. In *National Probation Service v Blackfriars Crown Court*,[25] Leggatt LJ attempted to clarify what McGowan J meant in the passage quoted above. His Lordship reasoned:

> when a community order imposing an unpaid work requirement is made, the order must specify as the date by which the unpaid work requirement must be complied with a date 12 months after the date of the order. [...] McGowan J was, as it seems to me, saying simply that it is not possible to make a community order with a sole requirement of performing unpaid work which has an end date later than the date by which the work is required to be completed (i.e. 12 months).[26]

In short, therefore, the following principles can be enunciated:

- A community order is a vehicle through which particular requirements are performed.
- As a result, a community order cannot last longer than the requirements within it.
- Where the court imposes a community order with a single requirement of unpaid work, the order can last no longer than 12

---

23 ibid, Schedule 9, para 1(1)(b).

24 ibid, Schedule 10, para 21(2).

25 [2019] EWHC 529 (Admin), [2019] 2 Cr. App. R. (S.) 24.

26 ibid, [33] (Leggatt LJ).

months. An application to extend the unpaid work requirement can be sought if required.

Extension of end date

The end date is capable of being amended by the court following an application by the offender or the Probation Service,[27] or in dealing with an offender for breach of a community order or following conviction for further offences.[28]

When does a community order cease to be in force?

A community order ceases to be in force:

- at the end of the end date, or
- when the offender has completed any unpaid work requirement imposed by the order.[29]

The effect of s.220(1)(b) is that a community order could theoretically continue ad-infinitum until the unpaid work requirement is complete.[30] A community order will also cease to be in force when it is revoked.[31]

---

27 Sentencing Act 2020, Schedule 10, para 20(1) (see Chapter 11).

28 ibid, Schedule 10, para 13(1) (see Chapter 6).

29 ibid, s.220(1). See also s.220(3).

30 *National Probation Service v Blackfriars Crown Court* [2019] EWHC 529 (Admin), [2019] 2 Cr. App. R. (S.) 24 at [19] (Leggatt LJ). See also *National Probation Service v Forbes* (Sheffield Crown Ct, 23 October 2023), at [29] (The Recorder of Sheffield, HHJ Richardson KC).

31 Sentencing Act 2020, s.220(2).

Key point

Knowledge of the end date of a community order is essential on account that the initiation of breach proceedings and applications made to revoke or amend will be restricted by the end date of the order. A similar position exists in respect of further offences for which the offender is convicted during the currency of the community order.

Suspended sentence orders

A suspended sentence order is a sentence of imprisonment.[32] However, under a suspended sentence order, the sentence of imprisonment is not to take effect unless:

- an activation event occurs, and
- a court, where it has the power to do so, subsequently orders that the sentence of imprisonment is to take effect.[33]

Reference to "an activation event occurs" means that the offender either:

- commits another offence in the United Kingdom[34] during the operational period of the order, or

---

32 ibid, s.289(1). "Imprisonment" is the term used for adult offenders (i.e. those aged 21 and over). The term "detention" is used for youth offenders aged 18-20 for which suspended sentence orders are equally available.

33 ibid, s.286(1). See also para 13 of Schedule 16 to the Sentencing Act 2020.

34 Whether or not it is punishable with imprisonment.

- contravenes any community requirement imposed by the order,[35] during the supervision period of the order.[36]

For the meaning of operational period and supervision period, see below.

Availability

A suspended sentence order is available in relation any sentence of imprisonment that is:

- at least 14 days; but

- not more than two years.[37]

Where an offender is sentenced for more than one offence, which are to be served consecutively, a suspended sentence order is not available if the sentence imposed is an aggregate of more than two years.[38] Therefore, it is wrong in law to suggest that two offences for which the court has imposed a sentence less than two years individually can each be suspended; the focus is on the total aggregate.

Combining a suspended sentence order with other orders

As discussed above, a court cannot make both a community order and a suspended sentence order at the same time.[39] Furthermore, as discussed

---

35 As will be discussed below, such community requirements are discretionary.

36 Sentencing Act 2020, s.286(3).

37 ibid, s.277(2).

38 ibid, s.277(4).

39 ibid, s.203. See also *R v Starie* (1979) 1 Cr. App. R. (S.) 172, (1979) 69 Cr. App. R. 239 (CA) and *R v Campbell* (1993) 14 Cr. App. R. (S.) 401 (CA).

above, a suspended sentence order can be imposed where an offender is already subject to a community order or suspended sentence order. The effect of such is that the offender will be subject to both orders at the same time and can be breached for both orders.

Additionally, a suspended sentence order should not be combined with a term of imprisonment,[40] nor should one be imposed where an offender is presently serving a term of imprisonment.[41] In neither circumstance is this course of action unlawful; there is no statutory bar upon passing concurrent sentences of imprisonment, the one immediate and the other suspended.[42] Rather, the Court of Appeal has simply regarded the course of action as being wrong in principle; it would not be a matter of good sentencing practice. In *R v Butters*,[43] Roskill J referred to such as "bad sentencing practice".[44] In *Sapiano*, Lord Parker CJ would explain that to impose a suspended sentence at the same time as imposing a term of imprisonment is a "wrong sentence" in two respects:

> first that it is really against the spirit and intention of the Act, because the main object of a suspended sentence is to avoid sending an offender to prison at all; secondly, it is wrong because in many circumstances it just will not work.[45]

Test to be applied

It is important to remember that a suspended sentence order is a sentence of imprisonment. Therefore, before the court can consider whether any sentence of imprisonment can be suspended, the court must first be

40 *R v Sapiano* (1968) 52 Cr. App. R. 674 (CA).

41 *R v Hammond* [1969] Crim. L.R. 500 (CA).

42 See McCullough J's comments in *R v Ipswich Crown Court* (1982) 4 Cr. App. R. (S.) 348 (CA) at 350.

43 (1971) 55 Cr. App. R. 515 (CA).

44 ibid, 521 (Roskill J).

45 *Sapiano* (n40) 675 (Lord Parker CJ).

satisfied that the custodial threshold has been passed, and must determine the length of such sentence.

In that regard, a four-stage approach must be followed:

1. The court must first consider whether the custodial threshold has been crossed.
2. The court must then consider whether a custodial sentence can be avoided.
3. If it does not so consider, the court must then determine the length of any such custodial sentence.
4. Having determined the length of the custodial sentence, the court can then proceed to consider whether any such sentence of imprisonment can be suspended.

We shall briefly consider each in turn.[46]

First, the court must consider whether the custodial threshold has been crossed. The custodial threshold is provided for in s.230(2) of the Sentencing Act 2020 and provides that the court must not pass a custodial sentence unless it is of the opinion that the offence (or combination of offences) was "so serious that neither a fine alone nor a community sentence can be justified for the offence."

Second, the court must consider whether a sentence of imprisonment is avoidable. In simple form, the crossing of the custodial threshold does not mean that the court is obliged to impose a custodial sentence. Where a community order could provide sufficient restriction on an offender's liberty (by way of punishment) while addressing the rehabilitation of the

[46] Advocates are advised to consider specialist practitioner texts for more detail on these elements.

offender to prevent future crime, the court should consider imposing a community order.[47]

If, however, the court does consider a sentence of imprisonment to be unavoidable, the court must then determine the appropriate length of sentence. In determining the appropriate length of sentence, the court must follow any sentencing guidelines which are relevant to the offender's case, unless the court is satisfied that it would be contrary to the interests of justice to do so.[48] In using the relevant sentencing guideline(s), the court will categorise the offence according to the offender's culpability in committing the offence, and any harm which the offence caused, was intended to cause, or might foreseeably have caused.[49] Having so determined the appropriate category for the offence, the court will identify the starting point and category range for that offence. The court will then consider, as appropriate, aggravating and mitigating factors, reduction for guilty plea, time spent on remand/ qualifying curfew, totality and any other relevant factor(s). Having considered all matters, the court is obligated to pass a custodial sentence which must be for the shortest term (not exceeding the permitted maximum) that in the opinion of the court is commensurate with the seriousness of the offence (or combination of offences).[50]

Finally, the court must consider whether the sentence can be suspended. Where any sentence of imprisonment is under two years, it is capable of being suspended. There is no statutory test for the court to apply when considering whether to impose a suspended sentence order. However, the Sentencing Council has published an overarching guideline on the *Imposition of community and custodial sentences*.[51] According to the

---

[47] A suspended sentence must not be imposed simply as a more severe form of community order.

[48] Sentencing Act 2020, s.59(1).

[49] ibid, s.63.

[50] ibid, s.231(2).

[51] Sentencing Council, *Imposition of community and custodial sentences* (1 February 2017).

guideline, the following factors should be weighed in considering whether it is possible to suspend the sentence.[52]

- *Factors indicating that it would not be appropriate to suspend a custodial sentence*
    - Offender presents a risk/danger to the public
    - Appropriate punishment can only be achieved by immediate custody
    - History of poor compliance with court orders
- *Factors indicating that it may be appropriate to suspend a custodial sentence*
    - Realistic prospect of rehabilitation
    - Strong personal mitigation
    - Immediate custody will result in significant harmful impact upon others

On a practical level, the court should also consider the length of time spent remanded in custody (or subject to a qualifying curfew) when deciding whether to impose a suspended sentence. In *R v Barrett,*[53] the Court of Appeal quashed a suspended sentence on account that had the offender been sentenced to immediate imprisonment to the statutory maximum for the offence they fell to be sentenced for, they would have been released soon after that sentence (the maximum sentence having been six months and the offender having spent four months remanded in custody already). This is because they had spent a substantial amount of time remanded in custody and were in effect "time served". Mr Justice

---

52 It is possible for one factor to outweigh multiple other factors: *R v Middleton* [2019] EWCA Crim 663, [2019] 2 Cr. App. R. (S.) 28.

53 [2010] EWCA Crim 365, [2010] 2 Cr. App. R. (S.) 86.

Keith would explain that whilst the conduct of the sentencing judge was noble, in that she sought to protect the public, the sentence was wrong in principle. His Lordship stated:

> by sentencing him as she did, she was in practical terms passing a sentence which was more severe in its impact on the appellant than the maximum sentence would have been. That was something which in our view the judge had to avoid. It could only have been avoided by passing sentences of imprisonment of immediate effect. Suspending those sentences was, in the circumstances, wrong in principle.[54]

It is therefore worth considering whether an offender can be sentenced as time served as opposed to imposing a suspended sentence order.[55]

Length of order

A suspended sentence order must specify the operational period, which is a period beginning with the day on which the order is made, of:

- at least six months, and
- not more than two years.[56]

Another way of phrasing this is that the suspended sentence order has a minimum length of six months and a maximum length of two years.

If a suspended sentence order imposes any community requirement(s), the order must also specify a "supervision period".[57] The supervision period relates to the period that the offender must complete the community requirements of the order and is thus the period where the

---

54 ibid, [6] (Keith J).

55 See also *R v Waters* [2008] EWCA Crim 2538.

56 Sentencing Act 2020, s.288(2).

57 ibid, s.288(3).

offender is subject to the oversight and supervision of the Probation Service and the court. The supervision period must be for a minimum period of six months, and can be no longer than two years (though the supervision period cannot be longer than the operational period).[58]

Therefore, where the court imposes a sentence of imprisonment, suspended for 18 months, the supervision period cannot exceed 18 months. However, where the suspended sentence order imposes an unpaid work requirement, the supervision period continues until the offender has completed the unpaid work requirement (though, once more, the supervision period cannot continue beyond the end of the operational period).[59]

In general, the supervision period will be the same as the operational period. However, in *R v Lees-Wolfenden,*[60] David Clarke J, giving the judgment of the Court, explained that the two periods need not be the same and warned against assuming such.[61] It is highly advisable, therefore, that the sentencing judge expressly states both the operational period and the supervision period. In *R v Levi*,[62] the Court of Appeal cautioned against failing to expressly state the length of the supervision period. Specifically, Holroyde J (as he then was), stated:

> It was a regrettable oversight by the learned judge not to identify in her sentence the length of the supervision period. It is in our view unfortunately an oversight which rendered those sentences unlawful for that reason.[63]

Importantly, *Levi* was an authority concerned with the former law under the Criminal Justice Act 2003 where community requirements were a

---

[58] ibid, s.288(4).

[59] ibid, s.288(5).

[60] [2006] EWCA Crim 3068; [2007] 1 Cr. App. R. (S.) 119.

[61] ibid, [13] (David Clarke J).

[62] [2011] EWCA Crim 2339.

[63] ibid, [25] (Holroyd J).

community requirements of the order (a "progress report") to be made to the responsible court before each review.[71]

Amendment following review

For a full discussion of the law relating to amendment of suspended sentence orders following review, see Chapter 11. In brief, s.294 of the Sentencing Act 2020 allows the court, following review of the progress report, to amend any of the community requirements of the suspended sentence order.[72] Furthermore, s.295 allows the court to dispense with the requirement for the offender to attend the hearing (and thus conduct the review on the papers alone), or dispense with the requirement of a hearing outright.

Review of community orders

Unlike suspended sentence orders, there is no general power for the courts to include a provision for review in respect of community orders. Rather, s.217 of the Sentencing Act 2020 empowers the Secretary of State by regulations to:

- enable or require a court making a community order to provide for the community order to be reviewed periodically by that or another court,
- enable a court to amend a community order so as to include or remove a provision for review by a court, and

---

71 ibid, s.293(2).

72 Subject to s.294(3) which requires the offender to consent to the amendment.

- make provision as to the timing and conduct of reviews and as to the powers of the court on a review.[73]

The Regulations may make the same provision in respect of community orders as is presently found in ss.293-295 for suspended sentence orders[74] (see above). The Secretary of State made such Regulations in respect of the former law under the Criminal Justice Act 2003[75] and the power to make regulations under s.217 is retained by the Police, Crime, Sentencing and Courts Act 2022.[76]

Review of orders qualifying for special procedures

Section 395A of the Sentencing Act 2020, as inserted by the Police, Crime, Sentencing and Courts Act 2022,[77] provides the courts with an additional power for periodic review of community requirements in suspended sentence orders and community orders 'qualifying for special procedures'. This power is entirely distinct from those already discussed.

Rather generally, an order qualifies for special procedures if the order—

- is of a description specified in regulations for the purposes of that provision, and

- is made within a period, or after a time, so specified.[78]

---

73 Sentencing Act 2020, s.217(1).

74 ibid, s.217(2).

75 The Community Order (Review by Specified Courts in Liverpool and Salford) Order 2006 (SI 2006/1006); The Community Order (Review by Specified Courts) Order 2007 (SI 2007/2162).

76 Police, Crime, Sentencing and Courts Act 2022, s.153 and Schedule 14.

77 ibid, Schedule 14, para 2.

78 Sentencing Act 2020, s.395A(1).

Reference to "a description specified" includes:

- the courts by which the orders are made (for example, courts sitting in particular places or areas),
- the persons who are subject to the orders (for example, persons of a particular sex),
- the offences to which the orders relate.[79]

These provisions do not extend to magistrates' courts and the Crown Court generally; rather, the Secretary of State must make regulations to permit particular courts / court centres to exercise such powers.

Orders qualifying for special procedures

In respect of suspended sentence orders, the Police, Crime, Sentencing and Courts Act 2022 inserted s.395A into the Sentencing Act 2020. This empowers a court to impose a provision of review into a suspended sentence order in the same terms as discussed above in ss.292-295 of the Sentencing Act 2020.

The aim of this provision is to improve offender compliance with community orders and suspended sentence orders and to reduce reoffending. The intention is to pilot the measure for an initial 18-month period, which will allow for close oversight by a court of particular sentences in the community. This will enable the court to be responsive to an offender's criminogenic needs and ensures that changes to the balance of incentives and sanctions can be made swiftly and directly by the reviewing judge.

In respect of community orders, the Police, Crime, Sentencing and Courts Act 2022 inserted ss.217A and 217B into the Sentencing Act

[79] ibid, s.395A(3).

2020. These provisions are largely identical to the provision of review for suspended sentence orders discussed above.

In both instances, the Police, Crime, Sentencing and Courts Act 2022 also inserted a specific penalty where an offender is found to be in breach of the requirements of an order following such review. This power is somewhat novel in that an offender can be committed to custody for a maximum period of 28 days.[80]

Regulations made

With effect from 26 June 2023, the Secretary of State made an order for piloting orders qualifying for special procedures.[81] This pilot extends only to three court centres, namely

- Birmingham Magistrates' Court,
- Liverpool Crown Court, and
- Teesside Combined Court Centre.[82]

The Regulations prescribe eligibility requirements for those offenders who may be made subject to an order qualifying for special procedures.[83] In particular, the Regulations provide that:

- the offender must be aged 18 or over at the date of conviction,

---

80 Sentencing Act 2020, Schedule 10, para 10(5)(ba); Schedule 16, para 13(1)(da). See Chapters 6 and 7 for full details of these powers on breach.

81 The Sentencing Act 2020 (Special Procedures for Community and Suspended Sentence Orders) Regulations 2023 (SI 2023/559).

82 ibid, Regulation 4.

83 ibid, Regulation 5.

- in the Birmingham Magistrates' Court, they may only be a female offender, and

- the offender cannot be subject to notification requirements, as defined at section 80(2) of the Sexual Offences Act 2003, at the date of conviction.

These Regulations establish certain categories of offences where an order qualifying for special procedures *cannot* be made. These include sexual offences and weapons offences.[84] An exception is made for first-time possession offences where these relate to knives or bladed weapons and the offender has not previously been convicted of a listed weapons offence or a possession of a knife or bladed article offence. In the case of first-time possession offences, the court will retain discretion to consider the suitability of the person to take part in the pilot scheme.[85]

With effect from 14 June 2024, the Secretary of State extended the pilot scheme to Bristol Crown Court.[86] The terms of the pilot in Bristol are identical to the pilot expressed above.[87]

Requirements in an order

As noted above, a community order, by its very name, is an order imposing one or more community order requirements.[88] The imposition of requirement(s), therefore, is an intrinsic aspect of a community order.

---

[84] ibid, Regulation 6.

[85] ibid, Regulation 7.

[86] The Sentencing Act 2020 (Special Procedures for Community and Suspended Sentence Orders) Regulations 2024 (SI 2024/654).

[87] With the exception that the restriction on female offenders at Birmingham Magistrates' Court does not apply.

[88] Sentencing Act 2020, s.200(1).

On the other hand, the imposition of community requirements in a suspended sentence order is entirely discretionary.[89] This is evident from the wording in s.286(2) of the Sentencing Act 2020 which states that a suspended sentence order "*may also* specify one or more available community requirements with which the offender must comply during the supervision period." (emphasis added) "May also" clearly demonstrates the discretionary nature of such requirements; it therefore being permissible for a court to pass a suspended sentence order without any community requirements at all (colloquially referred to as a "stand alone order").

For our purposes, we shall refer to both the requirements of a community order and the community requirements of a suspended sentence order by a suitable shorthand of the "requirements" of an order.

An introduction to the available requirements

The available requirements are listed in column one of the community order requirements table in s.201 of the Sentencing Act 2020[90] and column 1 of the community requirements table in s.287 of the Sentencing Act 2020.[91] The list of requirements are identical between community orders and suspended sentence orders:

- unpaid work requirement
- rehabilitation activity requirement
- programme requirement

---

[89] See *R v Fairweather* [2015] EWCA Crim 1027, [2005] 2 Cr. App. R. (S.) 56 [12] (The Recorder of Cardiff, HHJ Rees).

[90] In respect of community orders.

[91] In respect of suspended sentence orders.

- prohibited activity requirement
- curfew requirement
- exclusion requirement
- residence requirement
- foreign travel prohibition requirement
- mental health treatment requirement
- drug rehabilitation requirement
- drug testing requirement
- alcohol treatment requirement
- alcohol abstinence and monitoring requirement
- attendance centre requirement
- electronic compliance monitoring requirement
- electronic whereabouts monitoring requirement.

This is an exhaustive list; the court is not permitted to impose a requirement that is not listed as an "available requirement" above.[92] Furthermore, there are restrictions imposed on the availability of certain requirements;[93] these are dealt with below for each requirement that it is relevant for.

[92] Sentencing Act 2020, s.206(1); s.290(1).

[93] ibid, s.206(2); s.290(2).

Necessity for punishment

In respect of community orders, the Sentencing Act 2020 mandates that the court must impose at least one requirement "for the purpose of punishment."[94] This reflects the fact that many of the available requirements listed above aim to achieve purposes other than punishment, including the reform and rehabilitation of offenders.[95] Therefore, the court is obligated to impose at least one community order requirement of a punitive nature, such as unpaid work or a curfew.[96] This was evident in *AG's Ref (R v Singh)*[97] where the offender was sentenced for two offences of sexual assault to a 12-month community order with 40 days RAR. Lord Justice Singh explained that:

> [T]he imposition of only an RAR did not comply with the requirement of section 208(10) of the Sentencing Code in the circumstances of this case. It is not sufficient, as was submitted on behalf of the offender, that something has the *purpose* of punishment. Parliament clearly intended that there must be an additional requirement which *will* punish an offender. This can be, for example, an unpaid work requirement or a curfew requirement. In the circumstances of this case, merely to require an activity to be undertaken was not for the purpose of punishment. It was, as its term suggested, for the purpose of rehabilitation.[98]

---

94 ibid, s.208(10).

95 See above, "Principles and purposes of sentencing", for a discussion on the purposes of sentencing.

96 Though there does not appear be a condition that a requirement is imposed *solely* for the purposes of punishment; a requirement may feature a purpose in addition to punishment.

97 [2021] EWCA Crim 1426, [2022] 1 Cr. App. R. (S.) 48.

98 ibid, [31] (Singh LJ) (emphasis added). See *R v Hartland* [2023] EWCA Crim 790 for a reaffirmation of this.

The necessity for at least one requirement to be punitive in nature does not apply in two circumstances.

The first is where the court also imposes a fine.[99] This is so on account that a fine is a form of punishment in and of itself. However, it has been ruled that the imposition of a compensation order does not have the purpose of punishment of the offender; its purpose is compensating the victim(s).[100] In a pre-Sentencing Act 2020 authority, the Court of Appeal ruled that a three-year community order with an RAR and ATR was not considered as featuring an element of punishment.[101]

The second is where there are exceptional circumstances relating to the offence or to the offender which would make it unjust in all the circumstances for the court to:

- impose a requirement for the purpose of punishment in the particular case, *and*

- would make it unjust in all the circumstances for the court to impose a fine for the offence concerned.[102]

As is evident from the statutory language, this is a two-stage test. Not only must it be unjust to impose a punitive element, it must *also* be unjust to impose a fine.

In *AG's Ref (R v Singh)*, Singh LJ emphasised that to assist the judge in forming a view on this, authors of pre-sentence reports must, in appropriate cases, specifically address the question of whether there are exceptional circumstances to justify not imposing a requirement for the

---

99 Sentencing Act 2020, s.208(11)(a).

100 *AG's Ref (R v Singh)* (n97) [32] (Singh LJ).

101 *AG's Ref (R v Gregson)* [2020] EWCA Crim 1529, [2021] 2 Cr. App. R. (S.) 3. [26]-[28] (Thirlwall LJ).

102 Sentencing Act 2020, s.208(11)(b).

purposes of punishment.[103] Generally, the Probation Service would identify which requirements were "suitable" or otherwise not suitable for an offender and the impact of those requirements on offenders.

It will be helpful to provide two examples where the Court of Appeal has found there to be exceptional circumstances. The first example is *R v Cudd*[104] where Haddon-Cave LJ considered the sentencing judge to be in the best position to assess the question of exceptional circumstances having regard to the offender's age (80 at the time of sentence), his poor health and infirmity, and his limited financial means.[105] The second example is *R v Baldwin*[106] where William Davis J found that the fact that the offender had already served a significant custodial sentence (seven months' detention) constituted exceptional circumstances such that the offender had been punished for the offence, and "[i]n real terms the community order will not involve additional punishment."[107]

The restriction of "exceptional circumstances" may make it difficult for the court to pass a lawful community order where the requirements that would be otherwise imposed as a punitive element are considered as being unsuitable. In such circumstances, the court must not impose a suspended sentence order simply to get around the difficulties faced.[108]

---

[103] *AG's Ref (R v Singh)* (n97) [33] (Singh LJ).

[104] [2022] EWCA Crim 680.

[105] ibid, [18] (Haddon-Cave LJ).

[106] [2021] EWCA Crim 417, [2021] 2 Cr. App. R. (S.) 49.

[107] ibid, [23] (William Davis J).

[108] Sentencing Act 2020, s.230(2) (the court must still be satisfied that the custodial threshold has been crossed).

Key point

Given that the court must impose a punitive element unless it imposes a fine, or finds there to be exceptional circumstances, it is advised that where the court does not impose a punitive element nor a fine, the judge states in open court that there are exceptional circumstances and what they are.

There is no equivalent provision in respect of suspended sentence orders on account that (i) a suspended sentence order is treated as a sentence of imprisonment (and thus by its nature is punitive);[109] and (ii) the imposition of community requirements are a matter of discretion in any event.

Suitability of requirements

In respect of community orders specifically, the Sentencing Act 2020 prescribes an obligation on the courts to consider the suitability of requirements for a particular offender, and to have regard to the nature and seriousness of the offence when sentencing.

In respect of suitability, s.208(3) of the Sentencing Act 2020 requires the court consider whether, in its opinion, a particular requirement (or combination of requirements) is "the most suitable for the offender." Suitability is assessed with assistance from any pre-sentence report provided by the Probation Service[110] and the court is permitted to take into account any information about the offender which is before it at the time.[111] This may include any information from the advocates, the Probation Service, or the offender themselves.

[109] ibid, s.289(1).

[110] ibid, s.208(4).

[111] ibid, s.208(5).

In addition to considering the suitability of any particular requirements, the court must also have regard to any restrictions on liberty imposed by the order.[112] Specifically, any such restrictions must be (in the opinion of the court) commensurate with the seriousness of the offence (combination of offences).[113] For example, where the court imposes a prohibited activity requirement, the court must be satisfied that such a requirement is proportionate and any restriction of liberty imposed by that requirement is commensurate with the seriousness of the offence. A restriction on an offender's ability to enter licensed premises will most likely be disproportionate, as opposed to a restriction on the offender's ability to enter public houses, for example.

In assessing whether any such restrictions are commensurate with the seriousness of the offence, the court is obligated take into account all the information that is available to it about the circumstances of the offence (or combination of offences), including any aggravating or mitigating factors.[114] In addition, the court will be assisted by the views of the Probation Service in any pre-sentence report.[115]

Compatibility with other requirements

The Sentencing Act 2020 requires the court to consider the practicality of imposing multiple requirements as part of the sentencing exercise. In particular, the statute prescribes that before imposing two or more different requirements, the court must consider whether, in the circumstances of the case, the requirements are compatible with each other.[116] If at any time, the requirements of an order are no longer

[112] Though the court is not (subject to the requirement of punishment) obligated to impose any condition which restricts the offender's liberty (Sentencing Act 2020, s.208(9)).

[113] Sentencing Act 2020, s.208(6).

[114] ibid, s.208(7).

[115] ibid, s.208(8).

[116] ibid, s.208(12); s.292(3).

compatible, both the offender and the Probation Service may apply to court to amend any of the requirements of the order.[117]

Avoiding conflicts

As part of the sentencing exercise, the court must also ensure, so far as practicable, that any requirement imposed is such as to avoid:

- any conflict with the offender's religious beliefs,
- any conflict with any other court order to which the offender may be subject, and
- any interference with the times, if any, at which the offender normally works, or attends any educational establishment.[118]

If at any time, there has been a change in circumstances such that the requirements of an order conflict in any way described above, both the offender and the Probation Service may apply to court to amend any of the requirements of the order.[119]

Supervision of requirements

A community order, and a suspended sentence order which imposes any community requirement, must specify the area which is the offender's "home local justice area".[120] That area must be the local justice area in which the offender resides or will reside.[121]

---

[117] See Chapter 11.

[118] Sentencing Act 2020, s.208(13); s.292(4).

[119] See Chapter 11.

[120] Sentencing Act 2020, s.210(1); s.296(1).

[121] ibid, s.210(2); s.296(2).

Generally speaking, the court that made the order will be responsible for the supervision of that order (i.e. should the order be made by the Crown Court, it will be supervised by the Crown Court). Having "supervision" of the order in this context simply means that that respective court will be responsible for dealing with the offender should there be a breach of that order or applications to amend/revoke. However, where the Crown Court makes such an order, it may make a direction that the order is to be subject to magistrates' court supervision. This applies equally to community orders[122] and suspended sentence orders (so long as such orders impose any community requirement).[123]

Probation Reset

At this stage, it is necessary to discuss the impact of "Probation Reset" on the requirements of orders. Probation Reset was discussed in full in Chapter 1. For the purposes of this chapter, it is important to remember that an offender who has completed two-thirds of their court order may be eligible for Probation Reset which will mean that supervision of the offender will cease, and any RAR sessions will also cease. As discussed in Chapter 1, Probation Reset does not apply to a defined class of offenders.

Considering each requirement

The following shall provide a brief description of each requirement available to the court. Given that a court has the ability to amend requirements so as to replace them with a requirement of the same kind, and to impose further requirements following a probation breach, it is essential that an advocate knows the basic detail of each requirement.

[122] ibid, s.211(1).

[123] ibid, s.297(1).

Unpaid work requirement

An unpaid work requirement is a requirement that the offender must perform unpaid work in accordance with the instructions of the responsible officer.[124] Unpaid work is designed to be punitive in nature; though it is arguable that such a requirement is rehabilitative and capable of having reparative benefits also.

Where an unpaid work requirement is imposed, the offender must complete all hours of work within a 12-month period.[125] This is so regardless of the end date of the community order or expiry of the operational period. For example, where an offender is sentenced to a three-year community order (imposed on 12 August 2024), they must complete the unpaid work within 12 months (by 11 August 2025).[126] The minimum and maximum number of permitted hours is detailed below.[127]

An unpaid work requirement cannot be imposed unless the court is satisfied that

- the offender is a suitable person to perform unpaid work, and
- there is provision in the offender's home local justice area for the offender to complete the work.[128]

In determining whether the offender is suitable to perform unpaid work, the court must, if it thinks it necessary, hear from the Probation Service.[129] Suitability will reflect whether it is practical for the offender

---

124 ibid, Schedule 9, para 1(1).

125 ibid, Schedule 9, para 1(1)(b).

126 For applications to extend the unpaid work requirement beyond the initial 12-month period, see Chapter 11.

127 See below "Minimum and maximum limits in requirements".

128 Sentencing Act 2020, Schedule 9, para 3(1).

129 ibid, Schedule 9, para 3(2).

to complete the unpaid work and whether there is any practical consequence of such an order (e.g. employment or caring responsibilities may suffer).

Whilst it is correct that para 3(1) requires the court to assess the suitability of an offender for unpaid work, and the court may consider a multitude of views and opinions in coming to that opinion, "there is no requirement for the offender to consent to or indicate a willingness to carry out unpaid work before such an order can be made."[130]

Rehabilitation activity requirement[131]

A rehabilitation activity requirement (RAR) is a requirement where the offender must comply with any instructions given by the responsible officer to attend appointments and/or participate in activities. An RAR is designed to be rehabilitative,[132] and the Sentencing Act is clear that any instructions given by the responsible officer must be given with a view to promoting the offender's rehabilitation.[133] Though, the responsible officer can give instructions with a view to other purposes in addition to rehabilitation.[134]

As part of an RAR, the offender may be instructed to attend an appointment with the responsible officer or with someone else.[135] Further, when instructing the offender to participate in activities, the responsible officer may require the offender to participate in specified activities and (in doing so) comply with instructions given by the person

---

130 *R v Fairweather* [2015] EWCA Crim 1027, [2005] 2 Cr. App. R. (S.) 56 [12] (The Recorder of Cardiff, HHJ Rees).

131 Now subject to Probation Reset (see Chapter 1).

132 And for that reason, will not satisfy s.208(10) of the Sentencing Act 2020 if imposed alone as part of a community order.

133 Sentencing Act 2020, Schedule 9, para 5(1).

134 ibid, Schedule 9, para 5(2).

135 ibid, Schedule 9, para 5(3).

in charge of the activities, or to go to a specified place and (while there) comply with any instructions given by the person in charge of the place.[136]

It is important to note that it is for the responsible officer to instruct the offender as to what activities they are to carry out, and not the court. However, the court may be persuaded to impose an RAR where the Probation Service identify a particular activity as being both available and particularly suitable for the offender.[137]

The activities that a responsible officer may instruct the offender to participate in include activities forming an accredited programme, or activities whose purpose is reparative, such as restorative justice activities.[138]

Programme requirement

A programme requirement is a requirement that the offender must participate in an accredited programme at a particular place, and (in doing so) comply with instructions of the person in charge of the programme.[139] An "accredited programme" is one accredited by the Secretary of State,[140] and a "programme" means a systematic set of activities.[141] The Correctional Services Advice & Accreditation Panel (CSAAP) assists the Probation Service to accredit programmes by

---

[136] ibid, Schedule 9, para 5(4).

[137] This is in comparison with the former (and now repealed) "activity requirements".

[138] Sentencing Act 2020, Schedule 9, para 5(5). For the definition of restorative justice activity, see para 5(6) of Schedule 9 to the Sentencing Act 2020.

[139] ibid, Schedule 9, para 6(1).

[140] ibid, Schedule 9, para 6(2). The list of accredited programmes and a description of those programmes can be found at Gov.uk.

[141] ibid, Schedule 9, para 6(4).

reviewing programme design, quality assurance procedures and findings, and programme evaluations. They make recommendations about whether to accredit to the Accredited Programmes and Interventions Delivery Strategy Board (APIDSB). The Probation Service is accountable for decisions to accredit programmes.

Where a programme requirement is imposed, the court must specify the number of days on which the offender is to be required to participate in an accredited programme under the requirement.[142] It will then be for the responsible officer to decide which programme the offender is to participate and the place at which they are to do so.[143] It is not for the court to specify which programmes are to be completed. However, if such an order is made, the court *must* specify that an accredited programme needs to be undertaken; the court cannot delegate that role to the Probation Service.[144] A failure by the court itself to specify that a programme needed to be complied with, and to specify the number of days, would be a defect in the order and the order would be unlawful.[145]

> **Key point**
>
> Whilst the court cannot dictate which accredited programme an offender must undertake, they will inquire whether certain programmes can be completed within the period of the order imposed. It is essential for the advocate to have considered this and obtained the necessary information from the Probation Service prior to the hearing, if such information is not already available (e.g. in a pre-sentence report).

[142] ibid, Schedule 9, para 6(5)(a).

[143] ibid, Schedule 9, para 6(5)(b).

[144] *R v Price* [2013] EWCA Crim 1283, [2014] 1 Cr. App. R. (S.) 36 [8] (Elias LJ).

[145] ibid [9] (Elias LJ).

Prohibited activity requirement

A prohibited activity requirement is a requirement that obliges the offender to refrain from participating in specified activities on one or more particular days, or for a particular period.[146] The order must specify (with *exact clarity*) the activities from which the offender must refrain and the day or days on which, or the period for which, the offender must refrain from those activities.[147]

It is emphasised that the court must specify with clarity what the prohibited activities are on account that an offender cannot be in any doubt as to what is restricted. For example, a restriction on an offender's ability to enter "any licenced venue" will raise questions as to whether this includes only on-licence premises, or whether it also includes off-licence premises. Without such clarity, an offender would be prohibited from entering any store or shop that sold alcohol. Such a prohibition would be entirely disproportionate and would be unlikely to be intended by the sentencing judge. Clarity is therefore essential.

Importantly, a court may not impose a prohibited activity requirement unless it has consulted the Probation Service.[148] This may be by way of a pre-sentence report where a prohibited activity requirement is specifically discussed, or from an oral report in court.

[146] Sentencing Act 2020, Schedule 9, para 7(1).

[147] ibid, Schedule 9, para 7(2).

[148] ibid, Schedule 9, para 7(2). See also *R v Dunlop* [2015] EWCA Crim 1109 where this was not complied with.

Key point

Where a judge requests the view of the Probation Service regarding a prohibited activity requirement, the judge should be careful to ensure that the offender is not provided with a legitimate expectation that an order in the community will be imposed. The judge should be clear that all options remain open as part of the adjournment (unless, of course, the judge is satisfied that an order in the community is a definite).

In *R v Jacob,*[149] Bean J in the Court of Appeal explained that the "primary purpose" of a prohibited activity requirement is "not to punish the offender but to prevent, or at least reduce, the risk of further offending".[150] Mr Justice Bean further expressed that any such requirement must be proportionate to the risk of further offending.[151] By way of particular example, in *R v Dunlop*,[152] the offender was sentenced for the offence of violent disorder to 12 months' imprisonment, suspended for 24 months, with 200 hours of unpaid work requirement. In addition, the learned judge imposed a prohibited activity requirement, namely that the offender must not enter licensed premises for a period of 12 months. Whilst the focus of that appeal was the procedural errors involved,[153] the Court of Appeal concluded that the prohibited activity requirement imposed in that case was nevertheless disproportionate given the sentence as a whole.[154] Whilst, therefore, there is technically no limit on the restrictions that may be imposed, the court must nevertheless be

[149] [2008] EWCA Crim 2002, (2008) 172 J.P. 513.

[150] ibid, [9] (Bean J).

[151] ibid.

[152] [2015] EWCA Crim 1109.

[153] Namely that the views of the Probation Service had not been sought as required by para 8 of Schedule 9 to the Sentencing Act 2020.

[154] *R v Dunlop* (n152) [8] (Supperstone J).

satisfied that the restriction is proportionate and commensurate with the seriousness of the offence(s).

Curfew requirement

A curfew requirement is a requirement that the offender must remain at a particular place for particular periods ("curfew periods").[155] Curfew requirements may be imposed for punitive purposes or for the purposes of preventing further offending.

The curfew period and the place at which the offender must remain for each curfew period must be specified in the order imposed by the court.[156] The court is permitted to specify different places and different curfew periods for different days (e.g. an offender must remain at location A Monday-Friday, and location B on a weekend).[157]

The maximum and minimum curfew periods are dealt with below.[158] However, it is important to note at this stage that the court is not restricted when imposing a curfew requirement by the fact that the offender has been previously subject to a curfew as part of another court order (e.g. whilst remanded on conditional bail pending sentence or as part of conditions during a deferment of sentence).[159] In *SA*, HHJ Milford QC (giving the judgment of the Court) explained that the period of curfew prior to the imposition of the final court order was merely a part of the "history"[160] of the case. His Honour went further and stated:

> It was something which needed to be taken into account when looking at how onerous the community requirements

---

[155] Sentencing Act 2020, Schedule 9, para 9(1).

[156] ibid, Schedule 9, para 9(2).

[157] ibid, Schedule 9, para 9(3).

[158] See below "Minimum and maximum limits in requirements".

[159] *R v SA* [2011] EWCA Crim 2747.

[160] ibid, [19] (HHJ Milford QC).

> of the order were to be, but it was not a legal obstacle to imposing a curfew requirement at all[161]

Whilst this judgment concerned the now repealed s.204 Criminal Justice Act 2003, there is no reason to doubt that the same conclusion would be reached today. Indeed, para 9(5) of Schedule 9 to the Sentencing Act 2020 states that specified curfew periods begin "with the day on which the requirement first takes effect" (i.e. the date the community order or suspended sentence order is made). Furthermore, there is no requirement on the court to give credit for any time spent on curfew when imposing a community order or a suspended sentence order.[162]

Before imposing a curfew requirement, the court must obtain and consider information about each place proposed to be specified in the order,[163] including information as to the attitude of persons likely to be affected by the offender's enforced presence at that location.[164] For example, the Probation Service will not recommend that a curfew requirement is a suitable requirement where the offender has a history of domestic abuse and will be residing at any address with another person, or where there is a history of abuse in that household specifically.

Importantly, where the court imposed a curfew requirement, it must also impose an electronic compliance monitoring requirement.[165] Such a requirement is necessary to secure compliance with the curfew

---

161 ibid.

162 Unlike the requirement to do so when imposing a determinate sentence: see s.325 of the Sentencing Act 2020 and s.240A of the Criminal Justice Act 2003.

163 Sentencing Act 2020, Schedule 9, para 10(1).

164 ibid, Schedule 9, para 10(2).

165 See below for a full discussion on electronic compliance monitoring requirements.

requirement.[166] The court need not impose such an electronic compliance monitoring requirement in three distinct circumstances:

- where there is a person (other than the offender) without whose co-operation it will not be practicable to secure the monitoring, and person does not consent to the requirement,[167]
- where electronic monitoring arrangements are not available in the relevant area or where it is so available but the necessary provision cannot be made as to those arrangements,[168] and
- where the court otherwise considers it inappropriate to do so in the particular circumstances of the case.[169]

The power to vary a curfew requirement is discussed in full in Chapter 11.

Exclusion requirement

An exclusion requirement is a provision prohibiting the offender from entering a particular place (known as the "prohibited place")[170] for a particular period (known as the "exclusion period").[171] To clarify, it is plain on the construction of para 11 of Schedule 9 to the Sentencing Act 2020, that an exclusion requirement prevents an offender from entering

---

[166] Sentencing Act 2020, Schedule 9, para 10(3).

[167] ibid, Schedule 9, para 10(3)(a)(i); see also para 33 of Schedule 9.

[168] ibid, Schedule 9, para 10(3)(a)(ii); see also para 34 of Schedule 9.

[169] ibid, Schedule 9, para 10(3)(b).

[170] Which may be a general area as opposed to a specific location (see para 11(5) of Schedule 9).

[171] Sentencing Act 2020, Schedule 9, para 11(1).

an area *within* the United Kingdom.[172] As the then President of the QBD, Sir John Thomas, made clear in *Dragoman*:

> It cannot possibly, on any view, take effect as permitting a judge to exclude someone who is already in the United Kingdom from entering the United Kingdom.[173]

The Court in *Dragoman* also clarified that exclusion requirements are not designed to punish a particular offender;[174] the purpose is evidently to prevent the commission of further offences.

Both the prohibited place and the exclusion period must be stated in the order by the court,[175] and the court is permitted to impose a prohibition on more than one place, more than one exclusion period, and different prohibited places/ exclusion periods for different days.[176] The limits on exclusion requirements are detailed below.[177]

Given the restriction on the offender's movements and liberty, the court should conduct a full assessment as to whether any such exclusion would be workable.[178] As such, the court will wish to consider whether the offender takes a particular route for work, education, caring, religious, or other purposes that may disproportionately impede their freedom of movement.[179] The court may be more persuaded where an alternative route is available in cases of this sort.

---

[172] See *R (Dragoman) v Camberwell Green Magistrates' Court* [2012] EWHC 4105 (Admin) in the context of the predecessor to the Sentencing Act 2020.

[173] ibid, [10] (Sir John Thomas P).

[174] ibid.

[175] Sentencing Act 2020, Schedule 9, para 11(2).

[176] ibid, Schedule 9, para 11(3).

[177] See below "Minimum and maximum limits in requirements"..

[178] In the sense that the court would not want to set the offender up to fail.

[179] See *R v Jacob* [2008] EWCA Crim 2002.

As with a curfew requirement, where the court imposes an exclusion requirement it must also impose an electronic compliance monitoring requirement.[180] The same exceptions as with curfew requirements considered above are also relevant.[181]

Residence requirement

A residence requirement is a requirement that for a particular period (known as "the required period"), the offender must reside at a particular place (known as "the required place").[182] Importantly, unlike curfew requirements, the court has no power to specify multiple locations where the offender must reside during the required period. This order may be problematic, therefore, for an offender who resides at a variety of locations (e.g. for work purposes). However, the court does have the power to order that the offender must reside at the required place *but may*, with prior approval of the offender's responsible officer, also reside at some other place.[183] This may alleviate or mitigate any difficulties where an offender frequently resides are different places.

Before imposing a residence requirement, the court must consider the home surroundings of the offender.[184] This will include the impact of a residence requirement on other members of that household. In particular, where there is a history of domestic abuse, the court may be hesitant to impose a resident requirement.[185]

[180] Sentencing Act 2020, Schedule 9, para 12.

[181] ibid.

[182] ibid, Schedule 9, para 13(1)(a).

[183] ibid, Schedule 9, para 13(1)(b).

[184] ibid, Schedule 9, para 14.

[185] It is often the case that the victim of the offence subject to a court order will consent to the offender residing with them; the court should be wary to the suitability of that option.

When imposing the order, the court must specify the required place and required period. Importantly, a hostel or other institution may not be specified as the required place, except on the recommendation of the Probation Service.[186] Furthermore, if the court does permit the offender to reside at a different place, with prior approval of their responsible officer, the court must state that fact.[187] A defence advocate must be prepared to invite the court to state in the order that the offender may reside elsewhere with the permission of their responsible officer. This will be particularly important for offenders who live away for work purposes, e.g. in hotels around the country.

Applications to change the required place of the residence requirement are discussed in Chapter 11.

Foreign travel prohibition requirement

A foreign travel prohibition requirement is a requirement prohibiting the offender from travelling outside the British Islands.[188] The court may prohibit the offender from traveling to:

- a particular country or territory outside the British Islands,
- all countries and territories outside the British Islands, other than a country or territory otherwise excluded from the requirement, or
- all countries and territories outside the British Islands.[189]

---

[186] Sentencing Act 2020, Schedule 9, para 13(3).

[187] ibid, Schedule 9, para 13(2). Though there is no requirement to state the "other" place of residence; this is matter between the offender and their responsible officer.

[188] ibid, Schedule 9, para 15(1).

[189] ibid, Schedule 9, para 15(5).

Key point

In practice, the court will likely restrict the offender's ability to travel absolutely (i.e. restricting travel to any country or territory outside of the British Islands). This is to ensure compliance with the order. For example, it will be more difficult to manage and enforce an offender's compliance where they have the ability to travel to a prohibited country or territory via an intermittent country or territory.

This restriction may be imposed on a particular day or days, or for a particular period,[190] which the court must specify in the order and the area in relation to which the prohibition is to operate.[191] The limits on foreign travel prohibition requirements are detailed below.[192]

Mental health treatment requirement

A mental health treatment requirement (MHTR) is a requirement that the offender must submit, during a particular period or particular periods,[193] to mental health treatment, which may be:[194]

- in-patient treatment,[195]

[190] ibid, Schedule 9, para 15(1).

[191] ibid, Schedule 9, para 15(2).

[192] See below "Minimum and maximum limits in requirements".

[193] The Court may specify different treatment for different periods (Schedule 9, para 16(4)).

[194] Sentencing Act 2020, Schedule 9, para 16(1).

[195] Defined as "treatment as a resident patient in a care home, an independent hospital, or a hospital within the meaning of the Mental Health Act 1983, but not in hospital premises where high security psychiatric services are provided" (Schedule 9, para 16(2))

- institution-based out-patient treatment,[196] or
- practitioner-based treatment.[197]

"Mental health treatment" is defined as treatment which is by or under the direction of a registered medical practitioner or registered psychologist, and with a view to improvement of the offender's mental condition.[198] It is the offender's mental health at the time of sentence that is relevant.[199]

Where the court orders a MHTR, it must specify the period or periods during which the offender is required to submit to mental health treatment.[200] The court must also specify:

- the care home or hospital at which it is to be provided, if the mental health treatment is to be in-patient treatment,[201]
- the institution or place at which it is to be provided, if it is to be institution-based out-patient treatment,[202] and

---

196 Defined as "treatment as a non-resident patient at a particular institution or place" (Schedule 9, para 16(2))

197 Defined as "treatment by or under the direction of a particular registered medical practitioner or registered psychologist (or both)" (Schedule 9, para 16(2))

198 Sentencing Act 2020, Schedule 9, para 16(2).

199 *R v PS* [2019] EWCA Crim 2286, [2020] 2 Cr. App. R. (S.) 9.

200 Sentencing Act 2020, Schedule 9, para 16(3)(a).

201 ibid, Schedule 9, para 16(3)(b)(i).

202 ibid, Schedule 9, para 16(3)(b)(ii).

- the registered medical practitioner or registered psychologist (or both) by whom or under whose direction it is to be provided, if it is to be practitioner-based treatment.[203]

However, the court is not permitted to specify the nature of the treatment; that is a matter for the Probation Service.

Importantly for the purposes of Chapters 10 and 11 of this text, while an offender is under in-patient treatment, the responsible officer is to carry out the supervision of the offender only to the extent necessary for the purpose of revocation or amendment of the order.[204]

In order to impose a MHTR, the court must be satisfied of three requirements:[205]

- *The need for treatment condition:* The first requirement is that the court is satisfied that the mental condition of the offender requires treatment, may be susceptible to treatment, and does not warrant the making of a hospital order or guardianship order within the meaning of the Mental Health Act 1983.[206]

- *The arrangements condition:* The second requirement is that the court is satisfied that arrangements have been made, or can be made, for the treatment intended to be specified in the order.[207]

---

[203] ibid, Schedule 9, para 16(3)(b)(iii).

[204] ibid, Schedule 9, para 16(6).

[205] ibid, Schedule 9, para 17(1).

[206] ibid, Schedule 9, para 17(2).

[207] ibid, Schedule 9, para 17(3). Those arrangements include arrangements for the reception of the offender, where the offender is to be required to submit to resident treatment.

- *The consent condition:* Finally, the offender must express willingness to comply with the MHTR.[208]

See para 18 of Schedule 9 to the Sentencing Act 2020 for the circumstances where the treatment practitioner of a MHTR considers that part of the treatment can be better or more conveniently given by alternative arrangements.

Drug rehabilitation requirement

A drug rehabilitation requirement (DRR) is a requirement that during a period specified in the order (known as "the treatment and testing period") the offender:

- must submit to drug rehabilitation treatment, and
- for the purpose of ascertaining whether there is any drug in the offender's body during that period, must provide samples in accordance with directions given by the responsible officer, or the treatment director.[209]

A drug rehabilitation treatment is defined as treatment which is by or under the direction of a person who has the necessary qualifications or experience, and with a view to the reduction or elimination of the offender's dependency on or propensity to misuse drugs.[210] Such a requirement is therefore designed to be rehabilitative, and to prevent the commission of further offences; it is not designed to be punitive.

A DRR may take the form of:

[208] ibid, Schedule 9, para 17(4).

[209] ibid, Schedule 9, para 19(1).

[210] ibid, Schedule 9, para 19(2).

- resident treatment,[211]
- non-resident treatment.[212]

Where the court orders a DRR, it must specify:

- the treatment director,
- if the treatment is to be resident treatment, the institution or place where it is to be provided,
- if it is to be non-resident treatment, the institution or place where it is to be provided, and the intervals at which it is to be provided.[213]

However, the court must not specify the nature of the treatment as part of the order; the nature of the treatment is for the treatment director.

In order to impose a DRR, the court must be satisfied of four requirements:[214]

- *The need for treatment condition:* The first requirement is that the court is satisfied that the offender is dependent on drugs, or has a propensity to misuse drugs, and that the offender's dependency or propensity requires treatment and may be susceptible to treatment.[215]

---

211 Defined as "treatment as a resident in an institution or place".

212 Defined as "treatment as a non-resident at an institution or place".

213 Sentencing Act 2020, Schedule 9, para 19(5).

214 ibid, Schedule 9, para 20(1).

215 ibid, Schedule 9, para 20(2). As is evident from that requirement, there is no condition that the offender's dependency or propensity to misuse be an element of the offence that the offender is to be sentenced or was a factor

- *The arrangements condition:* The second requirement is that the court is satisfied that arrangements have been made, or can be made, for the treatment intended to be specified in the order.[216]

- *The suitability condition:* The third requirement is that the DRR has been recommended to the court as being suitable for the offender by the Probation Service (usually through a pre-sentence report).[217]

- *The consent condition:* Finally, the offender must express willingness to comply with the DRR.[218]

Where the court imposes a DRR, it must include provision for review if the treatment and testing period is more than 12 months.[219] Otherwise, the court has a discretion as to whether to include a provision for review.[220] Review and amendment of DRRs following review are discussed in full in Chapter 11.

Drug testing requirement

A drug testing requirement (DTR) is a requirement that during a period specified in the order, the offender must, for the purpose of ascertaining whether there is any drug or psychoactive substance in the offender's body during that period, provide samples in accordance with directions

---

to the commission of that offence (unlike an alcohol abstinence and monitoring requirement): see below, "Alcohol abstinence and monitoring requirement".

216 ibid, Schedule 9, para 20(3). Those arrangements include arrangements for the reception of the offender, where the offender is to be required to submit to resident treatment.

217 ibid, Schedule 9, para 20(4).

218 ibid, Schedule 9, para 20(5).

219 ibid, Schedule 9, para 21(1)(a).

220 ibid, Schedule 9, para 21(1)(b).

given by the responsible officer.[221] Importantly, this requirement is *only* available for offenders convicted on or after 28 June 2022.[222]

The responsible officer may give directions to the offender as to the type of samples to be provided (e.g. blood or urine), and the times at which, or circumstances in which, they are to be provided.[223]

Key point

It is common for advocates to misstate the obligation on the offender with a DTR. An offender is in breach of a DTR where they fail to provide a sample when directed; the use of illicit drugs is not a breach of the DTR.

In order to impose an DTR, the court must be satisfied of two requirements:[224]

- *The misuse condition:* The first requirement is that the court is satisfied that the offender's misuse of a drug or psychoactive substance caused or contributed to offence for which they are being sentenced, or is likely to cause or contribute to the commission of further offences by the offender.[225]

- *The availability of arrangements condition:* The second requirement is that the court has been notified by the Secretary of State that arrangements for implementing drug testing

221 ibid, Schedule 9, para 22A(1).

222 ibid, s.207(3A); s.291(3A).

223 ibid, Schedule 9, para 22A(3). The court has no power to direct when such samples are to be requested.

224 ibid, Schedule 9, para 22B(1).

225 ibid, Schedule 9, para 22B(2).

requirements are available in the offender's home local justice area (and the notice has not been withdrawn).[226]

Importantly, unlike DRRs (considered above), there is no requirement for the offender to consent to a DTR or express willingness to comply.

Alcohol treatment requirement

An alcohol treatment requirement (ATR) is a requirement that during a period specified in the order the offender must submit to alcohol dependency treatment.[227] Such treatment is defined as treatment which is by or under the direction of a person who has the necessary qualifications or experience ("the treatment director"), and with a view to reducing or eliminating the offender's dependency on alcohol.[228] As with DRRs, this requirement is designed to be rehabilitative, and to prevent the commission of further offences; it is not designed to be punitive.

An ATR may take the form of:

- resident treatment,[229]
- institution-based treatment,[230] or
- practitioner-based treatment.[231]

Where the court orders an ATR, it must specify:

---

226 ibid, Schedule 9, para 22B(3).

227 ibid, Schedule 9, para 23(1).

228 ibid, Schedule 9, para 23(2).

229 Defined as "treatment as a resident in an institution or place".

230 Defined as "treatment as a non-resident at an institution or place".

231 Defined as "treatment by or under the direction of the treatment director".

- the treatment director,
- whether the alcohol dependency treatment is to be resident treatment, institution-based treatment or practitioner-based treatment,
- if it is to be resident treatment, the institution or place where it is to be provided,
- if it is to be institution-based treatment. the institution or place where it is to be provided, and
- the intervals at which it is to be provided.[232]

However, the court must not specify the nature of the treatment as part of the order; the nature of the treatment is for the treatment director.

In order to impose an ATR, the court must be satisfied of three requirements:[233]

- *The need for treatment condition:* The first requirement is that the court is satisfied that the offender is dependent on alcohol and that the offender's dependency requires treatment and may be susceptible to treatment.[234]
- *The arrangements condition:* The second requirement is that the court is satisfied that arrangements have been made, or can be made, for the treatment intended to be specified in the order.[235]

---

[232] Sentencing Act 2020, Schedule 9, para 23(5).

[233] ibid, Schedule 9, para 24(1).

[234] ibid, Schedule 9, para 24(2).

[235] ibid, Schedule 9, para 24(3). Those arrangements include arrangements for the reception of the offender, where the offender is to be required to submit to treatment as a resident.

- *The consent condition:* Finally, the offender must express willingness to comply with the ATR.[236]

Unlike an alcohol abstinence and monitoring requirement (considered immediately below), there is no requirement that the offender's consumption of alcohol was an element of the offence or contributed to the offence with which the offender is to be sentenced.

Alcohol abstinence and monitoring requirement

An alcohol abstinence and monitoring requirement (AAMR) is a requirement that, during a particular period (known as "the abstinence and monitoring period"), the offender:

- must either (i) abstain from consuming alcohol entirely, or (ii) must not consume alcohol above a prescribed level, and

- must submit to monitoring in accordance with particular arrangements for the purpose of ascertaining whether the offender is complying with the order.[237]

Where the court imposes an AAMR, the court must specify the abstinence and monitoring period, the level of alcohol permitted to be in the offender's body during the abstinence and monitoring period, and the arrangements for monitoring.[238]

In order to impose an AAMR, the court must be satisfied of three requirements:[239]

---

[236] ibid, Schedule 9, para 24(4).

[237] ibid, Schedule 9, para 25(1). See also The Criminal Justice Act 2003 (Alcohol Abstinence and Monitoring Requirement) (Prescription of Arrangement for Monitoring) Order 2018 (SI 2018/210).

[238] ibid, Schedule 9, para 25(2).

[239] ibid, Schedule 9, para 26(2).

- *The relevance of alcohol condition:* The first requirement is that either the offender's consumption of alcohol is an element of the offence for which they are being sentenced,[240] or the court is satisfied that the offender's consumption of alcohol was a factor that contributed to the commission of that offence.[241]

- *The non-dependency condition:* The court must be satisfied that the offender is not dependent on alcohol.[242]

- *The availability of arrangements condition:* Finally, the court has been notified by the Secretary of State that arrangements for monitoring are available in the offender's home local justice area (and the notice has not been withdrawn).[243]

As a result of Article 3 of The Criminal Justice Act 2003 (Alcohol Abstinence and Monitoring Requirement) (Prescription of Arrangement for Monitoring) Order 2018, the arrangement for monitoring prescribed by the Secretary of State is monitoring by a transdermal electronic tag. Such tag is fitted to the offender's leg

Attendance centre requirement

This requirement is only available for offenders who were convicted prior to 28 June 2022 and were aged under 25 at the date of conviction.[244] On account of that, this text shall not discuss the requirement further.

[240] For example, driving whilst unfit through alcohol or over the prescribed limit, contrary to ss.4 and 5 of the Road Traffic Act 1988 respectively.

[241] ibid, Schedule 9, para 26(3).

[242] ibid, Schedule 9, para 26(4). Should the offender be so dependent, the court should instead consider an alcohol treatment requirement.

[243] ibid, Schedule 9, para 26(5).

[244] ibid, s.207(3); s.291(3).

Practitioners are advised to seek out a specialist sentencing text for a discussion on this requirement.

Electronic compliance monitoring requirement

An electronic compliance monitoring requirement (ECMR) is a requirement for securing the electronic monitoring of the offender's compliance with other requirements imposed by the order.[245] Reference to "other requirements imposed by the order" reflects the fact that an ECMR cannot be imposed unless the court also imposes at least one other available requirement.[246] This includes any requirement listed in the table of requirements in ss.201 or 287 of the Sentencing Act 2020, other than an AAMR[247] or an electronic whereabouts monitoring requirement. As noted above, an ECMR *must* be imposed for a curfew[248] or exclusion requirement.[249]

Any such compliance order must be during a period (known as "the monitoring period") specified in the order, or determined by the responsible officer in accordance with the relevant order.[250] Where an ECMR is imposed, the court must specify the person responsible for the monitoring.[251]

---

[245] ibid, Schedule 9, para 29(1).

[246] ibid, s.207(4); s.291(4).

[247] Which is specifically prohibited by para 29(4) of Schedule 9 to the Sentencing Act 2020. Though, see para 29(5) which states that an ECMR can still be imposed to monitor compliance with any other requirement.

[248] Sentencing Act 2020, Schedule 9, para 10(3).

[249] ibid, Schedule 9, para 12.

[250] ibid, Schedule 9, para 29(1).

[251] ibid, Schedule 9, para 31(1). See also, Regulation 7 of The Electronic Monitoring (Responsible Persons) (Miscellaneous) Regulations 2024 (SI 2024/340).

Where the court imposes an ECMR, the offender must:

- submit to being fitted with, or installation of, any necessary apparatus, and inspection or repair of any apparatus fitted or installed for the purposes of the monitoring,

- not interfere with, or with the working of, any apparatus fitted or installed for the purposes of the monitoring, and

- take any steps required by the responsible officer, or the person responsible for the monitoring, for the purpose of keeping in working order any apparatus fitted or installed for the purposes of the monitoring.

The offender must comply with these requirements as required from time to time by the responsible officer or the person responsible for the monitoring.[252]

Importantly, where the court proposes to impose an ECMR, but there is a person (other than the offender) without whose co-operation it will not be practicable to secure the monitoring, the requirement may not be included in the order without that person's consent.[253] There is a further restriction that the court must be notified by the Secretary of State that electronic monitoring arrangements are available in the relevant area (and the notice has not been withdrawn), and the court is satisfied that the necessary provision can be made under those arrangements.[254]

Electronic whereabouts monitoring requirement

An electronic whereabouts monitoring requirement (EWMR) is a requirement to submit to electronic monitoring of the offender's

[252] ibid, Schedule 9, para 32.

[253] ibid, Schedule 9, para 33.

[254] ibid, Schedule 9, para 34(1). See also paras 34(2)–(4) of Schedule 9.

whereabouts during a period specified in the order.[255] An EWMR cannot be used for the purpose of monitoring the offender's compliance with any other requirement included in the order; this is the purpose of an ECMR.

The same requirements listed above in respect of ECMRs, such as the responsibilities of the offender and the need for the court to specify a person responsible for such monitoring, apply equally to EWMRs, as do the restrictions noted above in respect of requiring another person's consent.

A court may not impose an EWMR unless:

- the court has been notified by the Secretary of State that electronic monitoring arrangements are available in the local justice area proposed to be specified in the order (and the notice has not been withdrawn),

- the court is satisfied that the offender can be fitted with any necessary apparatus under the arrangements currently available, and any other necessary provision can be made under those arrangements, and

- the court is satisfied that arrangements are generally operational throughout England and Wales (even if not always operational everywhere there) under which the offender's whereabouts can be electronically monitored.[256]

---

[255] ibid, Schedule 9, para 30.

[256] ibid, Schedule 9, para 35.

Minimum and maximum limits in requirements

It is essential for any advocate to be prepared to know whether a particular requirement of an order features a restriction on its imposition (i.e. a minimum or maximum length of time, number of hours etc).

Below is a list of all of the requirements that may be imposed and their respective restrictions.[257]

- *Unpaid work*:
    - Minimum period: 40 hours.[258]
    - Maximum period: 300 hours.[259]
- *RAR*: No minimum or maximum period.[260] This is on account that RAR days should be stated as an "up to" amount (i.e. the offender is not obligated to complete all RAR days; it is a determination for the Probation Service as to whether the offender has satisfied the objectives of sentencing from the number of days completed).
- *Programme requirement*: No minimum or maximum period.

[257] All requirements are subject to the same (self-explanatory) restriction in that any such requirement cannot run beyond the end date of a community order or the operational period of a suspended sentence order.

[258] Sentencing Act 2020, Schedule 9, para 2(1)(b)(i). Though note that the court may impose a minimum number of 20 hours when imposing an unpaid work requirement following breach of a community order not presently featuring an unpaid work requirement.

[259] ibid, Schedule 9, para 2(1)(b)(ii).

[260] Though from experience, the Probation Service would not normally advise a number over 60.

- *Prohibited activity requirement*: No minimum or maximum period.
- *Curfew requirement:*
    - Minimum period: two hours per day.[261]
    - Maximum period: 20 hours per day[262] and 112 hours in any seven-day period.[263]
    - A curfew may be imposed for no longer than two years.[264]
- *Exclusion requirement*:
    - No minimum period.
    - If the order is a community order, the exclusion period must not be more than two years.[265] There is no equivalent restriction for suspended sentence orders on account that the maximum length of the operational period of a suspended sentence order is two years.
- *Residence requirement*: No minimum or maximum period.
- *Foreign travel prohibition order*:

---

261 Sentencing Act 2020, Schedule 9, para 9(4)(a).

262 ibid, Schedule 9, para 9(4)(b). *N.B. This maximum number only applies where the offender is convicted on or after 26 June 2022. If the offender was convicted before this date, the maximum number of hours per day is 16 hours.*

263 ibid, Schedule 9, para 9(4)(c).

264 ibid, Schedule 9, para 9(5). *N.B. This restriction only applies where the offender is convicted on or after 26 June 2022. If the offender was convicted before this date, the maximum period of a curfew is 12 months.*

265 ibid, Schedule 9, para 11(4)(a).

  - No minimum period.
  - Maximum period: 12 months from the day the order takes effect.[266]

- *Mental health treatment requirement*: No minimum or maximum period.

- *Drug rehabilitation requirement*: No minimum or maximum period.

- *Drug testing requirement*: No minimum or maximum period.

- *Alcohol treatment requirement*: No minimum or maximum period.

- *Alcohol abstinence and monitoring requirement*:
  - No minimum period.[267]
  - Maximum period: 120 days.[268]

- *Attendance centre requirement*:
  - Minimum period: 12 hours.[269]
  - Maximum period: 36 hours.[270]

---

[266] ibid, Schedule 9, para 15(4).

[267] Unless one is prescribed by the Secretary of State: para 25(7)(a) of Schedule 9. At the time of writing, no such minimum period had been prescribed.

[268] Sentencing Act 2020, Schedule 9, para 25(4)(b).

[269] ibid, Schedule 9, para 27(3)(a).

[270] ibid, Schedule 9, para 27(3)(b).

  - An offender cannot be required to attend at an attendance centre, more than once on any day, or for more than 3 hours at a time.[271]

- *Electronic monitoring requirement* (including electronic compliance monitoring requirement and electronic whereabouts monitoring requirement): No minimum or maximum period.

<u>Transfer to Scotland and Northern Ireland</u>

Schedules 11 and 17 to the Sentencing Act 2020 make provision for the restriction, amendment and transfer of community orders and suspended sentence orders to Scotland and Northern Ireland.

Summary

This Chapter has covered a general overview of community orders and suspended sentence orders, and the requirements imposed under those orders. It has further discussed the responsibilities of both the responsible officer and the offender during the currency of an order. In this Chapter, we have discussed:

- The basic structure of court orders, including community orders and suspended sentence orders.

- The requirements that may be imposed as part of a community order or suspended sentence order, including their meaning, availability, and restrictions on the orders.

- The minimum and maximum periods to which those requirements may be imposed.

[271] ibid, Schedule 9, para 27(8).

CHAPTER THREE

THE INVOLVEMENT OF THE PROBATION SERVICE

Introduction

In this Chapter, we discuss the process that follows the imposition of a community-based court order. It follows on from Chapter 2 where we explored the two main community-based court orders (community orders and suspended sentence orders), and the various requirements that may be imposed as part of those orders.

In this Chapter, we deal with the practical aspects of such court orders following their imposition. We start by discussing the initial contact made with the Probation Service following the hearing and the booking of an induction appointment for the offender. We then proceed to discuss that induction appointment, and the contract agreement and induction pack considered at that appointment. We then consider the roles and responsibilities of the responsible officer and the offender during the currency of the order.

Key provisions

The relevant provisions are provided in the Sentencing Act 2020, as such:

- Community orders: Chapter 2
- Suspended sentence orders: Chapter 5

Procedure following imposition of sentence

The following details the procedure that will generally be adopted where an offender has been sentenced to an order in the community (whether it be a community order or a suspended sentence order).

Attending at the Probation office

Following the hearing where an offender is sentenced to either a community order or a suspended sentence order, the offender needs to obtain their induction appointment from the Probation Service.

Each court centre is different:

- In some court centres, a member of the Probation Service will be present in court during the sentence.
- In other court centres, the Probation Service will not have a presence in court and will require the offender to attend at their office situated in the court centre.

Regardless of whether a member of the Probation Service is present in court, the offender must ensure that they speak with the Probation Service before they leave the court building.

If the Probation Service was not present during the sentence, the advocate should inform the relevant officer of the details of the case. A simple checklist will be appropriate:

- *What court was the offender sentenced in?* (e.g. "Court 4")

  This will assist the officer in finding the offender's details with ease from the court list.

- *What was the offence(s) that the offender was sentenced for?*

  This will assist the officer in assessing the offender's risk prior to their induction appointment, and will determine whether the offender is allocated to a Probation Services Officer (PSO), or a Probation Officer (PO). For example, an offence involving domestic abuse will often require allocation to a Probation Officer given the risk involved.

- *What was the offender sentenced to?*

  Ensure the officer is told whether the offender was sentenced to a community order or a suspended sentence order, the length of the order, and any requirements imposed as part of the order.

In addition, the officer will also require the address and telephone number for the offender.

Key point

It is good practice and good advice for the advocate to accompany the offender to the Probation Service office and, if possible and convenient, remain with them whilst the officer schedules their induction appointment. The Probation officer will require details that the offender may not recall.

Once these details have been provided, the Probation officer will then book the offender an appointment with a PSO or PO. The appointment will be written down for the offender before they leave the court building, including the date, time and location of the appointment.

In some court centres, the Probation Service will not book an appointment with the offender whilst in court and will instead post a letter to the offender's address with information as to the induction appointment. This is especially so where an offender appears in a court centre that is outside of the offender's local justice area.

Induction appointment

At the induction appointment (also known as the "initial appointment"), the offender will meet a duty officer prior to being allocated their responsible officer, sign a contract, and complete an induction pack. At the induction, the offender will be allocated a Case Reference Number (CRN). This is a unique number assigned to an offender on the Probation Service's N-Delius system. Such references will have been created if the offender had a pre-sentence report prepared prior to sentence. CRNs follow the format of a letter followed by 6 digits (e.g. E631281).

CRNs are to be distinguished from case numbers ("S-numbers") which are allocated to an offender's case in the Crown Court where there is a breach or subsequent application to amend/ revoke.

Purpose of initial appointment

The induction appointment is designed to allow the responsible officer to work with the offender to develop their "sentence plan". This is a plan that sets out the goals and objectives of sentence that are aimed to help avoid future offending and to make positive changes to the life of the offender. The sentence plan will shape what the offender works on, who with, and when. It is this plan which is reviewed by the responsible officer against the offender's compliance to reflect the offender's progress with the objectives therein.

The regular occurrence of appointments will be discussed, including the period of time between appointments. Where an unpaid work requirement is imposed, the offender may agree to attend unpaid work once per week on any day, or may agree to attend on a particular day every week (e.g. "every Wednesday" until the requirement is complete). Discussions will be had regarding reasonable adjustments and the preferred method of communication between the responsible officer and the offender (e.g. face-to-face, telephone, text message etc).

Prior to the end of the induction appointment, the offender will be provided with any planned appointments for the future.

The responsible officer

The responsible officer must be

- an officer of a provider of probation services, or

- a person responsible for monitoring the offender in accordance with an electronic monitoring requirement imposed by the community order.[1]

They are defined in the Sentencing Act 2020 as the person who is "responsible for discharging the functions conferred by this Code on the responsible officer in accordance with arrangements made by the Secretary of State."[2] We deal with the responsibilities of the Probation Service and the responsible officer below, but in summary the functions of the responsible officer are to

- make any arrangements that are necessary in connection with the requirements imposed by the order, and

- promote the offender's compliance with those requirements.[3]

The responsible officer will ensure this by communicating with the offender regarding any planned appointments. For example, the responsible officer will often provide the dates and times of appointments in multiple mediums to ensure the best compliance (e.g. verbally informing the offender of their appointment, and repeating this by way of text message or posted letter).

---

1 Sentencing Act 2020, s.213(2); s.299(3).

2 ibid, s.213(1); s.299(2).

3 ibid, s.214(2); s.300(2).

In addition, in order to promote the offender's compliance, the responsible officer will seek to identify whether there are any barriers to the offender's compliance. They will seek to discuss any concerns that an offender may have with the order in order to ensure that they obtain the necessary support that is available. A common strategy adopted is for the responsible officer to mark absences as "acceptable", giving the offender the benefit of the doubt, so as to encourage the offender to attend in future. This strategy is often key to maintaining a rapport between the responsible officer and the offender.

The responsible officer will provide the offender with their contact details and will seek further details from the offender (including the details of an emergency contact).

Assessing risk

The responsible officer will also assess the various risks posed by the offender, using a tool called the Offender Assessment System (OASys). OASys is used to complete risk and assess the needs of an offender (i.e. why the offender offends and what can be done to reduce/ stop the offending). OASys is also used to identify whether the offender is a risk to themselves (i.e. whether they are likely to harm themselves) or a risk to other people.

When assessing risk, the responsible officer will have regard to a variety of factors, including:

- "Static risk factors": These are factors that do not change, for example the age of the first offence, the nature of offending etc.
- "Dynamic risk factors": These are factors that may fluctuate over time, such as substance misuse, accommodation, employment and other indicators of behaviour and thinking.
- "Acute risk factors": These are factors that can change rapidly, meaning that offending becomes more likely.

The Probation Service utilises a variety of risk tools. The following provides a few examples of these tools:

- Offender Group Reconviction Scale (OGRS): This is a tool that helps predict reoffending likelihood, using factors such as age, gender and criminal history. OGRS is used to guide decisions on probation delivery.
- General reoffending Predictor (OGP): This is a tool that assesses the likelihood of non-violent re-offending. This tool is only concerned with non-violent offences, and does therefore not cover offences of violence, or of a sexual nature, or offences involving harm to others such as arson and terrorism-related matters.
- OASys Violence Predictor (OVP): This is a tool used to assess the risk of re-offending for violent, non-sexual, offences.
- Risk of Serious Harm (RoSH): This is a tool used to assess the risk that an offender presents of serious harm to others, risks to children, risks to the offender, and risks relating to escape/ absconding. Such risk may be recorded as "LOW", "MEDIUM", "HIGH" or "VERY HIGH".

Those are just some examples of risk tools and indicators that the Probation Service may use.[4] The sheer variety of tools used are necessary on account that their focus is different (e.g. whilst RSR manages serious reoffending risks, OGRS guides broader rehabilitation efforts).

---

[4] Other examples include Risk Matrix 2000 (RM2000), OASys Sexual reoffending Predictor (OSP), Spousal Assault Risk Assessment (SARA), Active Risk Management System (ARMS), Asset, and Risk of Serious Recidivism (RSR).

Probation contract agreement

As part of the induction, the offender will be asked to sign a probation contract agreement. The terminology differs across services as to the name adopted for this agreement. Regardless of the name used, the document is an agreement between the offender and the Probation Service.

The agreement will set out the rights and responsibilities of the Probation Service, and of the offender whilst they are being supervised in the community by the Probation Service. The offender may be required to sign a separate contract/ agreement if they are subject to additional requirements.

By signing the contract, the offender declares that the agreement has been fully explained to them and they understand its contents. The offender confirms that they have had the opportunity to ask questions and agree to abide by the conditions and any other reasonable instructions that may be given to them. The offender also confirms by signing the contract that if they fail to comply, they may be returned to court for breach of the court order. The offender will be provided with a copy of the contract agreement for their own purposes.

The rights and responsibilities of the Probation Service and the offender are discussed below.[5]

Induction pack

Though practices may differ between different Probation Services, as part of the induction pack, the offender and their responsible officer will generally complete:

- *Self-assessment questionnaire:*

[5] See below "Responsibilities of the Probation Service".

The offender is asked to identify whether the offender requires assistance with a list of issues (such as "finding a good place to live", "gambling", "taking drugs", "losing my temper" and many more). The offender is also asked whether they consider if any of these issues are linked to their offending. The offender may be asked whether they think they will likely offend in the future and will be asked to explain why they take this view.

- *Consent form:*

  The Probation Service will likely request that the offender consent to sharing their personal information with other organisations and persons with a view to supporting the offender's progress. This consent form ensures that the offender can be referred to partner organisations (e.g. accommodation or finance support) without difficulty.

- *Priorities and Addressing Barriers to Engagement form:*

  Ideally as part of the induction meeting, the responsible officer will identify with the offender what they would like to achieve whilst on supervision, including their priorities. Such priorities may be obtaining support with finances and debt, accommodation support, registering for benefits, finding employment etc. The responsible officer will also seek to identify any barriers to the offender's engagement and compliance with the order, such as caring responsibilities, physical and mental health issues etc, and what can be done to help minimise the impact of these barriers.

- *Diversity and Inclusion form:*

  This form ensures the Probation Service comply with its legal responsibilities under the Equality Act 2010. It ensures that the Probation Service provides a fair and equitable service. The form is purely voluntary

- *Safeguarding and Wellbeing form:*

  This form is used by the Probation Service to ensure that the welfare and wellbeing of any child under the age of 18 who is living with the offender is ensured. The offender is asked whether there is any child under the age of 18 living with them, whether the offender has regular contact with any child under the age of 18, or whether the offender is expecting to have a baby or live with someone who is pregnant. If the answer is yes to any of those questions, the offender is required to provide appropriate details.

At the conclusion of the induction, the responsible officer will sign a witness statement confirming that they have conducted an induction interview with the offender.[6]

Responsibilities of the Probation Service

It is first necessary to discuss the responsibilities of the responsible officer and the Probation Service generally before turning our attention to the offender.

<u>Responsibilities under statute</u>

As discussed above, the responsible officer must make any arrangements that are necessary in connection with the requirements imposed by the order, and promote the offender's compliance with those requirements.[7]

In exercising those functions, the responsible officer must also ensure, as far as practicable, that any instruction given or requirement imposed by them is such as to avoid:

---

6 This witness statement is compliant with s.9 of the Criminal Justice Act 1967.

7 Sentencing Act 2020, s.214(2); s.300(2).

- any conflict with the offender's religious beliefs,
- any conflict with the requirements of any other court order to which the offender may be subject, and
- any interference with the times, if any, at which the offender normally works, or attends any educational establishment.[8]

Responsibilities under the contract

As part of the contract, the Probation Service will generally state that they (i.e. the responsible officer):

- will attend all appointments on time,
- treat the offender in a fair and respectful manner, with due regard for their needs (considering the individual circumstances of the offender and offer support as appropriate),
- respond to the offender's needs and agree to work with the offender to reduce risk,
- keep and maintain secure records about the offender to help the Probation Service make decisions about them and their progress.

Perhaps most significantly, the Probation Service's responsibilities will normally outline that they will take action, where necessary, if the offender does not comply with their sentence.

8 ibid, s.214(4); s.300(4).

Responsibilities of the Offender

As noted above, the contract signed by the offender, and the Induction Pack, makes clear what the responsibilities of the offender are during the currency of an order. In addition, the offender will be subject to statutory obligations. We shall discuss these in turn.

Responsibilities under statute

To begin with, it is important to refer to a statutory duty imposed on an offender.

Duty to keep in touch

In respect of both community orders, and suspended sentence orders, the offender is obligated to "keep in touch with the responsible officer in accordance with any instructions the responsible officer may give the offender from time to time."[9] This obligation is enforceable as if it were a requirement of the community order, or a community requirement of a suspended sentence order.[10]

"Keep in touch" will undoubtably require the offender to notify the Probation Service of any changes to contact details, including telephone number. The Probation Service will generally specify a time period in the contract as to when this must be done by. We discuss briefly below the requirement to obtain permission before changing residence. If, however, an offender becomes homeless or has no fixed abode, the requirement to "keep in touch" will also include a requirement to inform the Probation Service of this change of circumstance.

---

9 ibid, s.215(2); s.301(2). In respect of suspended sentence orders, such a requirement only exists if the suspended sentence order imposes one or more community requirements.

10 ibid, s.215(3); s.301(3).

An interesting question arises as to how the "keep in touch" requirement interacts with an offender's wish to go on holiday (whether in the UK or outside). An offender subject to a community order or suspended sentence order will be obligated to complete any requirement therein and must keep in touch with their responsible officer when doing so. To take a holiday may result in an offender missing an appointment, and thus be liable for breach. There is nothing in law that requires an offender to obtain either the responsible officer's or the court's permission before travelling away on holiday. However, to travel without first informing the responsible officer may amount to a breach of the requirement to keep in touch, and may also result in breach action should an appointment be missed. It is therefore advisable that the provision of holidays is discussed with the offender at the initial appointment, including the actions an offender must take. This open discussion will allow both parties to understand their responsibilities. Most commonly, upon such a request, the responsible officer can, in essence, suspend the supervision of the offender, and their requirements under the order for the period of time they are on holiday before they then return, and the requirements resume.

The extent to which the "keep in touch" requirement can be enforced was evident in *Richards v National Probation Service.*[11] In that case, the offender was sentenced to three months' imprisonment, suspended for 12 months. The offender was ordered to undertake 100 hours of unpaid work. As part of his induction appointment, the offender signed a contract with the Probation Service by which he agreed to abide by the terms of that contract. Two particular paragraphs of that contact were relevant to the Divisional Court, namely:

> (5) If I know I cannot keep an appointment in advance, I must inform my supervising officer as soon as possible, giving the reason.
>
> (6) Every failure to comply with these rules (or any other instructions as part of my order) will be treated as

[11] [2007] EWHC 2108 (Admin).

> unacceptable, unless my supervising officer decides otherwise. If I believe the failure is acceptable, I must provide the reason and supporting written evidence to my supervising officer, within seven days of the failure, for their consideration. My supervising officer will then decide if it is acceptable.

The offender failed to attend an unpaid work requirement but notified his responsible officer that he was not able to attend due to an employment commitment. The responsible officer requested evidence in accordance with para 6 of the agreed terms, above. The offender failed to provide such evidence within that period, and the responsible officer commenced breach proceedings against the offender.

Following legal arguments in the magistrates' court, the offender admitted the breach and the suspended sentence order was activated. The offender then appealed to the Divisional Court by way of case stated. On appeal, the offender submitted that whilst the responsible officer can require the offender to keep in touch, they cannot require the provision of evidence after the fact. The Probation Service, on the other hand, contended that such a requirement to provide evidence was part-and-parcel of the duty to keep in touch.

Lord Justice Thomas provided the judgment of the Court. At [24], his Lordship explained:

> a responsible officer is entitled to set conditions that require, as paragraph 5 did in this case, the offender to inform the officer in advance if he knows he cannot keep an appointment to do work. It seems to me that that plainly must fall within the words "keep in touch". It also seems to me that it would be entirely reasonable, and within what Parliament intended, that the officer could require that information to be in writing and to be supported by some third party evidence.

His Lordship continued:

> It follows, therefore, that where a Probation Officer requires an offender to inform him in advance of an appointment for which there is a good reason why he cannot attend and provide that information in writing together with supporting documentation, it is a reasonable requirement well within [the duty to keep in touch].[12]

However, his Lordship would distinguish this position from the situation where the Probation Service independently specified that evidence was to be provided after the event. His Lordship would explain:

> It cannot be right that [duty to keep in touch] can be read as enabling the responsible officer to request the information *ex post facto*, though, as is clear from what I have said, if the request is to provide the information in advance and a concession made to providing it later, that would be acceptable for the reasons I have given.[13]

In summary, therefore, it is perfectly proper for a Probation Service to require an offender to notify them in advance of a failure to comply, and that could include a requirement that this notice was to be in writing and with the provision of supporting documentation. However, an independent requirement to provide evidence following an apparent breach cannot be regarded as a requirement to keep in touch; it is simply a requirement to provide evidence.

Duty to obtain permission before change of residence

In addition, the offender has a duty to obtain permission before changing residence.[14] Such permission may come from the responsible officer or the court. This obligation has effect as if it were a requirement imposed

---

[12] ibid, [25] (Thomas LJ).

[13] ibid, [26] (Thomas LJ).

[14] Sentencing Act 2020, s.216(2); s.302(2).

by the court order.[15] The duty to obtain permission before changing residence is discussed in full in Chapter 11 in the context of applications to amend orders.

Responsibilities under the contract

Under the contract, an offender will be asked to agree that they will:

- Treat staff and other people on Probation in a fair and respectful manner. Fair and respectful will generally mean that the offender does not use offensive, discriminatory, abusive, threatening, aggressive or violent words/ behaviour during any Probation appointment, or activity.

- Engage with the agreed sentence plan, review progress being made and discuss openly what help can be provided to prevent reoffending/ discuss barriers to that goal.

- Respect the privacy of others during the order.

- Notify the Probation Service of any change in contact details or circumstances (e.g. becoming homeless).

- Permit the Probation Service to visit the offender at their home address.

- Be on time for appointments and carry out all reasonable instructions given.

- Notify the Probation Service as far in advance as possible if the offender knows that they will be unable to attend a scheduled appointment. The Probation Service will generally dictate the period of time within which the offender must do so. In addition,

[15] ibid, s.216(3); s.302(3).

the Probation Service will likely dictate that if the offender is unable to provide evidence of their failure to attend prior to the missed appointment, that they must do so within five working days of the absence.[16]

The contract will likely state that a breach of any of these responsibilities can result in breach of the order. However, it is important to note that the circumstances in which a breach can be initiated appear somewhat limited. As will be discussed in Chapters 6 and 7, a Probation breach may arise in two circumstances:

- Where the offender has failed to comply with a requirement of an order (which includes the duty to keep in touch, and a duty not to change residence without prior permission); or

- Where the offender has been convicted of a subsequent offence during the currency of a community order, or has committed an offence during the operational period of a suspended sentence order.

The law only makes provision for those two circumstances. Should the offender conduct themselves in a way that is inappropriate, but not in such a way that amounts to a breach of the requirements of an order, or results in a criminal offence, there is technically no power to breach the offender. For example, the contract states that the offender must treat Probation staff with respect. A failure to do so cannot result in a breach unless the offender has committed a criminal offence in doing so, or has breached a requirement of the order.

Take for example an offender, subject to a suspended sentence order, who sends their responsible officer a text message which is grossly offensive. This text message alone, whilst it may breach the contract agreement,

---

16 As discussed above, the Divisional Court in *Richards v National Probation Service* [2007] EWHC 2108 (Admin) suggested that a failure to provide evidence within five working days is capable of amounting to a failure to "keep in touch".

cannot itself amount to a breach of the community requirements of an order. Unless a liberal interpretation is given to the statute, the text message also cannot be treated as a failure to keep in touch.[17] The text message may amount to a criminal offence of malicious communications.[18] However, unless and until that matter progress to a criminal charge and ultimate conviction, the offender equally cannot be breached for their conduct. The options, therefore, appear limited.

Changing the facts of this example slightly: suppose the offender is attending an unpaid work requirement and conducts himself in an offensive and abusive manner. As a result of his conduct, the supervisor of the unpaid work requirement tells the offender to leave the site of the unpaid work. The supervisor then marks the offender's compliance for that unpaid work appointment as "attended but failed to comply". Equally, suppose during an RAR session, the offender conducts themselves in an inappropriate way such that the responsible officer, or provider of the RAR session, considers their conduct to be unacceptable and terminates the session. In this instance, they are likely to mark the offender's attendance as either "unacceptable absence" or "attended but failed to comply". In both examples, the offender's conduct, in not treating staff with respect, *can* amount to a breach of the order. In both instances, the record that the offender is marked as "unacceptable absence" or "attended but failed to comply" is a breach of the requirements of the order.

It would seem, at first blush therefore, that the offender can only be in breach where they are engaged in an appointment or activity. Returning to the first example, however. Could it be argued that the offender, in sending an offensive text message to their responsible officer has failed to "keep in touch" in accordance with ss.215(2) and 301(2) of the Sentencing Act 2020? On a literal interpretation, the answer would be no. This is on account that the offender has not failed to "keep in touch".

---

[17] See below.

[18] See, for example, s.1 of the Malicious Communications Act 1988 and s.127 of the Communications Act 2003.

In fact, they have done exactly that, but not in an appropriate way. However, reading the provision as a whole, there is an argument that the offender's conduct could breach the duty to keep in touch. The requirement could be interpreted as being circumstance or situation based.

It will be worth quoting the statute verbatim at this point; ss.215(2)[19] and 301(2)[20] state: "The offender must keep in touch with the responsible officer *in accordance with any instructions the responsible officer may give the offender* from time to time." (emphasis added)

It might be said that, on a generous interpretation of the statute, where an offender acts in an abusive or disorderly manner, they are not keeping in touch "*in accordance with any instructions the responsible officer*". Given the contract agreement, and the instructions in that agreement that the offender must behave in a certain manner, the provision could be read in any case as to say that the offender must (e.g.):

- "keep in touch with the responsible officer in a respectful manner"
- "keep in touch with the responsible officer in a non-offensive manner"
- "keep in touch with the responsible officer in a non-discriminatory manner", and so on.

Whilst this may be a generous interpretation of the statutory provision, it would ensure that offenders cannot act in an unsavoury way towards those responsible for their supervision without repercussions. Such a generous interpretation would likely be in accordance with Parliament's intentions that the offender is statutorily obliged to act in the manner

19 In respect of community orders.

20 In respect of suspended sentence orders.

befitting of someone serving a sentence in the community and being instructed by the responsible officer whilst doing so.[21]

Therefore, whilst the contract may state that the offender can be subject to breach proceedings for failing to comply with any aspect of the contract, the matter is not that straightforward. Without a generous interpretation of the provisions of the Sentencing Act 2020, there does not appear to be any such power in the Sentencing Act 2020. Without a broad interpretation, the various responsibilities covered in the contract agreement are not specified in the Sentencing Act 2020 as having the effect of being a "requirement" of an order.[22]

In summary, without an alternative provision providing such power or without a broader interpretation given to the meaning of "keep in touch", there does not technically appear to be any authority to breach an offender in circumstances where they do not act in accordance with their contract agreement.

Summary

This Chapter has covered the involvement of the Probation Service following the imposition of court orders. In this Chapter, we have discussed:

- The process following the imposition of a community order or suspended sentence order, including the induction appointment.

- The contract agreement signed by the offender and responsible officer and the sentencing goals and objectives set out in that agreement.

---

[21] Though, it may still struggle to overcome the judgment in *Richards v National Probation Service* [2007] EWHC 2108 (Admin).

[22] As the duty to keep in touch is (see ss.215(2) and 301(2)).

- The induction pack and the various documents considered and reviewed by the responsible officer and the offender as part of the induction appointment.

- The responsibilities on the responsible officer in statute to make the necessary arrangements and to promote the offender's compliance with the requirements, and their responsibilities under the contract.

- The responsibilities of the offender in statute, including a duty of the offender to keep in touch with their responsible officer, and their responsibilities under the contract.

- The enforceability of the offender's conduct.

PART TWO

PROBATION BREACHES

CHAPTER FOUR

GETTING AN OFFENDER TO COURT AND ISSUES OF BAIL

Introduction

In order for an offender to be brought before a magistrates' court or the Crown Court, there is a set procedure within Schedules 10 and 16 to the Sentencing Act 2020. When considering a probation breach, an advocate must ensure that the offender is lawfully before the court and the relevant procedure has been complied with.

This procedure is premised on the basis that the responsible officer is of the opinion that the offender has without reasonable excuse breached a requirement of a community order, or breached a community requirement of a suspended sentence order. This procedure is also relevant where the offender is to be brought before the court in respect of an application by the Probation Service to amend or revoke a community order/ suspended sentence order.[1]

Key provisions

The relevant procedure is provided in the Sentencing Act 2020, as such:

- Breach of Community Orders: Schedule 10.
- Breach of Suspended Sentence Orders: Schedule 16.

1 See Chapters 10 and 11.

Part 32 of the Criminal Procedure Rules (CrimPR) 2020 is also of assistance.

This chapter shall also briefly discuss getting an offender to court for commission of further offences during the currency of a court order. Such discussion is brief on account that it does not require action from the Probation Service; an offender will be brought before court for the new offence in the ordinary course of events, and will then be dealt with for the court order as part of that. The relevant discussion in this chapter will be committing the new offence, and the court order, to the Crown Court for sentence.

In addition to getting an offender to court, it is important for advocates to be able to deal with the question of bail should the proceedings not finalise at their first occurrence. This is dealt with at the end of the chapter.

Procedure for breach proceedings

The procedure for getting the offender to court is identical in respect of both community orders and suspended sentence orders, and can be stated as such:

1. A warning must first be provided to the offender.

2. The offender must be referred to an enforcement officer to consider the case.

3. Should the enforcement officer consider that the offender should be "breached", they should obtain a summons from a magistrates' court or the Crown Court to secure the attendance of the offender at court, or seek a warrant for the offender's arrest in the first instance.

Procedure for applications to amend or revoke

Where the Probation Service seek to have the court amend or revoke an order, or a requirement of an order, they must apply to the court to summons an offender or issue a warrant to ensure their attendance.

In respect of an application made by an offender, r.32.3(2) of the Criminal Procedure Rules (CrimPR) 2020 states that where the offender wants the court to exercise any power it has to revoke or amend an order, the offender must:

- apply in writing, explaining why the order should be revoked or amended; and
- serve the application on, the court officer, the responsible officer or supervisor, and as appropriate, the person affected.

This Chapter shall now focus on the procedure for getting an offender to court in respect of breach proceedings. The use of summons and warrants remains relevant, of course, for any application by the Probation Service for revocation or amendment. The chapter shall then consider the position on bail.

Warnings from the responsible officer

Where the responsible officer is of the opinion that the offender has without reasonable excuse breached either a requirement of a community order, or a community requirement of a suspended sentence order, they *must* either:

- Give the offender a warning,[2] or

[2] Sentencing Act 2020, Schedule 10, para 6(3)(a); Schedule 16, para 6(3)(a).

- Refer the matter to an enforcement officer.[3]

Where the responsible officer gives any such warning, they must record that fact.[4] In practice, this means that such records are held on the *N-Delius* system, and must be sent by post to the offender's registered address. In the Crown Court, such warnings will also be uploaded to the Digital Case System (DCS) and will be accessible to all involved in the case.

Content of warning

Any warning given by the responsible officer must include:

- A description of the circumstances of the breach,
- A statement that the breach is unacceptable, and
- A warning that if the offender again breaches a requirement of the order within the next 12 months, the offender will be liable to be brought before a court.[5]

The Probation Service uses a template form to complete the warning which includes all relevant details required by para 6(4). The warning letter also states the offender has the opportunity to explain their reason(s) for failing to comply, and provides a date upon which the offender must supply acceptable supporting evidence (normally five working days). The warning letter also provides the details of the responsible officer, and the date of the offender's next appointment.[6]

---

3 ibid, Schedule 10, para 6(3)(b); Schedule 16, para 6(3)(b).

4 ibid, Schedule 10, para 6(5); Schedule 16, para 6(5).

5 ibid, Schedule 10, para 6(4); Schedule 16, para 6(4).

6 Warnings letters are discussed in further detail in Chapter 5.

Discretionary and obligatory nature of referrals

It is evident from the wording of the legislation that the responsible officer has both a power (discretionary) and a duty (obligatory) in respect of the referrals to the enforcement officer.

The nature of this power and duty was explored by the Divisional Court in *West Yorkshire Probation Board v Robinson and Tinker.*[7] This case concerned the interpretation of para 4 of Schedule 12 and para 5 of Schedule 8 to the Criminal Justice Act (CJA) 2003. Those provisions are similar, though not identical, to the new provisions in the Sentencing Act 2020.[8]

In providing the judgment of the Court, Thomas LJ would explain the position as such:

> The plain purpose of the legislation is to give the probation officer a single discretion, so that he does not always have to bring the offender to court but can give a warning. But that one warning having been given, there is no discretion.[9]

Where the responsible officer is so satisfied with any explanation given, and supporting evidence, they will not refer the matter to the enforcement officer. Rather, they will attempt to reengage the offender and support them towards their next appointment. However, where the responsible officer is not satisfied with such explanation or evidence, they must either refer the matter to the enforcement officer, or (if this is the first warning within a 12-month period) continue to engage with the offender.

---

7 [2009] EWHC 2468/ 2517 (Admin), (2010) 174 J.P. 13.

8 As such, there is no reason to believe the authority does not remain of assistance today.

9 *Robinson and Tinker* (n7), [14] (Thomas LJ).

Choices available to the responsible officer

In summary, therefore, a responsible officer has three choices available to them:

1. Where the responsible officer considers that the offender has breached a requirement of the order, and has not been issued such a warning in the previous 12 months, they *may* give the offender a warning.[10]

2. Where the responsible officer considers that the offender has breached a requirement of the order, and has not been issued such a warning in the previous 12 months, but they consider that the breach is serious enough that breach proceedings should be initiated, they *may* refer the matter to an enforcement officer.

3. Where an offender has been given a subsequent warning within the previous 12 months in respect of the same order, beginning with the date on which the first warning was given, the responsible officer *must* refer the matter to the enforcement officer.[11]

It will be worthwhile to discuss the factors relevant to options one and two above.

Factors relevant to the decision of the responsible officer to warn or refer

In *West Yorkshire Probation Board v Cruickshanks*,[12] Leveson LJ would justify the mandatory nature of subsequent warnings and breach proceedings on the basis that they are "clearly intended to establish public confidence in the sentence by demonstrating that the orders cannot be

[10] Sentencing Act 2020, Schedule 10, para 6(3); Schedule 16, para 6(3).

[11] ibid, Schedule 10, para 6(2); Schedule 16, para 6(2).

[12] [2010] EWHC 615 (Admin), [2011] 1 W.L.R. 2154.

ignored with impunity."[13] In light of that quotation, the responsible officer must consider the seriousness of any alleged breach on their decision as to whether they should warn or refer.

As a starting point, a responsible officer will recall that there are a variety of reasons why individuals fail to comply with the requirements of a court order. Because of this, a responsible officer must ensure that an offender is provided with an opportunity to explain their failure to comply and offer any reasonable excuse.[14] It is clear, however, that responsible officers should avoid condoning repeated non-compliance.

Key point

In considering the seriousness of any such breach and whether to refer the matter to an enforcement officer as a matter of discretion, a responsible officer is likely to consider:

- The nature of the failure to comply, including whether they consider as a matter of professional judgement the failure to be serious, gross, wilful or fundamental to the order.

- The personal and domestic circumstances and responsibilities of the offender, including their physical and mental health, their employment and caring responsibilities, and any other factors that may impact on the offender's ability to comply.

- Whether the offender presents a risk of serious harm, or a likelihood of re-offending based upon their engagement and correspondence with the responsible officer. The more likely that such risk cannot be managed in the community, the more likely a referral should be made.

---

13 ibid, [14] (Leveson LJ).

14 Normally within five working days of the failure.

It is worth remembering the variety of circumstances by which an offender may be in breach of their probation order:

- Failing to comply with the requirements of a community order[15] or community requirements of a suspended sentence order.[16] For example, a failure to attend the unpaid work requirement or failure to comply with rehabilitation activity requirement (RAR) Days.

- Failing to attend general probation appointments or keep in touch with their responsible officer.[17] The requirement to keep in touch is enforceable as if it were a requirement of a community order,[18] or a community requirement of a suspended sentence order.[19]

- Failing to obtain permission before changing residence.[20] Where a community order or suspended sentence order is in force, the offender must not change residence without the permission of the responsible officer, or a court.[21] The requirement to first obtain permission is enforceable as if it were a requirement of a community order,[22] or a community requirement of a suspended sentence order.[23] A failure to notify that the offender is now of no fixed abode (NFA) may also result in a warning or referral.

---

15 Sentencing Act 2020, Schedule 10. See Chapter 6.

16 ibid, Schedule 16. See Chapter 7.

17 ibid, ss.215 and 301.

18 ibid, s.215(3).

19 ibid, s.301(3).

20 ibid, ss.216 and 302.

21 See Chapter 11.

22 Sentencing Act 2020, s.216(3).

23 ibid, s.302(3).

- Failing to comply with the Probation Contract Agreement.[24] This contract requires the offender to, for example, treat staff and other people on Probation in a fair and respectful manner, and notify the Probation Service of any changes to contact details including telephone numbers.

Effect of warning

In *West Yorkshire Probation Board v Robinson and Tinker*,[25] the Divisional Court dealt with the question of what the effect is on a first warning which was followed by a second warning and subsequent referral to an enforcement officer.

In brief, the issue was:

- Can the Probation Service still breach the offender in respect of the matter subject to a first warning, or

- Is the effect of the first warning to prevent the Probation Service from breaching an offender for that matter?

Thomas LJ was clear that he could not "see the basis for an argument" that the warning in respect of the first breach "had the effect of spending or dealing with that breach".[26]

His Lordship continued to explain that the statutory provision:

> ...does not say in any way (and I cannot construe the schedule as saying in any way) that the warning operates as a punishment. It is simply a warning that, if thereafter the

[24] See Chapter 3 for more details on the Contract and the generous interpretation required to find a breach in these circumstances alone.

[25] *West Yorkshire Probation Board v Robinson and Tinker* [2009] EWHC 2468/ 2517 (Admin), (2010) 174 J.P. 13.

[26] ibid, at [14] (Thomas LJ).

> offender complies and 12 months elapses, he may not be subject to having an information laid immediately, and the probation officer has a further discretion. In no way is the effect of the warning to expunge the initial breach. When a matter comes before the court, the court, in exercising its powers under paragraphs 8 and 9 respectively in each of the schedules, looks at the full circumstances of each breach in determining what to do, assuming, of course, that in respect of each breach it has determined that there has been a breach without reasonable excuse.[27]

What this means in practice is that where an offender has been the subject of a first warning, prior to the referral to the enforcement officer, the offender can be breached for both:

- the matter that gave rise to the original warning, and
- the subsequent matter that led to the statutory referral to the enforcement officer.

Duty of responsible officer following warning or referral

The issuance of a warning to an offender, or a referral to an enforcement officer, does not absolve the responsible officer of their duties in respect of the offender.

Responsible officers should continue to maintain contact with the offender and encourage continued engagement and compliance with the order. They should make every effort to re-engage the offender and ensure that any risk is appropriately managed. This will include engaging with other agencies, such as the police, multi-agency public protection arrangements (MAPPA), and social services as necessary.

---

27 ibid.

Role of the enforcement officer following referral

Where an offender has been referred to the enforcement officer by the responsible officer, the enforcement officer must:

(a) consider the case, and

(b) where appropriate, cause an information to be laid in respect of the offender's breach of the requirement.[28]

Considering the case

An enforcement officer is not obligated to lay an information before a magistrates' court or the Crown Court. They need only do so where it is "appropriate" to do so.[29]

Key point

In considering whether it is appropriate, the enforcement officer will consider such matters as:

- The offender's alleged breaches of the order, including the nature and number of such breaches,
- The offender's compliance with other aspects of their community requirements (e.g. where a community requirement includes unpaid work, their completion of that order to date),
- The offender's general compliance with Probation appointments, including planned office visits and telephone appointments, and

[28] Sentencing Act 2020, Schedule 10, para 7; Schedule 16, para 7.

[29] ibid, Schedule 10, para 7(b); Schedule 16, para 7(b).

- Any information relating to the offender's attitude or motivation to the court order.

The enforcement officer is responsible for quality assuring the breach material prepared by the responsible officer. This includes ensuring that the paperwork is correct and that the enforcement officer has sufficient evidence to proceed with the breach.

Having reviewed the information provided, the enforcement officer must decide whether to proceed with the breach on the basis presented by the responsible officer, or request additional information/ documents.

Laying information

Where the enforcement officer does consider it appropriate to proceed with breach proceedings, they must lay an information of such breach before the relevant court.[30]

Act of laying information

The act laying of an information is identical to the procedure adopted by the Crown Prosecution Service when laying an offence before the court.[31] This is expressly provided for in r.32.2(2)(a) of the CrimPR 2020 which states "a reference in those rules [r.7.2 and r.7.4] to an allegation of an offence included a reference to an allegation of failure to comply with an order" and "a reference to the prosecutor included a reference to the responsible officer or supervisor".

[30] See below "Choosing the proper venue".

[31] See r.7.2 and 7.4 of the Criminal Procedure Rules (CrimPR) 2020.

Simply, the act of "laying information" is the giving of a statement which informs the relevant court of the offence (for these purposes, breach of the requirements of an order).

In general, an information need not be in writing, unless the statute requires otherwise. As will be discussed below,[32] where the court issues a summons, there is no requirement for the information to be in writing. However, where the court issues a warrant in the first instance, the Sentencing Act 2020 requires the court to be first satisfied that any such information is "in writing and on oath".[33]

Timing of laying of information in suspended sentence order cases

In *West Yorkshire Probation Board v Cruickshanks*,[34] the Divisional Court was faced with the question of when an information must be laid before the court in respect of a suspended sentence order. Must the information be laid during the currency of the order (i.e. before the expiration of the operational period), or may it be laid at a later date?

Lord Justice Leveson explained:

> ...in my judgment, paragraph 7(2) of Schedule 12 to the 2003 Act does require an information to be laid before the end of the operational period of the sentence although there is no requirement that it be heard before then.[35]

Whilst this case was concerned with the interpretation of para 7(2) of Schedule 12 to the CJA 2003 Act, there is no reason as to why the

---

[32] See "Getting an offender to court".

[33] Sentencing Act 2020, Schedule 10, paras 8(2) and 9(2); Schedule 16, paras 8(2) and 9(2).

[34] *Cruickshanks* (n12).

[35] ibid, [15] (Leveson LJ).

provisions under the Sentencing Act 2020 should not be interpreted in the same way.

In short, therefore, in order to enforce a breach of community requirements of a suspended sentence order, the information must be laid before the magistrates' court or Crown Court *before* the expiration of the operational period. However, as the judgment makes clear, there is no requirement for the breach to be heard by the court *before* the expiration of that period.[36] This judgment makes practical sense where, for example, an offender fails to answer the summons and is, to use a colloquialism, "on the run" for a period of time beyond the expiry of the suspended sentence order. In such a situation, should the court not be permitted to deal with the breach, the court would essentially be toothless and the offender would have a certain way of avoiding action.

Timing of laying of information in community order cases

The Divisional Court in *Cruickshanks* did not explicitly deal with the issue of when an information must be laid in cases involving breach of the requirements of a community order. Lord Justice Leveson acknowledged that although the language in relation to the issue of a summons for non-compliance is effectively the same between suspended sentence orders and community orders, a difference exists between the expiry of those orders.[37]

Under the Sentencing Act 2020, a magistrates' court or the Crown Court can issue a summons or warrant against an offender where "a community order... is in force".[38] An information must, therefore, be laid whilst the

---

36 Though, see Chapter 7 for a discussion on the restriction of the court's powers in dealing with any such breach following expiration of the suspended sentence order.

37 *Cruickshanks* (n12), [16] (Leveson LJ).

38 Sentencing Act 2020, Schedule 10, paras 8(1) and 9(1).

community order remains "in force". By s.220(1) of the Sentencing Act 2020, a community order ceases to be in force:

(a) at the end of the end date (see s.209); or

(b) if later, when the offender has completed any unpaid work requirement imposed by the order.

The effect of s.220(1)(b) is that a community order could theoretically continue ad-infinitum until the unpaid work requirement is complete.[39]

Key point

The position is, therefore, as follows:

- Where the community order *does not* impose an unpaid work requirement, an information must be laid before the recorded end date of the community order.
- Where the community order *does* impose an unpaid work requirement, an information must be laid before the completion of the unpaid work requirement.

In a similar vein to suspended sentence orders, there seems no requirement for the breach proceedings to be heard before the end date of the community order, so long as the breach proceedings were *initiated* whilst the order remained in force. The Sentencing Act 2020 does not prescribe any such restriction on the court's ability to deal with such breaches. Further, the Sentencing Act 2020 appears to envisage the situation where breach proceedings are heard following the expiration of

39 *National Probation Service v Blackfriars Crown Court* [2019] EWHC 529 (Admin), [2019] 2 Cr. App. R. (S.) 24 [19] (Leggatt LJ). See also *National Probation Service v Forbes* (Sheffield Crown Ct, 23 October 2023) [29] (The Recorder of Sheffield, HHJ Richardson KC).

a community order. Paragraphs 10(10)[40] and 11(7)[41] of Schedule 10 to the Sentencing Act 2020 both provide that where a court is re-sentencing an offender for an offence, the court must revoke the community order "if it is still in force". Those paragraphs do not say that it is impermissible to deal with an offender where the order is no longer in force; rather, they simply provide that where the order is no longer in force, there is no order to revoke. However, that does not appear to prevent the court from dealing with the offender for any such breach.[42]

Choosing the proper venue

It is important that the enforcement officer and the advocates know the proper venue (or "correct court") at which an information should be laid. In summary:

- Where the order was made by a magistrates' court, the information must be laid before a justice of the peace.[43]
- Where the order was made by the Crown Court, the information must be laid before the Crown Court.[44]

This conforms with the Court of Appeal's judgment in *R v H*[45] which dealt with the former law under the Criminal Justice Act 2003. However, as is evident from paras 7 in Schedules 10 and 16 to the Sentencing Act 2020, the position has not changed. In *H*, HHJ Wait, giving the judgment of the Court, explained that:

---

40 Which deals with the powers of a magistrates' court following breach.

41 Which deals with the powers of the Crown Court following breach.

42 Though see Chapter 6 for the restriction on the court's powers in dealing with expired community orders.

43 ibid, Schedule 10, para 7(b)(i); Schedule 16, para 7(b)(i).

44 ibid, Schedule 10, para 7(b)(ii); Schedule 16, para 7(b)(ii).

45 [2013] EWCA Crim 2115.

> These paragraphs make it clear the summons for breach must be issued by the court that imposed the sentence and that same court must deal with the breach where the breach is one of requirement. Only the magistrates' court has power to deal with the breach of requirements of a suspended sentence imposed by that court. The power of the Crown Court to deal with a breach of a suspended sentence imposed by the magistrates is limited to breach by conviction of a further offence during the operational period…[46]

To highlight the importance of summoning an offender to the correct court, it is worth considering the facts of *R v H*:

- The offender was re-sentenced by a magistrates' court for breach of a community order to three months' imprisonment, suspended for 12 months with a community requirement of 100 hours unpaid work.

- The offender was summonsed to attend a magistrates' court for breaches of the community requirement by failing to attend his unpaid work requirement.

- The offender appeared before the Crown Court charged with an offence unlawful wounding,[47] for which he pleaded guilty on the day of trial. The offence was committed prior to the imposition of the suspended sentence order.[48]

- The offender was sentenced by the Crown Court to 30 months' imprisonment, and the suspended sentence order was activated in part (two months' imprisonment) consecutive in respect of the breach of requirement.

---

[46] ibid, [27] (HHJ Wait).

[47] Offences Against the Person Act 1861, s.20.

[48] Therefore, there was no breach by commission of a further offence.

On appeal, the Court of Appeal ruled that the activation of the suspended sentence order was unlawful. The Crown Court had no power to deal with the breach of the community requirements on account that it was a magistrates' court order, and the offender had been summonsed to the magistrates' court and not the Crown Court. In light of that, the two-month consecutive sentence of imprisonment was quashed.

Advocates must, therefore, be alive to the case of *H* and the necessity to ensure that the court only deals with matters that it has the power to do so.

General Rule on court centre

In addition to identifying the proper court (i.e. magistrates' court or Crown Court), the court venue should also be considered. The general rule is prescribed in para 5.12.6 of the Criminal Practice Directions (CrimPD) 2023. It provides that:

> Proceedings in respect of alleged breaches of community and other orders should be dealt with at the court centre where the order was imposed.

This procedural direction reflects the fact that, in general, the court making the order will have supervision over the offender and that order (i.e. an order made by the Crown Court will be supervised by the Crown Court). This is so unless the court makes a direction to the contrary.[49] When sentencing an offender to a community order or a suspended sentence order, the Crown Court may include a direction that the order is to be subject to magistrates' court supervision.[50] Where such a direction is made, a magistrates' court may deal with the offender as

[49] Specifically, the Crown Court; a magistrates' court has no such power to issue a direction on supervision to another court.

[50] Sentencing Act 2020, ss.211 and 297.

appropriate and thus an information can be laid before a magistrates' court.

Where, however, no such direction exists, the offender must be dealt with by the Crown Court for any breach and any such information must be laid before the Crown Court.

Summoning to a different court centre

Paragraph 5.12.7 of the CrimPD 2023 provides an exception to the general rule that proceedings should be brought at the court centre where the order was imposed. Paragraph 5.12.7 provides:

> An exception to that general rule should be made, however, to reflect the application of CrimPR Part 1, the overriding objective, and the key listing principles above, where the defendant's home is significantly closer to another court with jurisdiction to determine the proceedings, in which case those proceedings should be brought in that court.

Where this exception is utilised, the enforcement officer must explain the reasons for choosing a particular court centre to lay the information.[51]

Breaches reserved to particular judges

In addition, any breach may be reserved to a particular judge or a particular Crown Court centre. This will be detailed on the original order. Paragraph 5.10.13 of the CrimPD 2023 provides that:

> Allocation or committal for sentence following breach (such as a matter in which a community order has been made, or a suspended sentence passed), should, where possible, be

[51] CrimPD 2023, para 5.12.7.

listed before the judge who originally dealt with the matter or, if not, before a judge of at least the same seniority.

It is therefore important to confirm that any such breach proceedings are listed before the correct court centre or judge.

Key point

Where a breach has been listed before a court or judge different to that specified in the order, the advocate is advised to contact the Listings Office to advise whether the case has been unreserved by that judge or centre. If such is not possible due to particular time constraints, the matter should be raised with the judge for whom the case is listed before.

Information laid in the wrong court

It is possible that the above discussion is missed by the enforcement officer. It may not be clear, for example, that a particular judge or court centre has reserved breaches to themselves. Equally, there may have been an oversight that a direction of supervision by a magistrates' court was made by the Crown Court. What is the situation, then, where proceedings have been instituted in the "wrong court"?[52]

Should an advocate realise that proceedings have been initiated in the wrong court, they should make that known as soon as practicable to the Probation Service and to the Listings Office, as appropriate. Should the matter progress to the first hearing, the advocate should inform the judge of the issue. Realistically, there are two options open to the court:

[52] The use of the words "wrong court" is simply to demonstrate that an offender should have more properly been summonsed to another court or court centre.

- First, the court may request that the Probation Service summon the offender to the correct court. In essence, the Probation Service will be asked to withdraw the summons for the wrong court, and then asked to re-summon the offender to the correct court. If this course of action is taken, it is essential that any breaches are not put to the offender. Should the breaches be put and either denied or admitted, it then becomes inappropriate (and legally challenging) for the summons to be withdrawn and the offender to be summonsed elsewhere. Where breaches have been put, the second option should be preferred.

- The second option is for the case, once the offender has been summonsed to one court centre, to be transferred to another court centre. The CrimPD 2023 prescribes rules as to the situation where a case should be transferred from one court centre to another. Whilst it is not clear from the provisions whether the power of transfer applies to breach proceedings, there is no clear restriction against it. Paragraph 5.11.11 of the CrimPD 2023 states that "Transfer between courts on the same circuit must be agreed by the Resident Judges of each court, subject to guidance from the Presiding Judges of the circuit." This direction relates to cases on the same circuit; for cases on a different circuit, para 5.11.13 reads: "Transfer of sentences between circuits must be agreed between the Resident Judges of the courts concerned." A breach proceeding is not technically a "sentence" unless a breach is admitted and the offender is to be dealt with for the breach. It is questionable as to whether this provision therefore can apply. However, practice and experience would show that courts can, and do, transfer breach proceedings between centres. For example, an offender who fails to surrender to a summons in Derby, but is arrested on a community bench warrant in North Wales would generally be expected to be dealt with in Derby.

Where the matter requires an adjournment to return the offender to the proper venue, the court should consider the issue of bail.[53]

Lastly, where there is a dispute as to the proper venue in the Crown Court, para 5.12.7 of the CrimPD 2023 states that such dispute should be determined by the relevant Presiding Judges.

Getting an offender to court

Where an information has been laid before the magistrates' court, the justice of the peace may either:

- issue a summons requiring the offender to appear at the place and time specified in it, or
- if the information is in writing and on oath, issue a warrant for the offender's arrest.[54]

The same power exists in respect of an information laid before the Crown Court.[55] In the Crown Court, any such summons or warrants will also be uploaded to the Digital Case System (DCS) and will be accessible to all involved in the case.

Issuing a summons or warrant in Breach cases

Before we turn to the procedure for returning an offender to the court, it is first important to distinguish the use of a summons from a warrant. It is a decision for the responsible officer as to whether they should seek a summons or a warrant in the first instance; though it is important to note that ultimately the decision lies with the court.

[53] See below "Questions of Bail".

[54] Sentencing Act 2020, Schedule 10, para 8(2); Schedule 16, para 8(2).

[55] ibid, Schedule 10, para 9(2); Schedule 16, para 9(2).

Summons

A summons is used in circumstances where the Probation Service has an address registered in respect of the offender. The summons is a formal legal document requiring the attendance of the offender at a particular location (e.g. Sheffield Crown Court). The summons will state (inter alia):

- The court issuing the summons and the date of such issuance,
- The name, date of birth and address of the offender,
- The nature and date of sentence for the offence subject to the supervision of the Probation Service,
- The dates and details of the alleged breaches, and
- The date, time, and location that the offender must attend for the breach to be considered.[56]

Summons are standard forms used by the courts and are issued by either a Justice of Peace or an Officer of the Crown Court.

Key point

If an offender was sentenced before one Crown Court centre (e.g. Nottingham), but was summonsed to appear before another Crown Court centre (e.g. Derby), the advocate for the Probation Service should assess whether the offender ought to be summonsed to the same centre as sentenced them. In many cases, breaches of court orders will be "reserved" to particular judges or Crown Court centres; it is essential that practitioners are alive to this potential issue.

[56] See Chapter 5 for more details on the contents of a summons.

Warrants

A warrant in the first instance, also known as a "community warrant", is largely used in circumstances where the offender is of no fixed abode (NFA) or their whereabouts are presently unknown. In addition, where the responsible officer considers that the offender's risk of re-offending or the risk of harm to others cannot be managed in the community, they may consider a warrant in the first instance, over a summons, to be more appropriate.

Should a warrant be granted, it will state (inter alia):

- The court issuing the warrant and the date of such issuance,
- The name, date of birth and address (if known) of the offender,
- The nature and date of sentence for the offence subject to the supervision of the Probation Service,
- The dates and details of the alleged breaches,
- The details of the information laid by the enforcement officer, and
- A statement to the relevant Police Force to arrest the offender and bring them before the relevant court within 24 hours of their arrest.[57]

As is evident from the statutory language, a warrant requires proof that the information laid is "in writing and on oath".[58] The warrant issued will confirm that such information was laid in compliance with these requirements.

---

57 See Chapter 5 for more details on the contents of a warrant.

58 Sentencing Act 2020, Schedule 10, paras 8(2)(b) and 9(2)(a); Schedule 16, paras 8(2)(b) and 9(2)(b).

It is important to note that in the Crown Court, a community warrant can only be issued by a Crown Court judge. This is unlike a summons which can be issued by an Officer of the Crown Court. For this reason, the Probation Service will require the case to be listed before a Crown Court judge[59] to allow for the warrant to be granted.

<u>Issuing a summons or warrant in review cases</u>

A specific provision exists where the offender is subject to a community order or suspended sentence order which is subject to the review of the court in accordance with ss.217B[60] or 293A(1)[61] of the Sentencing Act 2020. These Orders were discussed in further detail in Chapter 2.

In brief, a summons or warrant can be issued by a magistrates' court or the Crown Court where:

- a community order is in force, or a suspended sentence order is subject to review,
- on a review hearing, a magistrates' court or the Crown Court is of the opinion that the offender has without reasonable excuse breached a requirement of the community order or suspended sentence order, and
- the court has not yet dealt with the breach.[62]

---

59 Which includes both Circuit Judges and Recorders.

60 In respect of community orders.

61 In respect of suspended sentence orders.

62 Sentencing Act 2020, Schedule 10, para 9A(2); Schedule 16, para 9A(2).

The summons or warrant must direct for the return of the offender to the court that issued the summons or warrant.[63] The power to deal with an offender as part of a review hearing is dealt within in Chapter 11.

Issuing a summons or warrant in cases where a further offence has been committed

This Chapter is concerned with getting an offender to court where they are in breach of the requirements of a community order or suspended sentence order. However, a power also exists in respect of both the magistrates' court and the Crown Court where the offender has been convicted of an offence during the operational period of a suspended sentence order.

Circumstances when to use the power

Generally, an offender will be before the court for the new offence in any event; the offender will be dealt with for the suspended sentence at the same time as the new offence. There is, therefore, no separate procedure required for getting the offender to court. However, there are two common circumstances where a necessity to get the offender to court is required:

- First, an offender may have been convicted of an offence committed during the operational period of a suspended sentence order, but the sentencing court was not aware of the existence of the suspended sentence order. This may be as a result of an oversight by the parties, or an error/ omission on the offender's antecedent record. In this instance, the offender will not have been dealt with appropriately and the court will want them to be returned for the suspended sentence order.

[63] ibid, Schedule 10, para 9A(3); Schedule 16, para 9A(3).

- Second, an offender may have been convicted of a further offence in Scotland or Northern Ireland (neither of whom has the power to deal with the suspended sentence order). In these circumstances, the Sentencing Act 2020 provides that the relevant court in Scotland or Northern Ireland must "give written notice of the conviction to the appropriate officer of the court by which the suspended sentence was passed."[64]

Getting the offender to court

Simply, where the offender:

- has been convicted in the United Kingdom of an offence during the operational period of a suspended sentence order, and

- has not yet been dealt with in respect of the suspended sentence order

the magistrates' court[65] or Crown Court[66] may issue a summons requiring the offender to appear at the place and time specified in the summons, or issue a warrant of their arrest. In the Crown Court, the offender can be summonsed or arrested under a warrant to attend at any Crown Court centre.[67] However, in the magistrates' court, the summons or warrant must direct the offender to appear or be brought before the court by which the suspended sentence was passed.[68]

Interestingly, there is no requirement for the Probation Service to lay an information in writing and on oath before the Crown Court can issue a

---

[64] ibid, Schedule 16, para 18.

[65] ibid, Schedule 16, para 20(2).

[66] ibid, Schedule 16, para 19(2).

[67] ibid, Schedule 16, para 19(3) (though they should be directed to attend at the court centre that imposed the suspended sentence order.

[68] ibid, Schedule 16, para 20(4).

warrant (unlike in cases of breach of the community requirements of an order considered above). However, in the magistrates' court, a summons cannot be issued under para 20 except on the laying of information, and a warrant cannot be issued except on the laying of information in writing and on oath.[69] This is so unless the magistrates' court is acting in consequence of a notice provided under para 18 (i.e. a notice from a court in Scotland or Northern Ireland).[70]

An equal power exists in respect of commission of further offences during the currency of a community order. Where the applicable court intends to revoke and resentence an offender for the community order, they must first summon the offender to the court.[71] Where an offender fails to appear on a summons in such a case, the applicable court may issue a warrant for their arrest.[72]

Returning an offender to the magistrates' court

The procedure for returning an offender to the magistrates' court depends on a variety of factors. The procedure differs for community order and suspended sentence orders. The following discussion should be read with regard to the discussions had above in respect of the CrimPD 2023.

Returning an offender for breach of a community order

Where a summons or warrant is issued in the magistrates' court in respect of a breach of a community order, that summons or warrant must direct that the offender appear or be brought before a magistrates' court.

---

69 ibid, Schedule 16, para 20(3).

70 ibid.

71 ibid, Schedule 10, paras 23(3) and 25(3).

72 ibid, Schedule 10, paras 23(4) and 25(4).

In general, an offender must be returned to any magistrates' court acting in the local justice area in which the offender resides, or, if it is not known where the offender resides, the offender's home local justice area.[73]

There are two exceptions to this general rule, and they apply in the following alternate circumstances:

- Where the community order imposes a drug rehabilitation requirement (DRR) which is subject to review, the offender must be returned to the magistrates' court responsible for the DRR,[74] or

- Where the community order qualifies for special procedures for the purposes of section 217A,[75] the offender must be returned to the magistrates' court that made the order.[76]

Returning an offender for breach of a suspended sentence order

In returning an offender to the magistrates' court for breach of a suspended sentence order, the general rule is that an offender must be returned to any magistrates' court acting in the local justice area in which the offender resides, or, if it is not known where the offender resides, the offender's home local justice area.[77]

---

73 ibid, Schedule 10, para 8(3)(b).

74 ibid, Schedule 10, para 8(3)(a).

75 See Chapter 2.

76 Sentencing Act 2020, Schedule 10, para 8(3)(aa).

77 ibid, Schedule 16, para 8(3)(b).

However, where a suspended sentence order is subject to review,[78] the offender must be returned to the magistrates' court responsible for that suspended sentence order ("the responsible court").[79]

Returning an offender to the Crown Court

Unlike the magistrates' court, the procedure for returning an offender to the Crown Court is more straightforward. This is because, unlike the magistrates' court, there is only one singular Crown Court (with multiple Crown Court centres).

In accordance with that basic principle of law, a summons or warrant must simply direct an offender to appear/ be brought before *the* Crown Court.[80] However, the summons should normally be returnable to the Crown Court centre that issued the summons.[81]

Committals for sentence

There may be circumstances where an offender appears before a magistrates' court in respect of a breach of a requirement of a Crown Court order. In a similar vein, where a defendant is charged with further offences during the currency of a Crown Court order, they will appear before a magistrates' court for their first appearance. In both instances, the issue becomes how the magistrates' court deals with the proceedings, and whether the case is transferred to the Crown Court.

Where the Crown Court passes a community order or suspended sentence order, the Court may direct that the order is to be subject to

---

78 ibid, s.293.

79 ibid, Schedule 16, para 8(3)(a).

80 ibid, Schedule 10, para 9(3); Schedule 16, para 9(3).

81 Criminal Practice Directions 2020, para 5.12.6.

magistrates' court supervision.[82] Where such a direction is made, the magistrates' court is in a position to deal with any breach(es) or conviction(s) for further offences. The following states the powers available to the magistrates' court when a direction for magistrates' court supervision is made.

Where an offender appears or is brought before a magistrates' court and it is proved to the satisfaction of the court that the offender has breached a requirement of a Crown Court community order, or a community requirement of a Crown Court suspended sentence order, the magistrates' court may commit the offender to the Crown Court (either in custody or on bail).[83]

Equally, where a Crown Court community order or suspended sentence order is in force in respect of an offender, and the offender is convicted of an offence by a magistrates' court, the magistrates' court may commit the offender to the Crown Court (either in custody or on bail).[84] It is, however, also necessary for the magistrates' court to separately commit the offender for sentence to the Crown Court for the further offence too;[85] the power to deal with the breach does not extend to the new offence unless separately committed.[86]

Naturally, even where the Crown Court has directed that the matter can be dealt with by a magistrates' court, the magistrates' court may still

---

82 Sentencing Act 2020, s.211 (in respect of community order supervision) and s.297 (in respect of suspended sentence order supervision).

83 ibid, Schedule 10, para 10(3); Schedule 16, para 10(3).

84 ibid, Schedule 10, para 24(2); Schedule 16, para 11(2).

85 ibid, ss.14-20. The most commonly used provisions are s.14 (where the magistrates' court consider their sentencing powers to be inadequate) and s.20 (where the magistrates' consider their powers to be adequate but consider it would appropriate for the Crown Court to deal with this offence alongside other offences).

86 See *R v De Brito* [2013] EWCA Crim 1134, [2014] 1 Cr. App. R. (S.) 38; *R v Harrison* [2022] EWCA Crim 1031 [16] (Jeremy Baker J); *R v Begg* [2023] EWCA Crim 102 [5] (Coulson LJ).

commit the offender to the Crown Court. Whereas, if no such direction has been made, the magistrates' court must commit the offender to the Crown Court (in custody or otherwise).

Information to be provided on a committal for sentence

Where the offender is convicted of an offence, and falls to be dealt with for breach of the suspended sentence order, the CrimPR 2020 prescribes the information that must be provided in a given case.[87] The information varies dependent on whether:

- the magistrates' court commits the offender to the Crown Court for sentence in respect of the suspended sentence order,
- the magistrates' court or the Crown Court adjourns the case to be dealt with by another court, or
- the magistrates' court or the Crown Court deals with an offender for a suspended sentence order.

In the first two circumstances, the court officers must, as soon as practicable, arrange the transmission from the convicting to the other court of a record of any relevant:

- certificate of conviction,
- magistrates' court register entry,
- decision about bail, for the purposes of section 5 of the Bail Act 1976,
- note of evidence,

[87] Criminal Procedure Rules 2020, r.28.10.

- statement or other document introduced in evidence,
- medical or other report,
- representation order or application for such order, and
- interim driving disqualification.[88]

In respect of the third circumstances, the court officers must, as soon as practicable arrange the transmission from the convicting to the other court of notice of the convicting court's order, and the recording of that order at the other court.[89]

Offender fails to appear

Where a summons has been issued, requiring an offender to appear before a magistrates' court or the Crown Court, and the offender does not appear in answer to the summons, the relevant court *may* issue a warrant for the offender's arrest.

This power applies in both the magistrates' court[90] and the Crown Court.[91] This power also exists in respect of community orders and suspended sentence orders subject to review.[92]

---

88 ibid, r.28.10(1)(a)(ii); r.28.10(2)(a).

89 ibid, r.28.10(1)(b); r.28.10(2)(b).

90 Sentencing Act 2020, Schedule 10, para 8(4); Schedule 16, para 8(4).

91 ibid, Schedule 10, para 9(4); Schedule 16, para 9(4).

92 ibid, Schedule 10, para 9A(4); Schedule 16, para 9A(4).

Applying for a warrant

In the first instance

In circumstances where an offender fails to attend, it is common for the advocate on behalf of the Probation Service to apply for a warrant for the arrest of an offender. Alternatively, the court may issue a warrant of its own motion.

> **Key point**
>
> Where an advocate intends to apply for a warrant, it is advisable that they consider the following:
>
> - The address stated on the summons, and whether it accords with the most recent address registered on the *N-Delius* system.
> - The offender's previous record for failing to surrender.
> - The nature of the failure to comply, and whether the offender has previous instances of breach of the order.
>
> These factors may prove valuable where the warrant is opposed.

Subsequent hearings

Where an offender attends at court and the matter is not finalised on the first occasion, the court may either simply adjourn the proceedings or remand the offender on bail/ in custody. In the former case, the offender is not under a duty to return to the court; the summons discussed above applies only to the hearing that is referred to in the summons. The court, therefore, cannot issue a bench warrant for the arrest of the offender (unlike if the offender had been remanded on bail).

The court also cannot issue a community bench warrant unless the court hears evidence on oath that the offender had been told to attend at court on that particular date (i.e. similar to a summons). This may apply where, for example, the responsible officer gives evidence on oath that they informed the offender to attend at court. If that is the case, the court may issue a community warrant for the arrest of the offender.

The key takeaway from this discussion is that where a case does not finalise at the first hearing, the court is strongly advised to remand the offender on bail pending further hearings.

Opposing a warrant

The power to issue a warrant for the offender's arrest is a discretionary power; the court is not obligated to do so. The decision as to whether to issue such warrant will largely depend on the accuracy of the details held by the Probation Service.

For example, where there is evidence that the Probation Service may have the incorrect address on their system, and thus the summons was issued to the incorrect address, the court may choose not to issue a warrant for the offender's arrest. This may occur where the offender has been in contact with the Probation Service and notified them of a change of address post the issuance of said summons, or where the offender is legally represented, and their advocate is aware of a different address to that stated on the summons. Equally, a warrant may be opposed where there is evidence to suggest that the offender did not, or could not have, received the summons. Alternatively, whilst the summons may have been received, it may be the case that the offender is unable to attend court on that given date due to illness or other difficulties.

Key point

It is essential for any practitioner defending in a probation breach to have full information relating to why an offender may not be in attendance at Court. The advocate should have a record of the offender's address (from previous dealings or from their instructing solicitors) and/or any details (and evidence) relating to their health or other circumstances which mean that they are unable to attend at court. Without such details, or assistance from the Probation Service, a defence advocate will struggle to oppose any application for a warrant for the offender's arrest.

No Bail Act offence

Importantly, where an offender is returned to the court, having been arrested on a warrant following a failure to answer to a summons, there is no offence for failing to surrender that can be put to the offender.[93] This is because the offender was not "released on bail in criminal proceeding" at the time, and thus there was no duty to surrender under the Bail Act.[94]

Whilst there is no direct authority on this point, a comparison can be drawn to the case of *R v Gourde.*[95] In this case, the offender had been released under investigation for conspiracy to rob and was subsequently issued with a postal requisition to attend court for his first hearing. The offender failed to attend, and a warrant was issued for their arrest. The offender was arrested and brought before the court. They were subsequently sent to the Crown Court for trial in respect of the conspiracy offence and pleaded guilty at the Plea and Trial Preparation Hearing. In the Crown Court, the offender was also dealt with for the failure to surrender at the first hearing; he was sentenced to a consecutive term of three months' imprisonment for the Bail Act offence.

On appeal to the Court of Appeal, the offender argued that no Bail Act offence had been committed as the offender was never on bail in the first place (they were released under investigation and due to appear by way of postal requisition). The Court of Appeal agreed and quashed a conviction for failing to surrender. Mrs Justice May would explain simply

93 Bail Act 1976, s.6.

94 ibid, s.3(1).

95 [2021] EWCA Crim 824.

that the offender was not on bail for the substantive offence, and thus could not be liable for failing to surrender.[96] In a similar vein, in *R v Mizan*,[97] the Court of Appeal quashed a conviction for failing to surrender where the offender had failed to attend for a deferred sentence.[98]

By analogy, therefore, where an offender is due to be appear before the court on a summons for breach of an order, they are not on bail. Therefore, they cannot be susceptible to a Bail Act offence if they fail to surrender.

A question may arise of: "well, what is the punishment if they fail to attend?" The simple answer is that the court is empowered to issue a community bench warrant for the offender's arrest and, if the matter does not finalise at the first hearing, may remand the offender into custody pending the next hearing. In short: the punishment for failing to answer a summons is the risk of being arrested on a warrant, and the risk of being thereafter remanded in custody.

Some exceptions

An offender who fails to appear having been granted bail on an adjournment is, however, susceptible to a Bail Act offence.[99] Likewise, where the court grants a community warrant backed for bail in the first instance, and the offender fails to appear having been arrested and then released on bail by the police, the offender will fall to be dealt with for the failure to surrender.

---

[96] ibid, [10] (May J).

[97] [2020] EWCA Crim 1553, [2021] 1 Cr. App. R. (S.) 51.

[98] By s.5(4) of the Sentencing Act 2020, where the court makes a deferment order, it cannot, on the same occasion, remand the offender (in custody or on bail).

[99] See below "Questions of Bail".

Key point

As will be discussed below, it is strongly advised that where an offender is not dealt with for a breach at the first hearing, and an adjournment is required, that the offender be remanded on bail (unconditional or otherwise). This will ensure that there is a consequence in circumstances where the offender fails to surrender.

Timeframe

It will be helpful to identify the general timeframe in proceeding with any breach. These timeframes are not provided in statute, but reflect best practice within the Probation Service:[100]

- The responsible officer should notify the offender of the potential for breach action **within two working days** of the alleged breach/ failure to comply occurring.
- The offender should then be provided with **up to five working days** to provide an explanation and appropriate evidence to demonstrate that the alleged breach/ failure to comply was reasonable.
- If no evidence is produced, or the produced evidence is not accepted, the responsible officer must refer the matter to the enforcement officer, and provide them with all details relating to the breach, **within eight working days** of the alleged breach/ failure to comply occurring.
- The enforcement officer must then consider the case and, if they consider it appropriate to progress this matter to court, should

[100] See Ministry of Justice and HM Prison and Probation Service, 'Enforcement of Community Orders, Suspended Sentence Orders and Post-Sentence Supervision Policy Framework' (2021).

lay the information before the court within two working days (**within ten working days** of the alleged breach/ failure to comply occurring).

These timeframes are designed to ensure that all probation matters are processed swiftly and efficiently.

Questions of Bail

It cannot be assumed that once an offender has been brought before the court that the case will be resolved at its first appearance. For example, a offender may appear before a magistrates' court and the magistrates' court commits the offender to the Crown Court to be dealt with. Alternatively, an offender may appear before the court and the court is not in a position to deal with the offender's case at the first opportunity.

In light of this, the court will consider the position regarding bail at the conclusion of proceedings. It is strongly advised that the advocate for the Probation Service invites the court to remand the offender on bail (conditionally or unconditionally) as opposed to simply adjourning the case. This will ensure that the offender can be dealt with if they fail to surrender on the subsequent occasion.

Principles of bail

The ordinary principles of bail apply equally to probation breaches as they do to criminal offences. As discussed above, r.32.2(2) CrimPR 2020 provides that the rules of court apply *as if* a reference in those rules to an allegation of an offence included a reference to an allegation of failure to comply with an order. That does not mean that probation breaches are criminal offences;[101] rather, for the purposes of the rules of court, they

[101] See Chapter 1.

are treated as if they were. For this reason, the court is required to consider the issue of bail at the conclusion of each hearing.

General right to bail

All advocates will know that, subject to a small number of exceptions, a presumption in favour of bail applies. Specifically, s.4 of the Bail Act 1976 provides that the presumption in favour applies to any person who appears or is brought before a magistrates' court or the Crown Court in the course of or in connection with proceedings for the offence.[102] However, such presumption does not apply in respect of proceedings on or after a person's conviction of the offence.[103]

What is the position, therefore, where an offender is brought before the court in respect of a probation breach?

Section 4(3)(b) of the Bail Act 1976, states that the presumption in favour of bail applies to an individual who, having been convicted of an offence, appears or is brought before a magistrates' court or the Crown Court under Part 2 of Schedule 10 to the Sentencing Act 2020.[104] The legislation does not specify whether the presumption in favour of bail continues following an admitted breach, or whether it ceases at that point. In a similar vein to the presumption ceasing to apply on or after a person's conviction, it is logical to suggest that the presumption does not apply following an admission or finding of a breach.

Furthermore, it is interesting to note that there is no equivalent provision in respect of breach of community requirements of a suspended sentence order. Could this be a legislative oversight or a deliberate omission meaning that breach of community requirements of a suspended sentence order does not benefit from the presumption in favour of bail?

---

[102] Bail Act 1976, s.4(2).

[103] ibid.

[104] i.e. breach of requirement of community order.

Powers of the courts in relation to bail

The Sentencing Act 2020 is limited in respect of the powers of the courts in respect of bail. This is likely to be simply a result of the fact that breaches of orders are treated as if they were criminal offences, and are thus subject to the ordinary rules of bail. There is limited provision in the Sentencing Act for decisions on bail, however.

In summary, both Schedules 10 and 16 to the Sentencing Act 2020 provide the magistrates' court with the power to commit an offender to the Crown Court where they are alleged to be in breach of the requirements of an order, or following the commission/conviction for further offences. This power is predicated on the basis that the order was made by the Crown Court and should be dealt with by the Crown Court. When exercising that power, a magistrates' court may either remand the offender in custody or on bail.[105] These provisions largely reflect the wording of the powers of the magistrates' court when committing an offender for sentence.[106]

The is no equivalent provision for bail in the Crown Court. However, as discussed above, this is likely to be a deliberate omission on account that the general principles of bail apply in the normal way.

Bail Act offence

As discussed above when dealing with offenders who fail to appear in answer to a summons, there is no offence of failing to surrender (colloquially referred to as a "Bail Act offence"). Likewise, where the court simply adjourns the proceedings as opposed to remanding the offender, there is no Bail Act offence. This is because the offender was

105 Sentencing Act 2020, Schedule 10, paras 10(3) and 24(2); Schedule 16, paras 10(3)(b) and 11(2)(a).

106 See ss.14-20 of the Sentencing Act 2020.

not subject to bail, and under no obligation to surrender in accordance with s.3(1) of the Bail Act 1976.

However, where an offender has appeared before the courts and their case is adjourned for a period of time (e.g. to test their compliance), then the court will normally remand that individual on bail (conditionally or unconditionally). The court will identify the next date at which the offender is required to attend and will inform the offender of this in open court. Should the offender then fail to attend that stated date, they will in those circumstances have committed an offence of failing to surrender.[107]

There are two forms of Bail Act offences:

- Section 6(1): This offence applies where an offender has been released on bail and fails without reasonable cause to surrender to custody.

- Section 6(2): This offence applies where an offender has been released on bail and fails to attend at first due to having a reasonable cause, but then subsequently fails to surrender to custody at the appointed place as soon after the appointed time as is reasonably practicable.

Should the offender fail to attend as required in compliance with their general duty to surrender on bail, they commit a criminal offence, a warrant may be issued for their arrest, and they may be remanded in custody following execution of that warrant.

---

[107] Bail Act 1976, s.6.

Summary

This Chapter has covered the key processes and procedure in getting an offender to court. When considering whether the correct legal processes have been applied in getting an offender to court, consider:

- Whether a warning has been issued to the offender by the responsible officer, and a record of that fact has been made.
- Whether the enforcement officer has laid information before the relevant court.
- Whether the relevant court has issued a summons to the correct address compelling the offender's attendance, or a warrant of their arrest otherwise.
- Whether the offender has been returned to the correct court listed in the summons or warrant.

An offender who fails to attend on a validly issued summons may have a warrant issued for their arrest.

A case may not finalise at the first hearing, thus requiring the court to consider the position of bail in respect of the offender.

CHAPTER FIVE

PREPARING A BREACH CASE OR APPLICATION

Introduction

In this Chapter, we focus on the necessary preparation that goes into proceedings for a probation breach. Whether one is acting for the Probation Service, or the offender, it is essential that the advocate feels fully prepared for any hearing. This chapter guides readers through the various documents that will feature in an alleged breach and the steps necessary by an advocate in preparing for such hearing.

> **Key provisions**
>
> There are no legislative provisions specifically relevant to the preparation of a breach case. Advocates are directed to be familiar with the provisions in Schedules 10 and 16 to the Sentencing Act 2020 as appropriate.

Our discussion shall consider each document that an advocate should expect to see in preparing a breach case, and other documents that would assist in said preparation. As part of that discussion, it will then consider what steps should be taken by an advocate prior to the hearing.

Document checklist

A Probation Breach will feature a number of documents as a minimum. There may also be additional documents provided dependent on the approach adopted by local providers.

As a minimum, advocates would expect to see:

- Summons.
- Breach warnings.
- Breach report.
- Memorandum of conviction and associated court order.
- Up-to-date record of antecedents.
- Case file (or at the least the MG5) for the original case subject to the court order.
- Pre-sentence report for the original case subject to the court order (should there be one).
- HMPPS Warrant Risk Assessment Form.
- HMPPS Suicide Risk Form.

These documents are the minimum required in order for an advocate to prepare any breach proceedings. For our purposes, and often in practice, they shall be referred to as the "Breach Pack".

In addition to the above list, however, an advocate is also encouraged to obtain the following documents:

- Induction pack and HMPPS contract.
- Any other evidence considered relevant to the proceedings.

The Induction pack and HMPPS contract should be obtainable from the Probation Service within the court centre, and any other relevant evidence separate to the Probation Service can be obtained from the Crown Prosecution Service.

We will consider each of these documents in turn.

Summons

In the previous chapter, we discussed the procedure for getting an offender to court. We discussed in detail the law relating to court summons and the obligations on parties to a case in respect of that summons.

When preparing for any breach proceedings, it will be necessary to check the accuracy of a number of matters. They include:

Personal details of the offender

Has the summons been correctly addressed? Is there any reason to believe that the address is incorrect? Perhaps the advocate has had previous dealings with the offender; in which case, the advocate should check the registered address with the Probation Service (or if defending, the instructing solicitors).

The alleged breaches:

The summons will identify what the alleged probation breaches are, e.g. "*On [DATE] you failed, without reasonable excuse, to comply with the Rehabilitation Activity Requirement of your order, in that you failed to attend, as instructed, for a Rehabilitation Activity office appointment and did not provide an acceptable explanation*".

It is necessary to check that the date and circumstances of the breach are consistent with the Breach Report (see below).

It will be the summons/warrant that is put to the offender in court (see Chapters 6 and 7). It is therefore essential that the information is accurate.

Date and time to appear

It is important to ensure that the summons states the correct date and time that the offender is due to attend before the Court. In the previous chapter, we discussed the circumstances where a warrant can be issued for the arrest of an offender where they have been issued with a summons, and they do not appear in answer to that summons.[1]

Before any such warrant can be issued, the court must be satisfied that the summons has been properly executed. The date and time of the answer to the summons must therefore be clear and accurate.

Key point

Given that the court list will only be generated the day before any breach hearing, all summons will likely be issued for 10am on that day. However, in practice, a case may be heard at any time during the court's busy list. Whilst an offender should therefore be in attendance by 10am, even if their case is not to be heard before 2pm, it is often reasonable to wait until 2pm before a bench warrant is sought.

Equally, should the case be listed at 9.30am (as seen in some court centres), a bench warrant should not be considered until the time of answer to the summons (10am) has passed.

Signature

Lastly, one must ensure that the summons has been signed by the appropriate person (either a JP or an officer of the Crown Court). This signature certifies that the summons has been properly executed and posted to the offender.

[1] Sentencing Act 2020, Schedule 10, para 8(4) and 9(4); Schedule 16, para 8(4) and 9(4)

Breach Warnings

As discussed in the previous chapter, breach proceedings may only be initiated following a singular warning (that is considered sufficiently serious/ appropriate to refer) or following the second/final warning (where it is obligatory to refer the matter). In any case which has therefore progressed to breach stage, it is expected that the Breach Pack will contain the relevant warning(s) issued to the offender.

Content of Breach Warning

A Breach Warning is a letter addressed to the offender, sent in the post to the address registered with the Probation Service. It is common for probation practitioners to notify the offender as part of their regular contact that a breach warning has been issued.

The Breach Warning will be headed either "Breach Warning" or "Final Warning" dependent on the circumstances, and will include:

- Personal details of offender (including name and address registered with the Probation Service).

- The Case Reference Number (CRN) associated with the offender and the Probation Service.

- The date of the warning.

- The details of the failure to comply (including the nature of the failure (e.g. "Failed to attend planned appointment"), the date of the failure, and the reason for the Breach Warning (e.g. "Failed to attend as instructed").

- A clear and unambiguous statement that "This failure to comply is unacceptable" with an explanation of the duties/ obligation of the offender under the terms of a court order.

- A statement explaining what the offender should do having received the Breach Warning. This advises the offender to contact their responsible officer immediately to explain their reasoning for failing to comply and to provide any supporting evidence for the failure (generally within five working days of the failed appointment). If the offender fails to provide an explanation and/or supporting evidence, it is made clear that the failure to comply will remain "as a breach of this Order".

- A statement as to what may happen should there be a further warning/breach. This includes a statement that the offender will receive a summons through the post directing them to attend court.

The Breach Warning will end with the contact details of the responsible officer, which ensures that the offender is in no doubt as to who they should get into contact with.

Once more, it is good practice to check the Breach Warnings to ensure that the circumstances of any alleged breach are consistent between them, the summons, and the breach report.

Breach report

Perhaps the most important document as part of the Breach Pack is the breach report. This is a document produced on a template form by the responsible officer for the offender.

Content of the breach report

At the top of the breach report is a summary of the alleged failure to comply. This will be a very succinct statement of the alleged breach, such as: "Failed to attend RAR appointments on 01/02/2024 and 12/02/2024. [Offender's name] failed to provide any acceptable evidence or explanation within five working days of these failures."

Following that opening summary, the breach report is broken-down into seven sections:

Section 1: "Details of the offender"

This will include the name of the offender, their date of birth, and the address and telephone number registered with the Probation Service (if any). The breach report will also identify the Case Reference Number (CRN) for the offender; this is the unique reference number attached to the offender that allows the Probation Service to identify and locate the offender on the N-Delius system.

Section 2: "Details of the responsible officer"

This will include the name of the responsible officer, the Probation Region within which they work (e.g. Yorkshire and Humberside), and their office address, phone number and email address.

Section 3: "Details of original offence"

This will include a statement of the original offence(s) (e.g. "going equipped for stealing"), the sentencing court, the date of sentence, the sentence imposed (including length of custodial period if the order was a suspended sentence), and any requirements imposed (e.g. "DRR – 12 months").

Section 4: "Amendments to the order".

This will include any previous breaches or other amendments to the order. If any, the former should identify the details of the amendment (e.g. "10 further RAR days"), the reasons for the amendment (e.g. "Breach by failing to attend scheduled RAR appointments") and the date the amendment was made.

Section 5: "Details of breach"

Section 5 is the most important part of the breach report. It provides the key information relevant to the breach and any supporting evidence. Section 5 itself is broken down into distinct sub-sections which require attention.

The first sub-section is labelled "Why is the offender in breach?"

This will include any information and appropriate analysis as to the details of the conduct or behaviour of the offender that has triggered breach action. It should include a rationale for the breach decision, detailing any reasons provided by the offender in respect of any absences of behaviour. If reasons have been provided, the responsible officer should explain why those reasons were not accepted.

The form should also detail the induction appointment of the offender (including the date and the fact that the rules and requirements of the order were explained) and whether any diversity factors have impacted on the breach.

If the relevant breach is a failure to attend, the report should ideally identity:

- The nature of the appointment missed (e.g. unpaid work)
- The date of the appointment.
- The circumstances in which the appointment was given, including the date and medium of communication (e.g. "This appointment was given on 26/01/2024 in person, and a reminder was sent via text on 27/01/2024").
- Whether an explanation / supporting evidence was provided (and if so, why it was not acceptable).

The second sub-section is labelled "What steps have been taken to prevent this breach?"

In this part, the responsible officer will identify what attempts have been made to engage and re-engage the offender. It will note whether the offender has identified any barriers to their compliance, and whether the offender has made any constructive attempts to discuss any concerns they may have in complying with the order. This part is focused on ensuring that the offender has had the opportunity to seek necessary support in completing their court order successfully.

It will also note what communications have taken place between the responsible officer/ relevant provider and the offender, and how those communications have taken place (e.g. encouraging discussions over the telephone as opposed to via letter). Any rescheduling of appointments to fit around work or child obligations will also be noted.

A common action taken by the Probation Service to prevent breaches and encourage compliance is to mark absences as "authorised". The desired effect is that the offender will feel that the Probation Service is seeking to support them and not prosecute them. The results, of course, are mixed.

The third sub-section is labelled "Compliance with the order to date".

This sub-section of the form details the offender's compliance and engagement with the requirements of their order and with general probation appointments. The form will state the total number of hours/ days/ appointments to be completed for each requirement, and the defendant's compliance thus far (e.g. for a requirement of 150 hours of unpaid work, it may read "unpaid work: 15:30 hours completed, 134:30 hours remaining"). If there are any noteworthy compliance issues, the responsible officer will state them here, for example "Curfew – During the four-week curfew, the offender committed multiple breaches/ violations by remaining out of their required residence for days at a time".

It is worth clarifying a particular issue that relates to rehabilitation activity requirement (RAR) days at this stage. It is common for an offender's Breach Report to show minimal compliance with RAR days (e.g. "0 out of 25"). Advocates should not take this figure at face value for a number of reasons:

- Where an order imposes multiple community requirements, it is common for the Probation Service to prioritise other requirements (e.g. unpaid work) over RAR. There are several reasons for this: First, some requirements, such as unpaid work, must be completed within a strict period of time (12 months). Second, as discussed in Chapter 2, an RAR should be expressed in a court order as an "up to" figure. This is because an RAR is to be directed by the Probation Service who will determine how many RAR sessions an offender should complete. That number may vary dependent on the offender's level of engagement during the currency of an order.

- An appointment may be offered to an offender as a dedicated RAR appointment, which will be recorded without difficulty on the N-Delius system. However, an appointment may involve features of an RAR nature (e.g. Thinking Skills), but will not be recorded or registered as an official RAR session. In light of that, an offender may have completed several RAR-style sessions, but those sessions may not be recorded on the Probation Service's system.

For those reasons, an advocate should feel confident in explaining to the court why an offender may have complied well with other aspects of their order, but not with RAR.

Regarding overall compliance with probation appointments, the form will detail:

- Appointments offered

- Appointments attended and complied (also called "Attended OK")

- Appointments attended but failed to comply

- Appointments not attended but recorded as an acceptable absence ("AA")[2]

- Appointments not attended and recorded as an unacceptable absence ("UA").

These notes on compliance are as of the date of the breach report (which can be found at the end of the form). As discussed later in this chapter, it is essential that an advocate obtains an update on this compliance prior to the hearing.

Key point

Ensure that the numbers add up! Whilst it obvious to state, it is common for the number of appointments offered to not correlate with the number of appointments attended, acceptable and unacceptable absences etc. If the numbers do not add up, check with the Probation Service in court to see if there are any appointments marked as "not yet recorded".

This sub-section will also identify any previous breaches and any enforcement action taken.

The final sub-section is labelled "Has the risk of serious harm changed since the order was imposed?"

As detailed in Chapter 3, as part of the induction process, the responsible officer will assess the risk posed by the offender. This risk is generally detailed in a pre-sentence report (should there be one). However, the responsible officer is also responsible for monitoring this risk and amending such risk as is necessary.

2 The Breach Report will often detail on what basis the Probation Service consider any such absences to be "acceptable". If it does not, the advocates should clarify on what basis any absence is marked as acceptable.

The question posed in the breach report requires a "Yes" or "No" answer from the responsible officer. If the answer is "No", there is no further detail required. However, if the answer is "Yes", the responsible officer must indicate the risk of serious harm assessed at the outset of the order, and a summary of any changes to this, including any evidence for this. Further details on the offender's relative risk can be found in the Warrant Risk Assessment Form (see below).

Section 6: "Recommendation"

This sub-section of the form details what the responsible officer recommends should happen as a consequence of the breach proceedings. In Chapters 6 and 7, we consider the powers available to the court upon breach of the requirements of a community order and breach of the community requirements of a suspended sentence order.

The form offers the responsible officers three options:

- "The order is continued"
- "The community order is revoked and the offender be re-sentenced"
- "Custody is activated for the suspended sentence"

Whichever option the responsible officer chooses, they must provide detailed comments to support their recommendation. Whilst the decision on breach is a matter for the court, the Court of Appeal has been clear that the view of the Probation Service should be given considerable weight and one of the key questions at any breach proceedings is: Does the Probation Service feel its work with the offender may usefully continue?[3]

---

3 *R v Aslam* [2016] EWCA Crim 845, [2016] 2 Cr. App. R. (S.) 29 [13] (HHJ Cooke QC).

A full explanation for the recommendation made is therefore essential.

Unless the breach is particularly serious, or the offender's level of compliance is low, the Probation Service will commonly recommend that the order can continue. This is especially so if it is the offender's first breach. If the responsible officer recommends that the order should continue, they should also identify what action is suitable to be taken to mark the breach. The responsible officer will identify what requirements the offender is suitable to undertake (whether they be new requirements or further work on a particular requirement). For example, the responsible officer may say that an offender is unsuitable for a curfew due to domestic abuse risks, is also unsuitable for unpaid work due to their mental health, but is suitable for a financial penalty or (further) RAR days.

In addition, the responsible officer should identify the impact of custody on the offender, including any impact on accommodation, employment, health and caring responsibilities.

Key point

If the recommendation of the responsible officer is further unpaid work hours, consider how long the order has remaining and whether it is possible for the offender to complete the further hours in the time remaining. Consider whether an extension to the unpaid work requirement is necessary, or whether an extension to the end date of the community order, or the operational period of a suspended sentence order, itself is required.[4]

[4] See Chapter 11 for full details on extending the unpaid work requirement and extended court orders more generally.

Section 7: "Witness availability"

This final sub-section of the form details any dates of pre-booked leave for the responsible officer or any other witness over the next 12 weeks. This information is essential in case the alleged breaches are not accepted by the offender. Should the breaches be disputed, the responsible officer (or another member of a service provider) may be required to give evidence in a contested hearing.[5]

Much like an MG10 detailing the witness availability for a general criminal trial, Section 7 should be used to avoid any dates unavailable to the responsible officer or other witness.

Updated Breach Report

As is common in breach proceedings, a judge may choose to adjourn or defer taking action following an admitted breach in order to test the offender's compliance. Generally, where a case is adjourned, it will be done so for a minimum period of six to eight weeks (or any period the court considers appropriate). During that time, the offender will be told by the court what its expectations are (e.g. to not miss a single appointment).

It is common, therefore, for the Probation Service to be directed to produce an updated breach report. This report should focus on the time period between the date on which the case was adjourned and the return date. The updated report should provide an up-to-date account of the offender's compliance with the order (e.g. appointments attended etc).

5 See Chapter 8.

Key point

It is possible that the Probation Service may not produce an updated breach report. This may be so for a number of reasons. It is important, therefore, for an advocate to take the initiative and obtain an update personally from the probation practitioners within the court centre.

Memorandum of conviction and/ or court order

The original court order/ sentence should be included in any Breach Pack. This will identify the offence(s) for which the offender has been sentenced, the date of the sentence, and the nature of the order (including details on any requirements imposed).

One particular detail of importance is the position in respect of supervision of the particular order. As discussed in Chapter 4, it is important to ensure that the breach proceedings have been brought before the correct court centre. The court order will identify whether the case is reserved to a particular judge, or whether there is a direction for supervision by another court. If the order is silent as to this, then the case should be brought before the court centre that originally sentenced the defendant. As advised in Chapter 4, if the case appears to be before a court centre or judge different to that specified on the order, an advocate should contact Listings as appropriate.

Antecedent history

An up-to-date antecedent record for an offender is important to any breach proceedings.[6] It is possible that a defendant may have been convicted of further offences during the currency of a community order or committed further offences during the operational period of a suspended sentence order without action having been taken on those

[6] A print out from the Police National Computer (PNC) will be necessary.

orders. Alternatively, action may have been taken but the relevant order was permitted to continue. In any regard, the court must have a clear picture as to the offender's most recent antecedent history.

In addition to a recent PNC, an advocate is strongly advised to speak to a member of the CPS at court and ask for them to check whether the offender has any outstanding cases on the CPS Compass ("CMS") system.

CPS Case File / MG5

The first additional document (or collection of documents) that would be essential to any practitioner is the original case file for the offence which is subject to a court order. Alternatively, an advocate may feel able to deal with a probation breach solely with the MG5 (i.e. the police summary) for the offence.

The original case file / MG5 is valuable for a number of reasons:

- In respect of community orders, should the judge wish to revoke and re-sentence the offender, the judge will need to be provided with the facts of the original case (unless the breach judge was the original sentencing judge and recollects the facts). Without the MG5, the advocates would not be in any position to assist. The MG5 alone, however, may not be sufficient when, for example, the judge requires assistance with categorisation of the original offence.[7]

- In respect of suspended sentence orders, the Sentencing Guidelines on *Breach of a Suspended Sentence Order,*[8] identify that the court must consider whether the new offence is (i) similar in type and gravy to the offence which the suspended sentence order

[7] It often being difficult to properly categorise either culpability or harm without witness statements (including victim personal statements).

[8] Sentencing Council, 1 October 2018.

was imposed, (ii) is of a less serious nature but still requiring a custodial sentence, or (iii) is one that does not require a custodial sentence. Without the case file or MG5, an advocate could not properly assist the court with this.

If the Breach Pack does not contain the MG5 or original case file, this can be obtained from the CPS officers in court.

Pre-sentence report

Pre-sentence report for the original offence

In circumstances where the court is considering revoking and re-sentencing a community order, or considering whether it is unjust to activate a suspended sentence order, the pre-sentence report from the original offence (if any) will be of assistance. The pre-sentence report will identify the personal circumstances of the offender, the risk they posed at the time the report was drafted, and the suitability of sentencing options.

It will be useful to compare the breach report with the pre-sentence report and note any differences or changes due to the passage of time. Suppose, for example, a pre-sentence report noted difficulties that an offender may have with unpaid work, and the court imposed such a requirement anyway as part of a suspended sentence order. Now, the offender is in breach for failing to attend the unpaid work requirement and the Probation Service note that the absences are due to the difficulties identified in the pre-sentence report. This may amount to a defence to any breach action (a reasonable excuse for failing to comply) or, alternatively should any breaches be admitted, it may amount to a reason as to why it would be unjust to activate the suspended sentence order.

Pre-sentence report for the new offence

Should an advocate seek a pre-sentence report in respect of an offender who has breached the community order or suspended sentence order by committing a further offence? The answer to that question will ultimately depend on the length of time that has elapsed between the original offence which was subject to an order, and the new offence. In general, such a pre-sentence report will not be necessary as, in the majority of cases, there will have been a pre-sentence report for the purposes of the original offence. This view is supported by *The Better Case Management Revival Handbook* which states that where an offender has been convicted of a further offence during the period of a community order, or has committed an offence during the operational period of a suspended sentence order, "it will usually be sufficient to order a progress report from the supervising officer to supplement an existing PSR."[9] In light of that, advocates are encouraged to obtain an update from the Probation Service prior to the hearing,[10] or request an updated breach report.[11]

HMPPS Warrant Risk Assessment Form

A standard document included in the Breach Pack will be the Warrant Risk Assessment Form. This form details the present risk posed by the offender according to the opinion of the responsible officer for the purposes of a warrant for their arrest. This form is often overlooked by practitioners on account that its primary purpose is to assist the Probation Service when considering the execution of a warrant. However, the form

---

9 Judiciary of England and Wales, *The Better Case Management Revival Handbook* (January 2023), p12.

10 See below "Obtaining an update prior to the hearing".

11 See above "Updated Breach Report".

does hold value as presenting an important insight into the views of the Probation Service as to the risks involved with the offender.[12]

The Warrant Risk Assessment Form is devised as a tick-box exercise with an opportunity for further comment as appropriate. The responsible officer is asked to comment on the following matters:

- Is the offender subject to MAPPA procedures? "MAPPA" stands for "multi-agency public protection arrangements" and concerns arrangements that are in place between the police, probation and prison services for the management of violent and sexual offenders and terrorist offenders, in the community.[13]

- Is the offender assessed as posing a high risk of serious harm? This is a risk to both themselves and to others. There is no definition of serious harm, but should be treated in the same way as risk of harm is treated in pre-sentence reports.

- Is the offender assessed as posing a high risk of absconding? This will assist the police in understanding what resources may be required in executing the warrant.

- Is the offender particularly vulnerable? Vulnerability may arise as a result of physical or mental health conditions, or particularly difficult circumstances (e.g. victims of domestic abuse).

If the answer to any of these four questions is "Yes", any warrant for the arrest of the offender must be allocated to the police for execution as opposed to the responsible officer (though in practice, warrants will generally always be executed by the police).

---

12 See Chapter 3 for a fuller discussion on the tools utilised by the Probation Service to assess the offender's risk.

13 The establishment of MAPAA is provided for in s.325 Criminal Justice Act 2003.

The responsible officer is also asked to answer:

- Is the offender known to carry or use weapons?
- Does the offender have a history of assaulting police?
- Does the offender misuse drugs and/or alcohol?

Naturally, these questions impact on the potential concern for the safety of officers executing a warrant, but can equally be of assistance to the court when considering a potential breach and whether the risks associated with the offender can be managed in the community.

HMPPS Suicide Risk Form

The final document of relevance to the Breach Pack is the Suicide Risk Form. This form should indicate any relevant history that the offender has associated with suicide, any references made by the offender to suicide, any history of psychiatric treatment, and any knowledge of current psychiatric treatment underway.

This form is designed to assist the Probation Service, courts and other agencies to best understand what human intervention may be appropriate in the circumstances. For the purposes of breach proceedings, it will assist practitioners in understanding whether an offender can be properly managed in the community given any potential risks at play.

Induction pack and HMPPS contract

As discussed in Chapter 3, at the induction appointment with the Probation Service, the offender will be required to complete an induction checklist and a HMPPS contact. The contents of that contract are discussed in full in that chapter.

For the purposes of this chapter, the induction pack and HMPPS contract will assist advocates in understanding the terms of agreement made with the Probation Service, and the obligations on each party to the proceedings.

Please note that in certain cases, an induction pack may not be available where the initial appointment was undertaken prior to the renationalisation of the National Probation Service in December 2020. Prior to that date, practices varied and there was no guarantee an induction pack would be utilised. Given the time that has passed since such renationalisation, these limited cases will only apply to community orders that have outstanding unpaid work on them.[14]

Obtaining an update prior to the hearing

Whilst the advocates rely heavily on the Breach Report when considering the offender's compliance, their preparation must not cease with the Breach Report alone. Rather, the advocates should seek an update from the Probation Service prior to the hearing as to the offender's compliance. Advocates are also advised to speak with a member of the Crown Prosecution Service (CPS).

Obtaining an update from the Probation Service

General update

The Court will be particularly assisted to see what progress the offender has made with the requirements of the order, or their attendance at events, between the date of the Breach Report and the court hearing. It will naturally be viewed positively should an offender have re-engaged with the Probation Service in light of the breach, and the risk to their liberty. A court will be especially pleased to hear an advocate inform them that (e.g.) "since the date of the Breach Report, the offender has been offered ten further appointments and has attended all ten". Whilst not

[14] See Chapter 2 on the indefinite nature of community orders with an unpaid work requirement.

all cases may present such a positive level of re-engagement, the up-to-date compliance of an offender is a key aspect of the court's decision-making process.

The defence often suggest that the breach proceedings alone have given the necessary "shock" to an offender and that they are now, as a result, re-engaged and dedicated to complete the order imposed. Equally, an offender's continued lack of engagement will be used by the advocate for the Probation Service to demonstrate that the offender is unmotivated and the order is unworkable as a result. It is vital, therefore, that the advocates obtain a clear picture as to the offender's most up-to-date record of compliance.

Key point

When seeking an update from the Probation Service, have to hand the offender's name, date of birth and, if possible, their CRN. All of these can be found in the Breach Report. These three things will ensure that the Probation Service can swiftly find the offender on the N-Delius system and provide the advocate with a quick update.

Future appointments

As part of this update, the advocates should request details of the offender's future appointments. Should the court allow an order to continue, they will warn the offender that they must continue to comply with the order and, should they breach the order again, they may not be so lucky on the next occasion. As part of this warning, the court will generally appreciate being informed of an offender's scheduled future appointments so that the offender can be informed of them in open court. Should an offender fail to attend those named appointments, the court will have a record or a note that the offender was told, in open court, of the appointment(s).

Recall

The Probation Service will also be in a position to inform the advocate whether an offender has been recalled to prison, having been released on licence. Of course, this is naturally only applicable where the offender is serving a term of imprisonment, in addition to a community-based court order. However, given the restriction in s.225 of the Sentencing Act 2020 on the court when sentencing offenders who have been released on licence, it is of vital importance that the court knows whether an offender has been recalled.

Information from the CPS

The court will wish to know whether an offender has committed any further offences since the community-based order was imposed. This includes offences which have resulted in a conviction, and offences which have been charged.

An advocate is highly recommended, therefore, to speak to a member of the CPS in court to ascertain whether the offender has any live or outstanding cases against them. By "live" cases, we mean cases that have been charged, but not finalised. An offender's pending prosecutions can be found on a Prosecutor's PNC; however, this is not always an accurate reflection of what charges an offender presently faces.

As such, it is advisable that the advocate requests that the CPS member conducts a search on the Compass ("CMS") system for any live cases (referred to as "related cases" given that they relate to that offender). Where the offender does have outstanding/ live cases, it is advisable that the advocate obtain from the CPS:

- The Unique Reference Number (URN) for that case file.[15]
- Details of the alleged offence, including the offence name, and the date of the alleged commission.[16]
- Details of any case progression or history thus far and dates in the future (e.g. the offender has their first hearing in the magistrates' court two weeks' after the breach hearing).

Where an offender is due to appear before the court at a future date, in connection with further offences, the breach court may seek to adjourn proceedings to await the outcome of the further offences. The defence advocate may be expected to assist the court with the likely position of the offender (i.e. whether they will be pleading guilty or proceeding the matter to trial). Such information will be of assistance to the court in determining the correct course of action.

Key point

Whilst the defence advocate may garner favour in circumstances where they can assist the court with an insight into the offender's intention regarding the new offences, they should not place themselves in a difficult position. The advocate may not be privy to the case file for the new offences and is unlikely to be in a position to advise the offender on the evidence against them. For those reasons, an advocate should not feel pressured to offer an offender advice on the new offences, nor should they feel pressured to assist the court with the offender's intended plea to the new offences.

---

15 This will allow the Judge to access the case file for those new offences (should a case file exist on the Crown Court Digital Case System, Common Platform or Xhibit.

16 In cases of suspended sentence orders, the court will be particularly interested to know whether any new offence was allegedly committed during the operational period of the suspended sentence order, or whether it pre-dated that order.

Defence instructions

The above information has been largely focused on information relevant to both parties, or specifically the advocate for the Probation Service. If one is defending a potential breach, the advocate must obtain an understanding from the offender whether the breach(es) will be admitted or denied.

The former will require the advocate to consider how they may possibly mitigate any such breach, and the latter will require the advocate to identify the real issue in the case (i.e. how the offender is not in breach or has a defence to that breach).[17] Should the breach be denied, the advocate must also consider what evidence the defendant may have to support their claim. For example, suppose the defendant claims to have contacted the Probation Service to inform them that they could not attend their scheduled appointment. In this case, the advocate will want to have evidence that the offender did indeed contact (or attempt to contact) the Probation Service.

Obtaining legal aid

In many cases, an offender is unrepresented in court and an advocate will stand in to act as their counsel. In other cases, an advocate will be instructed at short notice to defend a breach where there has been no opportunity to apply for legal aid. In these instances, the defence advocate should also remember to seek a representation order in respect of the proceedings.

Scope of legal aid

The Legal Aid, Sentencing and Punishment of Offenders Act (LASPO) 2012 makes clear that the scope of the criminal legal aid scheme includes

---

[17] See Chapter 8 for contested breach hearings.

"proceedings before a court for dealing with an individual convicted of an offence, including proceedings in respect of a sentence or order."[18]

All alleged breaches of a community order or suspended sentence order, whether made by a magistrates' court or the Crown Court, will therefore fall within the scope of criminal legal aid. The Criminal Legal Aid (General) Regulations 2013[19] provides that "proceedings for dealing with an individual who is alleged to have failed to comply with an order of the magistrates' court or the Crown Court" are not to be regarded as incidental to the criminal proceedings from which they arise.[20] As a result, a new legal aid application is required.

Application for legal aid

The application for legal aid in respect of breach cases varies according to the court at which the breach will be heard.

- In a magistrates' court, the application will be subject to the Interests of Justice test and the magistrates' court means test.
- In the Crown Court, the application is subject to the Interests of Justice test only; it is not means tested.

The Crown Court has the power to grant legal aid to an unrepresented offender in circumstances where the proceedings "arise out of an alleged failure to comply with an order of the Crown Court and it appears to the court that there is no time to instruct a provider".[21] In essence, a Crown Court judge (which includes Recorders) can exercise its power to grant a representation order in breach proceedings where they consider it is in

---

18 LASPO 2012, s.14(b).

19 The Criminal Legal Aid (General) Regulations 2013 (SI 2013/9).

20 ibid, Regulation 20(2)(b).

21 The Criminal Legal Aid (Determinations by a Court and Choice of Representative) Regulations 2013 (SI 2013/614), Regulation 6(b).

the interests of justice for the offender to be represented. Should an adjournment be required, the representation order will continue to any future proceedings relating to the breach.

Final checklist

To end this chapter, it will be beneficial to provide a simple checklist of facts that every advocate should know in preparation for a breach case:

- Date and details of alleged breaches.
- Date and details of original court order, including any requirements imposed.
- Brief details of the facts of the original offence subject to the relevant court order (and categorisation for the purposes of sentence).
- Details on the offender's compliance with the requirements of the order, and general Probation Service appointments, as of the date of the breach report.
- Details on the offender's compliance with the requirements of the order, and general Probation Service appointments, as of the date of the hearing.[22]
- Details of the recommendation(s) of the Probation Service regarding the breach, including their view on the level of compliance shown by the offender ("LOW", "MEDIUM", "HIGH").[23]

22 To allow the court to see the difference in the offender's compliance between the breach and the hearing.

23 See Chapter 9 on assessing compliance.

- Details of any future scheduled appointments or events for the offender.
- Whether there are any live/ outstanding cases for the offender.

Summary

This Chapter has covered the documents necessary to prepare for breach proceedings. In this Chapter, we have discussed:

- The documents necessary for the adequate preparation of a breach case, including the breach report, summons, warnings, list of antecedents, etc.
- An advocate should be alive to any inconsistency in the paperwork, including dates or alleged breaches.
- An advocate should ensure that they seek an update from the Probation Service prior to any hearing.
- An advocate should obtain any necessary details/ information from the CPS which may assist the court.
- A defence advocate should have their lay client's clear instructions, and should, if necessary, make an application for a representation order.

CHAPTER SIX

BREACH OF COMMUNITY ORDERS AND CONVICTIONS FOR FURTHER OFFENCES

Introduction

In this Chapter, we consider breaches of community order requirements and the conviction of further offences during the currency of a community order. Unlike suspended sentence orders, a conviction for further offences during the currency of a community order does not amount to a breach of a community order. For those purposes, it is important to maintain a distinction in both procedure and language when it concerns breaches and further convictions.

Key provisions

The relevant provisions are provided in the Sentencing Act 2020, as such:

- Breach of requirement of a community order: Schedule 10, Part 2.
- Conviction of further offence during a community order: Schedule 10, Part 5.

This chapter attempts to adopt a logical sequence to breaches of a community order, and further convictions, and a structure which will be the most beneficial to practitioners. In light of that, the Chapter is broken down as such:

- Breach of requirement of a community order.

- Conviction of further offence during a community order.
- The procedure adopted at a breach hearing.
- The powers of the court following an admission/ finding of breach.

It is hoped that this structure will follow the sequence of events as it plays out in the practitioner's preparation: First they will consider whether the breach/ conviction is made out in law (the first two sections of this chapter), then they will prepare for the hearing itself (the third section of this chapter), and then they will consider what powers are available to the court (the final section of this chapter).

Let us consider each in turn.

Breach of requirement of a community order

As discussed in Chapter 2, a community order is, by its very nature, an order imposing one or more community order requirements.[1] Any failure to comply with the requirements without reasonable excuse may result in breach action being taken.

In this section, we shall discuss the pre-requisites in order to be breached for failing to comply with the community order requirements.

Conditions applicable

Before we consider the powers of a magistrates' court and the Crown Court in dealing with any such breach, it is necessary to understand the pre-requisites or conditions before any such power can be exercised.

It will be of assistance to break our discussion down into three matters:

---

1 Sentencing Act 2020, s.200(1).

1. There must be a "breach"
2. The breach must be of a "requirement of the community order"
3. The breach must be "without reasonable excuse".

We shall take each in turn.[2]

There must be a breach

The court must be satisfied that the offender has "breached" a requirement of the community order without reasonable excuse.[3] The Sentencing Act 2020 provides that any reference to "breach of a requirement" is a reference to "any failure of the offender to comply with a requirement imposed by the order."[4]

Meaning of "breach"

The reference to "failure... to comply" would suggest that an offender can only breach a community requirement by omission. However, the distinction between an act and omission is not strictly necessary. On any interpretation, an offender's conduct could be interpreted as an act or a failure to act. Take for example:

- An offender is required to attend their unpaid work requirement. They fail to attend and do not provide any explanation for their non-compliance.

---

2 We discuss this more fully in Chapter 7 in the context of suspended sentence orders. The following adopts a more streamlined approach.

3 Sentencing Act 2020, Schedule 10, paras 10(1)(b) and 11(1)(b).

4 ibid, Schedule 10, para 1(2).

- An offender is required to attend a Rehabilitation Activity Requirement (RAR). They attend, but are abusive to staff and refuse to engage.

In both examples, the offender could be said to have failed to comply (omission) or deliberately made a decision not to comply (an act). It is for that reason, it is said that the distinction is not necessary; it must simply be proven that the offender has failed to comply.

Timeframe of breach

A community order must specify a date (the "end date") by which all the requirements in it must have been complied with.[5] This end date must not be more than three years after the date of the order.[6] Any requirements imposed must therefore be completed before the end date of the order. As discussed in Chapter 2, where a community order imposes an unpaid work requirement, the community order only ceases to be in force when the offender has completed any unpaid work requirement imposed by the order.[7]

<u>The breach must be of a community requirement</u>

In order to bring breach proceedings, an offender must have failed to comply with a requirement of the community order. The Sentencing Act 2020 makes clear that a breach of a community order requirement includes:

- A failure to comply with any community order requirement imposed as part of the community order.

---

5 ibid, s.209(1).

6 ibid, s.209(2).

7 ibid, s.220(1)(b) and (3).

- A failure to keep in touch with the responsible officer in accordance with such instructions as the responsible officer may give the offender from time to time.[8]

- A failure to obtain permission from the responsible officer or court before changing residence.[9]

In chapter 3, we discussed whether a breach of the Probation Service contract could amount to a failure to comply for the purposes of breach proceedings. We concluded unless one were to take a generous interpretation of the duty to keep in touch, a failure to comply with the contract alone (e.g. inappropriate behaviour) cannot amount to a breach. We provided a detailed example in Chapter 3 to demonstrate this point, and readers are advised to return to that example.[10]

<u>The breach must be without reasonable excuse</u>

Finally, the court must be satisfied that any such breach has been committed "without reasonable excuse". The reference to "reasonable" would suggest that the test is an objective one; asking whether the reasonable person would consider an explanation for the failure to comply to be an acceptable one.

Whether there has been a failure to comply will be entirely case-and-fact specific. Common excuses provided by offenders include:

- Work commitments

---

8 ibid, s.215(2). This obligation is enforceable as if it were a community requirement imposed by the community order. (see s.215(3) Sentencing Act 2020).

9 ibid, s.216(2). This obligation is enforceable as if it were a community requirement imposed by the community order. (see s.216(3) Sentencing Act 2020).

10 Chapter 3.

- Caring responsibilities
- Physical or mental health difficulties
- Difficulties with addiction
- Difficulties with homelessness
- Difficulties in communication with Probation Service.

This list is not exhaustive, nor will any of these excuses be automatically regarded as "reasonable". The individual circumstances of any excuse must be considered and assessed by the court. If the offender claims to have a reasonable excuse, and that is not accepted by the Probation Service, a contested hearing will be required.[11]

Readers are advised to refer to Chapter 7 for a more detailed account on reasonable excuses as they apply to incapability to comply, appeals,[12] and reasonable refusals to comply with a treatment requirement.[13]

Conviction for further offences

An offender who is convicted of a further offence during the currency of a community order runs the risk that the community order is revoked and they are resentenced for the original offence.

Importantly, and unlike breach of the requirements of a community order, where an offender is convicted of further offences during the currency of a community order, the court is permitted to take no action against the offender. Furthermore, unlike breach of community order

[11] See Chapter 8.

[12] See *West Midlands Probation Board v Sadler* [2008] EWHC 15 (Admin), [2008] 1 W.L.R. 918 (also cited as *West Midlands Probation Board v Sutton Coldfield Magistrates' Court*).

[13] For the latter of which, see Sentencing Act 2020, Schedule 10, para 12.

requirements, the hearing for conviction of further offences must be held whilst the community order remains in force. It is vital to keep these considerations in mind as we proceed through this part of the chapter.

Conditions applicable

Before we consider the powers of a magistrates' court and the Crown Court, it is necessary to understand the pre-requisites or conditions necessary before any such power can be exercised. These conditions are two-fold:

1. The community order must be in force.
2. The offender must be convicted of an offence.

Community order is in force

The first requirement is different to that of breach of community order requirements.

Community order must be in force

The court only has the power to act on the conviction of a further offence where the community order remains in force. This is clear in para 22 of Schedule 10 to the Sentencing Act 2020 which states that the powers of magistrates' courts following subsequent conviction apply where "a community order ("the existing community order") is in force in respect of an offender". A similar provision is found in para 25(1) of Schedule 10 in respect of the Crown Court.[14]

[14] "where a community order is in force in respect of an offender".

Quite simply, therefore, the community order must be in force at the time an offender is dealt with for the conviction. This can produce different results, for example:

- Offender convicted of a further offence during the currency of a community order, but sentence adjourned to a date post the end date of the community order. The court no longer has the power to deal with the original offence.

- Offender committed a further offence during the currency of a community order, and pleaded not guilty to that offence. By the time the offender is found guilty of that offence after trial, the end date of the community order has passed. The court no longer has the power to deal with the original offence.

- Offender convicted of a further offence during the currency of a community order, and is sentenced on the same date. The court has the power to deal with the original offence.

In the first two examples, whilst the court cannot take action in respect of the original offence, the court can treat as an aggravating factor that the new offence was committed during the currency of the community order.

When does a community order cease to be in force?

By s.220(1) of the Sentencing Act 2020, a community order ceases to be in force:

(a) at the end of the end date; or

(b) if later, when the offender has completed any unpaid work requirement imposed by the order.

The end date must not be more than three years after the date of the order,[15] unless the order was amended to extend the length of the order.[16] A community order also ceases to be in force when it is revoked.[17]

> **Key point**
>
> The first question that should be asked, therefore, is whether the community order remains in force. Advocates should first check the end date listed on the original order. If that date has passed, the advocates should then check whether there was an unpaid work requirement imposed as part of the order. If there is such a requirement, then the advocate should check if all of the hours have been completed. If they have not, the community order remains in force. If the end date has not yet passed, advocates should consider how much longer the order has effect so as to ensure the court is fully aware of its inability to deal with the original offence should the end date expire before sentence.

Requirement of a conviction

The second requirement is perhaps a more interesting concept. The court has the power to deal with an offender where they have been *convicted* of an offence whilst the community order is in force. There are two separate concepts to play here:

- First, there must be a "conviction",

---

15 Sentencing Act 2020, s.209(2).

16 ibid, Schedule 10, para 20(1). As discussed in Chapter 11, such extension may be for no longer than six months, but may result in the end date being longer than three years. An order may only be extended once.

17 ibid, s.220(2).

- Second, the "conviction" must be during the currency of the community order.

Necessity of a conviction

The legislation is very clear in its wording for both a magistrates' court and the Crown Court: the power applies where the offender "is convicted of an offence".[18] A conviction may follow as a result of a guilty plea, or a guilty verdict following trial.

As discussed in Chapter 1, a failure to comply with the requirements of a community order, or the community requirements of a suspended sentence order is not a criminal offence. Therefore, the court cannot exercise its powers in respect of convictions for further offences where the offender is simply in breach of an order by failing to comply.

What is the situation where an individual commits a further offence but is dealt with by way of absolute or conditional discharge?[19] Section 82(2) of the Sentencing Act 2020 provides that an offence which results in an order for an absolute discharge, or a conditional discharge, will not be deemed a "conviction" for any purpose.[20] On that basis, a conviction for a further offence which has been dealt with by way of absolute or conditional discharge does not allow the court to deal with the original offence under the community order.[21]

---

18 ibid, Schedule 10, paras 22(b) and 25(1)(a).

19 Which must be distinguished from the situation where a further offence is committed during the period of conditional discharge (for which see Schedule 2 to the Sentencing Act 2020).

20 Other than the purposes of the proceedings in which the order is made, and in the case of an order for conditional discharge, any subsequent proceedings which may be taken against the offender under Schedule 2 of the Sentencing Act 2020.

21 See Chapter 7 for a more detailed discussion of absolute and conditional discharges in respect of suspended sentence orders.

Timing of conviction

What is evident from the wording in the Sentencing Act 2020 is that the offender must be *convicted* of an offence during the currency of the community order. It is not sufficient, nor is there a requirement, for the further offence to have been *committed* during the currency of the community order. This was made clear by William Davis J in *R v Kakakhan* as such:

> The position was that whilst this offence had been committed during the currency of the order, the offender had not been convicted during the currency of the order. For the court to have power to deal with him in the way the judge did require the conviction to be sustained whilst the order was current.[22]

This is distinct from the power in respect of suspended sentence orders, where the court can deal with any further offence which was *committed* during the operational period of the suspended sentence order. It is not necessary for a suspended sentence order to still be in force at the time of conviction/ sentence, provided that it has not been previously activated.[23]

The effect of this can seem somewhat absurd: Where an offender commits an offence during the currency of a community order but, for whatever reason,[24] is only convicted of said offence following the

---

22 *R v Kakakhan* [2020] EWCA Crim 1236 at [12] (William Davis J). The same conclusion was reached in *R v JR* [2022] EWCA Crim 1839 [19] (Farbey J).

23 *R v Sproul* [2018] EWCA Crim 2034; *R v Beirne* [2020] EWCA Crim 1433. See Chapter 7 for a more detailed discussion.

24 For example, where the offender pleaded not guilty and there is a delay in bringing the trial, or a delay generally.

cessation of said order, the court has no power to deal with the community order. The legislation simply does not permit it.[25]

However, when sentencing for the new offence, the court will treat the commission of the further offence during the currency of the community order as an aggravating factor.[26]

Procedure for dealing with an offender

Before we consider the powers available to the court for a breach of the community order requirements or a conviction for a further offence during the currency of a community order, we should first consider the procedure to be adopted.

Dealing with the offender at the correct court

It is important to clarify whether a magistrates' court or the Crown Court should deal with the community order following a breach of a community order requirement or further conviction. This section should be read in conjunction with Chapter 4.

Breach of community order requirements

The offender will generally be subject to the supervision of whichever court imposed the community order, whether that be a magistrates' court

[25] The Sentencing Council Guideline *Totality* (1 July 2023) states: "The power to deal with the offender depends on the offender being convicted while the order is still in force; it does not arise where the order has expired, even if the additional offence was committed while it was still current."

[26] "Failure to comply with current court orders" in the relevant Sentencing Council Guideline.

or the Crown Court. This was made clear by the Court of Appeal in *R v H*[27] where HHJ Wait, giving the judgment of the Court, explained that:

> the summons for breach must be issued by the court that imposed the sentence and that same court must deal with the breach where the breach is one of requirement. Only the magistrates' court has power to deal with the breach of requirements of a suspended sentence imposed by that court.[28]

Whilst the Court of Appeal was concerned with suspended sentence orders, it applies equally to community orders.

For that reason, breaches of community orders made by a magistrates' court can *only* be dealt with by a magistrates' court. The power of the Crown Court to deal with a community order imposed by the magistrates' court is limited to convictions for a further offence during the operational period.[29]

As discussed in Chapter 4, the position is more complicated for orders of the Crown Court. In accordance with *R v H*, where the community order was made by the Crown Court, any breaches can only be dealt with by the Crown Court. However, should the judge who made the community order include a direction that the order was to be subject to magistrates' court supervision,[30] the magistrates' court may deal with the offender in respect of the community order.

---

27 [2013] EWCA Crim 2115.

28 ibid, [27] (HHJ Wait).

29 See below.

30 Sentencing Act 2020, s.211(1). See also Sentencing Act 2020, Schedule 10, para 3(b).

Conviction for further offences

Naturally, where a community order was made by a magistrates' court, the offender will be present at that court by way of postal requisition or in police custody. This is because all criminal cases begin in the magistrates' court. The court must conduct proceedings in the usual way (i.e. taking the offender's plea). Where the community order was made by a magistrates' court, the court may deal with the original offence at the same time as dealing with the new offence.

Where the community order was made by the Crown Court, a magistrates' court has no power to deal with the original offence subject to the community order. The issue, therefore, is how does the original offence find its way to the Crown Court?

An offender may make their way to the Crown Court in the ordinary way where, for example, the further offence is indictable only or the offence is sent to the Crown Court for trial.[31] In this case, para 25(1)(a) of Schedule 10 allows the Crown Court to deal with the offence following conviction. What is the situation, however, where the defendant pleads guilty, or indicates a guilty plea to a further offence[32] and is thus "convicted" in the magistrates' court?

By para 24(2), the magistrates' court will arrange for offender to appear before the Crown Court (colloquially referred to as "committing" them to the Crown Court).[33] Where the court does so, it must send the Crown Court such particulars of the case as may be desirable.[34]

---

31 This is reflected in Schedule 10, para 25(1)(a) to the Sentencing Act 2020.

32 A summary-only or either-way offence.

33 This is different from the court's powers to commit for sentence in ss.14-20 of the Sentencing Act 2020.

34 ibid, Schedule 10, para 24(5).

If the magistrates' court chooses commit the offender to the Crown Court, they may either remand the offender in custody[35] or release them on bail until the offender can be brought before the Crown Court.[36] However, the magistrates' court may not exercise the power in para 24 unless the offender has been summoned to appear before it.[37] If the offender fails to appear in answer to a summons, the court may issue a warrant for the offender's arrest.[38]

Upon commission by the magistrates' court under para 24, the Crown Court then has the power under para 25 to deal with the offender. However, the power in para 25 only allows the Crown Court to deal with the original offence subject to the community order; the Crown Court has no power under para 25 to deal with the subsequent offence/ further conviction.[39] It is therefore necessary for the magistrates' court to separately commit the offender for sentence to the Crown Court for the further offence too.[40]

The following reflects the most likely position:

- Where the magistrates' court considers their sentencing powers to be inadequate in respect of the new offence, they will commit the offence to the Crown Court under s.14 of the Sentencing Act 2020.

---

35 ibid, Schedule 10, para 24(2)(a).

36 ibid, Schedule 10, para 24(2)(b).

37 ibid, Schedule 10, para 24(3).

38 ibid, Schedule 10, para 24(4).

39 See *R v De Brito* [2013] EWCA Crim 1134; [2014] 1 Cr. App. R. (S.) 38.

40 Sentencing Act 2020, ss.14-20. The most commonly used provisions are s.14 (where the magistrates' court consider their sentencing powers to be inadequate) and s.20 (where the magistrates' consider their powers to be adequate but consider it would appropriate for the Crown Court to deal with this offence alongside other offences).

- Where the magistrates' court considers their sentencing powers to be adequate in respect of the new offence, they will commit the offence to the Crown Court under s.20(1)(c) of the Sentencing Act 2020.

> **Key point**
>
> In practice, this means that the Legal Adviser must be alive to the issue that both para 24(2) of Schedule 10 to the Sentencing Act 2020, and ss.14-20 of the Sentencing Act 2020 must be utilised to commit both the original offence and the subsequent conviction to the Crown Court. These options are reflected in para 25(1) of Schedule 10 to the Sentencing Act 2020.

Unlike the magistrates' court, the Crown Court is not restricted to dealing only with community orders imposed by that Court. Where an offender is before the Crown Court convicted of an offence during the currency of a magistrates' court community order, the Crown Court is empowered to deal with the offender for the new offence, and the offence subject to the community order.

Procedure at court

For a full discussion of the procedure to be adopted at court, please see Chapter 7. The procedure adopted for suspended sentence orders is virtually identical to community orders.

Powers of court following breach of requirement

Having now considered the legal principles relevant to breaches of the requirements of a community order, convictions for further offences, and the procedure to be adopted at the hearing, we can now consider the powers available to the court. Readers will notice that we have separated our discussion of the powers into:

- Powers of court following breach of requirement
- Powers of court following conviction for further offence.

It will be necessary to first explain why this has been done.

Distinguishing breach of requirement from conviction

It must be made clear from the outset that the powers of the court in dealing with a breach of community order requirements is distinct from the powers of the court where an offender is convicted of a further offence. This is because a conviction for a further offence does not constitute a breach of a community order. It is for this reason that our discussion has been separated.

It will be useful at this stage to identify what those differences are:

- Where an offender is in breach of a requirement of the community order, the court *must* take action on that breach. Whereas, where an offender is convicted of a further offence whilst the community order remains in force, the court *may* take action where it is in the interests of justice to do so.

- Where an offender is in breach of a requirement of the community order, the court has a multitude of powers available to it including issuing a fine, extending the order, imposing more onerous requirements and revoke/re-sentence. Whereas, where an offender is convicted of a further offence whilst the community order remains in force, the court's only powers are to revoke the order outright or revoke and re-sentence.

Overview of powers following breach of requirement

Where a court is satisfied that the offender has breached a requirement of a community order, it must deal with the offender in accordance with paras 10(5)[41] or 11(2)[42] of Schedule 10 to the Sentencing Act. The powers are identical between both the magistrates' court and the Crown Court.

In dealing with a breach of a community order requirement, the court must do one of the following:[43]

- Order the offender to pay a fine not exceeding £2,500,
- Amend the terms of the community order so as to impose more onerous requirements,
- In particular circumstances, commit the offender to prison for a period not exceeding 28 days, or
- Re-sentence the offender for the offence in respect of which the order was made.

Reference to the court imposing a criminal courts charge[44] is to be ignored on account that from 24 December 2015[45] the sum payable was reduced to £0 (effectively abolishing the criminal courts charge).

---

41 In respect of a magistrates' court.

42 In respect of the Crown Court.

43 Sentencing Act 2020, Schedule 10, paras 10(5) and 11(2).

44 ibid, Schedule 10, paras 10(6) and 11(3).

45 As a result of The Prosecution of Offences Act 1985 (Criminal Courts Charge) (Amendment) Regulations 2015.

Court must take action

Before we consider each of these powers in turn, it is important to note that the court is obligated to take one of the actions in paras 10(5) or 11(2). The court is *not* permitted to take "no action" in respect of the breach. The court may take a combination of actions to mark the breach (e.g. the court may order a fine, and impose more onerous requirements).

No power to revoke outright

Importantly, however, there is no power on breach to revoke the community order outright; the legislation does not provide that as an option. This is unlike where an offender is convicted of a further offence. The court may only exercise its powers to revoke where an application is made to do so.[46]

Compliance with the order

The Sentencing Act 2020 is clear that in dealing with an offender for a breach, the court "must take into account the extent to which the offender has complied with the requirements of the community order."[47]

As discussed in Chapter 9, the level of compliance by the offender with their order will be used by the court to determine the appropriate penalty. For example, the Sentencing Council Guideline *Breach of a community order*[48] provides that where the offender has shown a "high level of compliance", the court should not consider re-sentencing the offender for the offence subject to the community order. Rather, the Guideline recommends imposing/adding a curfew requirement, additional RAR or unpaid work or a Band A Fine.

---

[46] See Chapter 10.

[47] Sentencing Act 2020, Schedule 10, paras 10(7) and 11(4).

[48] Sentencing Council, *Breach of a community order* (1 October 2018).

There are a number of appellate authorities where the court has considered the offender's compliance with their order when assessing which power to utilise. In *R v Webster*,[49] Hughes J would acknowledge the need to take account of the offender's compliance when dealing with a breach. His Lordship emphasised that:

> It does not however follow that there is any exact arithmetical relationship between the hours worked and the reduction in sentence which is to ensue. Moreover, it seems to us that the court is entitled in assessing the credit which is to be given for the hours worked and the extent to which the order has been complied with, to have regard to the defendant's approach to the order and the extent to which he has tried to comply with it. Provided that the sentence is measured by the original offence, it is not, as it seems to us, punishing simply for breach of the community service order to take those factors into account when assessing the credit to be given for part performance of the community sentence.[50]

This judgment is reflected in the Sentencing Guideline *Breach of a community order*, which focuses not only on the offender's numerical compliance with the order, but also on their attitude towards the order and the impact of any completed or partially completed requirements on the offender's behaviour. There are a number of authorities discussed in Chapter 7 in the context of suspended sentence orders where the Court of Appeal has afforded no reduction to offenders who, whilst completing requirements focused on rehabilitation, have learned nothing from their requirement.[51]

---

49 [2001] EWCA Crim 699.

50 ibid, [7] (Hughes J).

51 See, for example, *R v Abdille* [2009] EWCA Crim 1195, [2010] 1 Cr. App. R. (S.) 18; *R v Collins-Reed* [2012] EWCA Crim 2036, [2013] 1 Cr. App. R. (S.) 95.

In *R v Aslam*,[52] HHJ Cooke QC, giving the judgment of the Court of Appeal would explain:

> What is important at a breach hearing is: has there been any re-offending? Has risk been reduced? Does the Probation Service feel its work with the offender may usefully continue?[53]

Those questions may assist the court in determining what action to take following a finding of breach.

In the case of *R v Poulton,*[54] the offender was subject to a community order and was in breach of that order by failing to attend their unpaid work requirement. The offender was also before the court having been convicted of a further offence during the currency of the community order. To mark the breach, the sentencing judge imposed a sentence of 18 months' imprisonment for the original offence, consecutive to the new offence. The offender appealed against this part of his sentence, considering it to be manifestly excessive. Whilst the offender had performed only a few hours of the unpaid work requirement, he had complied with the supervision and Thinking Skills Programme requirements of the order. The Court of Appeal agreed and ruled that the sentencing court was required to take account of the offender's limited compliance with the order. The Court gave the offender a "modest reduction"[55] to mark his compliance; reducing the 18 months' imprisonment to one of 12 months' imprisonment and ordering it to run concurrently to the new offence.

In *R v Williams,*[56] the offender was made the subject of a community order with an unpaid work requirement. She was also ordered to pay

---

[52] [2016] EWCA Crim 845, [2016] 2 Cr. App. R. (S.) 29.

[53] ibid.

[54] [2013] EWCA Crim 1453.

[55] ibid, [12] (Griffith Williams J).

[56] [2019] EWCA Crim 1092.

compensation for the fraud she committed. The offender failed to attend two of her unpaid work appointments and was breached by the Probation Service. By the date of the breach hearing, the offender had completed 16.4 hours out of the 80 hours unpaid work. The judge re-sentenced the offender to two months' imprisonment. The offender appealed to the Court of Appeal on account that the sentencing judge erred in principle in revoking the community order and re-sentencing the offender, had failed to take a proper account of the mitigation in relation to the breaches, and had failed to consider whether immediate custody was the only sentencing option. The Court of Appeal agreed; Simon LJ ruled that:

> the sentence of immediate imprisonment at the first breach hearing in the instant case was wrong in principle. There were compensation orders in place; and the appellant was in employment, which would enable her to pay the compensation. She was of previous good character and there had been partial completion of 20 per cent of the work requirement. Furthermore, she had only breached on two occasions and there was email correspondence evidencing a continuing willingness to carry out the unpaid work requirement, albeit on terms which suited her and her employment. Significantly, the probation service was not suggesting that she should be sentenced to imprisonment. On the contrary, it suggested a fine as an appropriate sanction. The recorder's very short sentencing remarks did not address any of these points.[57]

In respect of the issue that custody was not the only option, Simon LJ explained that the sentencing judge:

> also failed to consider whether immediate custody was the only option in relation to the breaches. In our view, it was plainly not. These were breaches that called for the appellant to be brought back to court so that the consequences of her

[57] ibid, [13] (Simon LJ).

> casual and inadequate approach to the sentence could be made clear to her by a financial penalty or the imposition of additional hours of unpaid work. A sentence of immediate imprisonment was wrong in principle.[58]

The Court of Appeal substituted the term of imprisonment with a conditional discharge.

We shall now consider each power available to the court in turn; we have adopted the structure of the Sentencing Act 2020 in respect of the powers available.

Fine

The first power available is for the court to order the offender to pay a fine.[59] The fine payable by the offender cannot exceed £2,500, irrespective of the offender's financial position. A fine imposed in breach of a community order requirement is to be treated for the purposes of any enactment as being a sum adjudged to be paid by a conviction.[60]

Effect of power on community order

The effect of a fine is that the order will continue. It is important, therefore, that where the court imposes a fine the judge warns the offender that the order remains in effect, and they are obligated to continue to comply with the order.

---

[58] ibid, [14] (Simon LJ).

[59] Sentencing Act 2020, Schedule 10, paras 10(5)(a) and 11(2)(a).

[60] ibid, Schedule 10, paras 10(8) and 11(5).

Impose more onerous requirements

The next power available to the court on breach is to amend the terms of the community order so as to impose more onerous requirements.[61] The power to impose more onerous requirements includes:

- Imposing requirements not otherwise imposed, and
- Extending the duration of requirements already imposed.

Where the court imposes more onerous requirements, the court is also permitted to extend the duration of the community order generally. We shall consider these three powers in turn.

Imposing new requirements not otherwise imposed

The first option available is for the court to impose a requirement that had not previously been imposed under the community order. For this purpose, the court can impose any requirements which it could include as if the offender had just been convicted of the offence in respect of which the order was made and it were then making the order.[62]

Specifically, the court may only impose a requirement that is listed in column 1 of the community requirements table in s.201 of the Sentencing Act 2020. The list of requirements are:

- unpaid work requirement
- rehabilitation activity requirement
- programme requirement

[61] ibid, Schedule 10, paras 10(5)(b) and 11(2)(b).

[62] ibid.

- prohibited activity requirement
- curfew requirement
- exclusion requirement
- residence requirement
- foreign travel prohibition requirement
- mental health treatment requirement
- drug rehabilitation requirement
- drug testing requirement
- alcohol treatment requirement
- alcohol abstinence and monitoring requirement
- attendance centre requirement
- electronic compliance monitoring requirement
- electronic whereabouts monitoring requirement.

By way of specific note, where the court marks a breach by imposing an unpaid work requirement to a community order, the court must order a minimum of 20 hours.[63] This is different from the circumstances where the court imposes an unpaid work requirement generally, for which the minimum numbers of hours is 40.[64] However, as noted below, there

63 ibid, Schedule 10, para 13(4).

64 ibid, Schedule 9, para 2(1)(a)(i).

remains a requirement that the aggregate hours cannot exceed 300; that is unchanged by the presence of a breach.

> **Key point**
>
> The views of the Probation Service as to the suitability of requirements should be sought before the court imposes any requirement not already imposed. Ideally, the suitability of requirements should be included in the Breach Report. If no such suitability is stated, the court is advised to seek the views of the Probation Service before acting on the breach.[65]

Extending the duration of requirements already imposed

The second power available to the court is to extend the duration of any requirement already imposed. In essence, this means that the court is permitted to increase the number of hours or days imposed as part of a community order (i.e. add to the requirements already imposed).[66] For example, should a community order impose 150 unpaid work hours, the court may impose any number of further hours (up to a total of 300).[67]

Extending the duration of the community order generally

The final power available to the court, in the context of imposing more onerous requirements, is provided in para 13(1)(b) of Schedule 10. This provision states that where the court imposes more onerous requirements, it may "substitute a later date for the end date". This power

---

65 The court must not impose a requirement (or combination of requirements) unless the court is of the opinion that it is the most suitable for the offender (s.208(3) of the Sentencing Act 2020).

66 Subject to any limit imposed by Schedule 9 to the Sentencing Act 2020.

67 Practitioners should ensure that where an offender has completed, or is close to completing, two-thirds of their order, the court should not impose further RAR due to Probation Reset (see Chapter 1).

more simply means that the court can extend the duration of the community order.

Key point

Simply extending the length of the order is not a standalone option for dealing with a breach;[68] the court must first impose more onerous requirements (by adding a requirement not otherwise imposed or adding to the requirements already imposed).

There are a number of principles to note at this stage:[69]

- The maximum extension permitted is six months.[70]
- An extension may allow a community order to continue beyond the statutory maximum of three years. [71]
- There is no minimum period that the court must extend the order by.
- Once the power to extend the community order has been exercised, it cannot be exercised again by any court.[72]

---

68 This is made clear in the Sentencing Council's *Breach of a community order* guideline (1 October 2018).

69 Which are fully developed with examples in Chapter 11.

70 Sentencing Act 2020, Schedule 10, para 13(2)(a).

71 ibid, Schedule 10, para 13(2)(b).

72 ibid, Schedule 10, para 13(3). This includes where the order has previously been extended by application (Sentencing Act 2020, Schedule 10, para 20(4)).

Restrictions

Paragraph 13(5) of Schedule 10 to the Sentencing Act 2020 provides that the power to impose more onerous requirements is subject to any provision that applies to the court in making a community order as if the court were making the order. In essence, the court is restricted in the same way as the sentencing court would be when imposing the order.[73]

Effect of power on community order

The effect of imposing more onerous requirements is that the order will continue. It is important, therefore, that where the court does so, the judge warns the offender that the order remains in effect, and they are obligated to continue to comply with the order.

Commit the offender to custody

The next power available to the court is to commit an offender to custody.[74] The power to commit the offender to custody is subject to the following conditions:[75]

- the community order must qualify for special procedures,[76]

[73] For which see Schedule 9 to the Sentencing Act 2020.

[74] The power being added by Schedule 14(1), para 13(6) of the Police, Crime, Sentencing and Courts Act 2022.

[75] Sentencing Act 2020, Schedule 10, paras 10(5)(ba) and 11(2)(ba).

[76] Reference to "special procedures" simply means that the community order is subject to review in accordance with s.217A(1) (see Chapter 2 for further detail of community orders subject to such review).

- the offender must be before the court for breach of the community requirements of the suspended sentence order,[77] and
- the offender must be aged 18 or over.

Should these conditions be satisfied, the court may order the offender to be committed to prison[78] for such period as the court considers appropriate, not exceeding 28 days.[79]

The Sentencing Act also directs readers to "see also paragraph 13A". Paragraph 13A provides that no more than three orders committing an offender to custody may be made in relation to the same community order.[80] In this regard, where this power is exhausted, the court will be obligated to take one of the other actions.

Effect of power on community order

The effect of committing an offender to custody is that the order will continue. It is important, therefore, that where the court does so, the judge warns the offender that the order remains in effect, and, upon their release from custody they are obligated to continue to comply with the order.

---

77 This means that the power to commit to custody is not available where the offender is before the court for the conviction of further offences during the currency of a community order.

78 Or a Young Offender Institution in the case of a person under the age of 21 (Sentencing Act 2020, Schedule 10, para 13A(1)(a)).

79 Sentencing Act 2020, Schedule 10, paras 10(5)(ba) and 11(2)(ba).

80 ibid, Schedule 10, para 13A(3).

Re-sentence

The final power available to the court is to re-sentence the offender for the original offence.[81] Where the court re-sentences an offender, the court *must* also revoke the community order if it is still in force.[82]

Considering the matter afresh

When re-sentencing, the judge should consider the matter afresh; this means that the judge may be minded to find that the custody threshold has been passed, and immediate custody is the only option in the circumstances. However, it is essential to remember that the court *must* be satisfied that the custodial threshold has been crossed, i.e. "the offence, or the combination of the offence and one or more offences associated with it, was so serious that neither a fine alone nor a community sentence can be justified for the offence."[83]

In considering whether to re-sentence to custody, specifically, the court must have regard to the Sentencing Council's Guideline *Imposition of community and custodial sentences.*[84] This Guideline reminds practitioners that passing the custody threshold does not mean that a custodial sentence should be deemed inevitable. Custody should not be imposed where a community order could provide sufficient restriction on an offender's liberty (by way of punishment) while addressing the rehabilitation of the offender to prevent future crime. In essence, the court must remind themselves that custody should be a measure of last resort, reserved as a punishment for the most serious offences.

---

81 ibid, Schedule 10, paras 10(5)(c) and 11(2)(c).

82 ibid, Schedule 10, paras 10(1) and 11(7). See below for details on the court dealing with a breach during an expired community order.

83 ibid, s.230(2).

84 Sentencing Council, *Imposition of community and custodial sentences* (1 February 2017).

As discussed above, the offender's compliance with the community order should be taken into account when considering what action to take.

Options open to the court when re-sentencing

It is a common misconception that where the court is considering exercising its power to re-sentence, the court must make the sentence more onerous. For example, the court when re-sentencing an offender on a community order must impose either a suspended sentence order, or a term of imprisonment. This is not the case.

The court must consider the matter afresh and consider what the appropriate penalty is for the offence, irrespective of the offender's compliance with the order. Therefore, it is permissible for the court to revoke a community order, and re-sentence an offender to a further community order. Likewise, it is possible to re-sentence an offender to a penalty which is less serious than a community order (e.g. a discharge (absolute or conditional)). In many cases, the court will re-sentence the offender to a short term of imprisonment, which is commensurate with time spent remanded in custody (therefore meaning that the offender is sentenced to a term of imprisonment that has already been served). The simple notion is this: there is no requirement or expectation that the offender be re-sentenced to a more serious penalty: the full range of disposals remain available to the court.

Re-sentencing where offender previously told custody threshold not crossed

Re-sentencing to custody may cause difficulties where the first sentencing judge told the offender that the custody threshold had not been crossed. In *R v Bishop*,[85] the offender had been sentenced to a community order with an unpaid work requirement. When sentencing the offender in the first instance, the sentencing judge told the offender that the offence *did not* cross the custody threshold. It later came to light that the offender

[85] [2004] EWCA Crim 2956.

could not complete the unpaid work requirement due to ill health. The judge on the second occasion (who was different from the judge on the first occasion) took a different view; the second judge considered that the custody threshold *had* been passed. The second judge therefore re-sentenced the offender to a period of imprisonment. The Court of Appeal concluded that it was "wrong in principle" to re-sentence an offender to custody where a community order was revoked due to the ill-health of the offender.[86] Mr Justice Gibbs explained that:

> The fact is that by the time the judge came to re-sentence this appellant he was doing so against the background in which the Recorder had already made a finding on the same issue, namely the seriousness of the offence. [...] Accordingly, in our view the appellant was entitled to expect that no order would be made against him, nor sentence passed, which was inconsistent with the spirit of that finding.[87]

His Lordship sought to distinguish cases where the offender had deliberately or neglectfully broken the terms of the community order, from those where the offender was incapable of completing the order due to ill health. In the former scenario, Gibbs J expressed that "that in itself might have justified the subsequent court considering afresh the appropriate sentence for the original offence and taking a more severe view".[88] In the latter scenario, however, his Lordship would conclude:

> Under those circumstances, it was in our judgment not properly open to the judge dealing with him subsequently to re-examine the seriousness of the original offence. The appellant was entitled to expect that the judge would approach the matter on broadly the basis adopted by the

---

[86] ibid, [11] (Gibbs J).

[87] ibid.

[88] ibid, [12] (Gibbs J).

> Recorder. Under those circumstances, we feel compelled to quash the suspended sentence of three months.[89]

Bishop was followed by the Court of Appeal in *R v Boniface.*[90]

These authorities must be viewed in light of the Sentencing Act 2020 which now provides that where the court is re-sentencing an offender, and the court is of the opinion that the offender has "wilfully and persistently breached the requirements of the community order", the court may impose a custodial sentence even if it is not of the opinion that the custody threshold has been crossed.[91] Where an offender's lack of compliance is regarded as "wilful and persistent", it is somewhat irrelevant where the original sentencing judge placed the offence in terms of thresholds.

Assistance from prosecutor

The Court of Appeal in *R v Clarke,*[92] made it clear that where the court is re-sentencing an offender for an original offence, the court must be assisted by the prosecutor. In particular, Toulson J, providing the judgment of the Court, stated:

> Where an offender who is subject to a community service order is bought to court for breach and is liable to be re-sentenced for the original offence, the prosecution should be in a position to put before the court not only the facts of the breach but also the facts of the original offence—at least in outline—together with any relevant information about his

89 ibid, [13] (Gibbs J).

90 [2006] EWCA Crim 682.

91 Sentencing Act 2020, Schedule 10, paras 10(9) and 11(6).

92 [1997] 2 Cr. App. R. (S.) 163 (CA).

> co-defendants, their antecedent histories and the sentences passed on them.[93]

If there is insufficient information to assist the court with re-sentencing, it may be appropriate to seek an adjournment.[94] This was the view of the Court of Appeal in *R v Reynolds*,[95] where the offender had failed to attend his unpaid work requirement (having completed only 22 out of 120 hours) as part of a suspended sentence order. At the breach hearing, the Probation Service requested an adjournment so that they could investigate why the offender had not attended for several appointments post the breach report. The sentencing judge refused this adjournment and activated the suspended sentence in part (22 weeks' imprisonment; a reduction from six months' imprisonment to reflect compliance). On appeal, the Court of Appeal ruled that:

> the recorder should have adjourned in order that further investigations into the post breach history could be made. He would then have been in a position to make his decision on the full facts and give the appellant credit for all the hours of unpaid work which he had done.[96]

The Court of Appeal reduced the activation period to the 50 days which the offender had already served, thus justifying their immediate release.

Re-sentencing multiple offences/ orders

It is common for an offender to be subject to multiple court orders at the same time (e.g. multiple community orders). Where an offender appears before the court for breach, it is likely that they will be in breach of both

---

93 ibid, 167 (Toulson J).

94 See *Allen v West Yorkshire Probation Service Community Service Organisation* [2001] EWHC 2 (Admin).

95 [2015] EWCA Crim 1796, [2016] 1 Cr App R (S) 33.

96 ibid, [9] (Lang J).

orders.[97] In such a case, the court is empowered to re-sentence the offender for all offences, across multiple community orders. When re-sentencing an offender, the court is empowered to impose a singular sentence as a replacement for several distinct sentences.

Suppose an offender was subject to three separate community orders and now appears before the court in breach of those orders. The court is empowered to re-sentence the offender on all three community orders and can impose a singular sentence for all three community orders. For example, the court could revoke all three community orders, and impose a singular community order to tie everything together. There is no requirement or obligation for the court to re-sentence an offender to three separate penalties to reflect the three separate community orders.

Time spent on remand and qualifying curfew

Where the court re-sentences an offender to a term of imprisonment, any time spent remanded in custody, or time spent subject to a qualifying curfew on conditional bail, will count towards any sentence of imprisonment. A full discussion on time spent remanded in custody,[98] or on qualifying curfew[99] is had in Chapter 7.

Restriction on re-sentencing

In re-sentencing an offender, the court may deal with the offender in any way in which it could deal with them as if they had just been convicted by or before it of the offence.[100] This means that an offender before the magistrates' court or Crown Court is subject to the same possible sentence as they would have been when they were first before that court

---

97 See *R v Butt* [2012] EWCA Crim 462.

98 Criminal Justice Act 2003, s.240(ZA).

99 Sentencing Act 2020, s.325.

100 ibid, s.402(1).

for sentence. However, where the Crown Court is re-sentencing an offender subject to a magistrates' court community order, or a Crown Court community order that was restricted to the powers of a magistrates' court, the Crown Court would be restricted to the powers of the magistrates' court.[101]

Equally, where a court is re-sentencing an offender for a summary-only offence, in addition to other summary-only offences, the court is limited to a total aggregate of six months' imprisonment.[102] As previously discussed, the Crown Court has no power to deal with an offender for breaches of community order requirements imposed by a magistrates' court, and vice versa.

Re-sentencing and minimum terms

Where a court re-sentences an offender to custody, any restrictions on the imposition of custody apply as normal. For example, the minimum term of detention for an offender aged between 18-21 is 21 days;[103] this applies just the same where a young offender is re-sentenced from a community order to a term of detention in a Young Offender Institution.

Cannot re-sentence and impose a further penalty

Whilst the court is permitted to combine a number of the penalties prescribed in the Sentencing Act (e.g. revoke and issue a fine), the court must be careful not to punish the offender twice.

Suppose, for example, an offender breaches the requirements of a community order and comes before the court. The court revokes the order and re-sentences the offender for the original offence to three

---

[101] ibid, s.402(2).

[102] Magistrates' Courts Act 1980; *R v Palmer* [2019] EWCA Crim 2231, [2020] 1 Cr. App. R. (S.) 54.

[103] Sentencing Act 2020, s.263(2).

months' imprisonment. The court then also imposes one month's imprisonment for the actual breach of the order itself. This latter part of the court's decision is unlawful. The act of re-sentencing the offender for the original offence *is* the same as the action taken on the breach of the order. To phrase it another way: the consequence/ punishment of breaching the order is the re-sentence itself; there is only one matter before the court, not two. To impose two separate penalties – one for the original offence, and the other for the breach – is to doubly punish the offender.

This is, of course, to be compared to cases where the offender falls to be sentenced for a new offence of which they were convicted during the currency of the community order. In this circumstance, the offender is to be dealt with separately for both the breach and the further offence.

Wilful and persistent breaches

Where the court is re-sentencing an offender, and the court is of the opinion that the offender has "wilfully and persistently breached the requirements of the community order",[104] the court may impose a custodial sentence even if it is not of the opinion that the custody threshold has been crossed.[105] Wilful and persistent non-compliance is dealt with separately in full below.

Aggravating the original offence

Suppose an offender falls to be re-sentenced for an offence following a failure to comply with the requirements of a community order; can the court, when re-sentencing, aggravate the original offence as a result of the non-compliance?

---

[104] Sentencing Act 2020, Schedule 10, paras 10(9) and 11(6).

[105] See s.230(2) of the Sentencing Act 2020.

We have seen above that where an offender is considered to have wilfully and persistently breached the requirements of the community order, the court may impose a custodial sentence when re-sentencing even where the offence itself does not cross the custody threshold.[106] In that respect, the court can, in effect, aggravate the original offence.

The Court of Appeal had ruled prior to the introduction of the Sentencing Act 2020 that the court should not aggravate the original offence when re-sentencing. In *R v Webster*,[107] Hughes J would explain that:

> a court dealing with a man [for an original offence subject to a community order] is sentencing for the original offence rather than punishing for breaking the community service order [...]. Accordingly, however frustrating repeated disobedience to a community sentence may be, the sentence which is imposed must be measured by the original offence.[108]

More recently, in *R v Veloz-Parra,*[109] the offender was made the subject of a community order and breached that order on three occasions. On the third occasion, the offender was re-sentenced to imprisonment. By the date of re-sentence, the offender had completed 62 hours out of the total of 175 hours of unpaid work ordered. The sentencing judge took the view that the repeated failure to attend for unpaid work was a factor capable of aggravating the original offence; the offender appealed.

---

106 Sentencing Act 2020, Schedule 10, paras 10(9) and 11(6). This is repeated in the *Breach of a community order* Sentencing Guideline (1 October 2018).

107 [2001] EWCA Crim 699.

108 ibid, [6] (Hughes J). See also *R v Clarke* [1997] 2 Cr. App. R. (S.) 163 (CA).

109 [2012] EWCA Crim 1065.

In the Court of Appeal, Pitchford LJ concluded that the sentencing judge had not taken the "right approach".[110] His Lordship then explained the proper approach to sentencing that should be taken:

> The task is first to identify the appropriate sentence for the original offence and then to give credit, if it is due, for the extent to which the offender has complied with the requirements of the community order.[111]

Rather than aggravate the original offence, the Court of Appeal concluded, therefore, that the offender should be given appropriate credit (even if limited) for their compliance.[112]

This approach was confirmed by the Court of Appeal in *R v Gemza*[113] in the context of credit for guilty plea. In *Gemza*, the offender had been made the subject of a community order which featured, according to the Court of Appeal, a "blatant and deliberate"[114] history of non-compliance, and the offender generally showed a "wanton disregard for community orders and the importance of compliance."[115] In re-sentencing the offender, the judge afforded them between 15-20 per cent credit for their guilty plea to the original offence, despite the fact that they had pleaded guilty at the first opportunity.[116] On appeal to the Court of Appeal, His Honour Judge Goldstone QC (The Recorder of Liverpool) provided the sole judgment for the Court. His Lordship would explain:

> It is not clear what factors influenced the judge to adopt this approach. We think that the judge may have considered it

---

[110] ibid, [10] (Pitchford LJ).

[111] ibid.

[112] Which was clear in the Court of Appeal's judgment in *R v Clarke* [1997] 2 Cr. App. R. (S.) 163 (CA) 166 (Toulson J).

[113] [2017] EWCA Crim 730.

[114] ibid, [12] (The Recorder of Liverpool, HHJ Goldstone QC).

[115] ibid.

[116] Thus justifying a reduction of 1/3.

> appropriate to reduce the level of credit because of the appellant's lack of compliance with the order which put her in breach of the community order. If so, the judge fell into error. Failure to comply with the requirements of an order cannot aggravate the original offence [referring to *Veloz-Parra*]; nor can it of itself disentitle an offender to the normal credit.[117]

Given these authorities were decided prior to the Sentencing Act 2020, it is questionable as to what extent they remain relevant. The Sentencing Act 2020 provides that in dealing with the offender for non-compliance with a community order requirement, the court must "take into account the extent to which the offender has complied with the requirements of the community order."[118] This is repeated in the Sentencing Council's Guideline *Breach of a community order*,[119] which provides the court with a variety of options in respect of penalty for breach dependant on the offender's level of compliance with the order.[120]

There is a distinction to be drawn, however, between using the offender's non-compliance to aggravate the original offence, and using their non-compliance to determine the appropriate penalty for breach of the order. They are two separate considerations.[121] The former suggests that the court should, for example, increase the starting point of the original offence based upon the offender's lack of compliance. With the exception of wilful and persistent breaches noted above, this simply cannot be correct. Neither the Sentencing Act 2020, nor the Sentencing Council Guidelines on *Breach of a community order* provide the court with the

---

[117] *Gemza* (n113) [16] (The Recorder of Liverpool, HHJ Goldstone QC).

[118] Sentencing Act 2020, Schedule 10, paras 10(7) and 11(4).

[119] Sentencing Council, *Breach of a community order* (1 October 2018).

[120] See Chapter 9.

[121] As recognised by the Court of Appeal in *R v Clarke* [1997] 2 Cr. App. R. (S.) 163 (CA), 166 (Toulson J).

power to increase the length of a re-sentence to reflect the offender's non-compliance.

It is submitted, therefore, that where an offender has wilfully and persistently shown non-compliance with the order, the court can aggravate the original offence in that they can impose a custodial sentence which would not otherwise have been justified. However, beyond such wilful and persistent non-compliance, the court cannot aggravate the original offence. Rather, the court uses the offender's non-compliance to determine the appropriate penalty in respect of the breach.

Appeals

Where an offender is re-sentenced for an original offence in the magistrates' court, they may appeal to the Crown Court against that re-sentence.[122] This provision is simply designed to preserve the automatic right to appeal that an individual convicted by a magistrates' court has to the Crown Court.[123] Of course, should an offender wish to appeal against a re-sentence in the Crown Court, they will require leave to appeal in the ordinary way.[124]

Wilful and persistent non-compliance

As noted above, where an offender is deemed to have demonstrated a wilful and persistent non-compliance with the order, the court may re-sentence them to a custodial sentence for the original offence, even if the offence did not cross the custody threshold. The issue that falls at this stage is the meaning of "wilful and persistent non-compliance".

Neither the Sentencing Act 2020, nor the Sentencing Council Guideline, *Breach of a community order*, offer assistance as to the meaning of wilful

---

122 Sentencing Act 2020, Schedule 10, para 10(11).

123 See Magistrates' Courts Act 1980, s.108.

124 See Criminal Appeal Act 1968, s.9(1).

and persistent non-compliance, or how to assess it. It is evident from the Guideline that there are three concepts at play:

- "wilful"
- "persistent"
- "non-compliance"

It will be worth looking at each in turn. Before that, it is advised that the views of the Probation Service should be sought as to whether they consider the offender's non-compliance to be wilful and persistent. It is further advised that the sentencing judge should invite submissions from the advocates in the case before concluding that the offender has shown wilful and persistent non-compliance. Certainly, the advocate for the offender should be permitted to make representations on wilful and persistent non-compliance first before any decision is made.

Wilful

The presence of the word "wilful" suggests that the offender has made a deliberate decision to not comply with the requirement of the order. Indeed, the word "wilfully" has been defined by the criminal courts in a variety of cases.

In *AG's Reference (No 3 of 2003)*,[125] Pill LJ approved the definition of the term from Webster J in *Graham v Teesdale*[126] as "deliberately doing something which is wrong knowing it to be wrong or with reckless indifference as to whether it is wrong or not".[127] This was the approach taken by the Court of Appeal in *R v JD*,[128] and *R v Sheppard (James*

---

125 [2004] EWCA Crim 868.

126 (1981) 81 LGR 117.

127 *AG's Ref (No 3 of 2003)* (n125) [28] (Pill LJ).

128 [2008] EWCA Crim 2360.

Martin).[129] Lord Keith in *Sheppard (James Martin)* explained that wilful means "deliberate". From these authorities, "wilful" can be understood as meaning either

- an awareness of a risk (akin to recklessness), or
- a lack of care (akin, in some respects, to intention).

There must, therefore, be an element of deliberate non-compliance on part of the offender (i.e. a deliberate decision to not engage with the order).

Persistent

The requirement of "persistent" non-compliance demonstrates that the order must have been in effect for a sufficient period of time that the offender can be said to have persistently failed to comply. Various Sentencing Guidelines use "persistent" to increase the seriousness of an offence.[130] Persistence requires repeat behaviour. An evident failure to comply towards the start of the order may not permit the court to find any such non-compliance to be persistent. On the other hand, a blatant disregard for a longer-standing period of the order may permit the court to find such persistence.

Non-compliance

It is inadvisable to attach numerical figures to any calculation of compliance, but the court will be assisted by the Probation Service in understanding the number of appointments attended by the offender, and their attitude and engagement during those appointments. Indeed,

---

[129] [1981] AC 394.

[130] For example, "persistent breach" in the context of breach of a restraining order, or "persistent and prolonged assault" in the context of several non-fatal offences against the person.

the presence of "low level of compliance" in the Sentencing Guideline suggests that the offender has engaged marginally with the order (e.g. attending the odd appointment, or completing a small number of unpaid work hours). "Non-compliance" would therefore seem to suggest that the offender has engaged in no appointments whatsoever, or their engagement is so insignificant that it is negligible.

Some examples

What may be regarded, therefore, as wilful and persistent non-compliance? Some examples may include:

- The offender has repeatedly failed to attend their initial appointment.[131] The offender has been contacted via telephone and letter by their responsible officer and has not engaged with any communication.

- The offender has attended several unpaid work sessions but on each occasion is sent away by the unpaid work provider on account that they have failed to comply with the instructions provided. Whilst the offender has attended, they are marked on all occasions as "attended but failed to comply".

- The offender attends appointments with their responsible officer but is abusive and offensive at each appointment. They are told that they must engage responsibly and with respect. Despite that warning, the offender continues to be disrespectful and verbally aggressive at all appointments. All appointments are therefore marked as "attended but failed to comply"

- The responsible officer has made repeated attempts to engage the offender, and those attempts have been repeatedly met either with silence or a negative attitude.

---

[131] Often referred to as their Induction.

Importantly, these are just examples. A court must deal with an offender on the facts of their case; the facts of other cases will be of limited assistance.

What powers do the courts not have?

The final discussion necessary under this section is to explain what powers the courts do not have when faced with a probation breach. This section is primarily designed to ensure that errors are not made by parties to the case when dealing with any such breach.

The following details what powers the court does not have.

- The court cannot take "no action" in respect of the breach; the court must utilise one of its powers in paras 10(5) or 11(2).

- The court cannot simply revoke a community order following breach. Revocation is only possible where the offender is re-sentenced for breach of community order requirements, the offender is convicted of a further offence during the currency of the order, or upon application by the Probation Service or the offender.

- There is no power to impose a second victim surcharge when re-sentencing an offender for the original offence.[132] Breach of court orders do not, standalone, attract the victim surcharge.

- In a similar vein, where the offender was disqualified from driving at the same time the community order was imposed, the court

[132] *R v Abbott* [2020] EWCA Crim 516; *R v George* [2015] EWCA Crim 1096, [2015] 2 Cr. App. R. (S.) 58. The breach itself does not attract a surcharge.

has no power to impose a second disqualification if the offender is re-sentenced (and the original order revoked).[133]

Powers of court following conviction for further offence

As noted above, the powers of the court in respect of convictions for further offences are different to breaches of the community order requirements. This is because, as discussed above, conviction of further offences during the currency of a community order is not classed as a breach of the community order.

Powers of the court in overview

Where the community order remains in force, and the offender has been convicted of a further offence, a magistrates' court or the Crown Court may:

- revoke the community order, or
- both revoke the community order, and re-sentence the offender for the offence in respect of which the order was made.[134]

Such a power may only be exercised if it appears to the court to be in the interests of justice to do so, having regard to circumstances which have arisen since the order was made.[135] This means that the court may take no action against an offender where the court is of the opinion that it is not in the interests of justice to revoke the order.

133 *R v Coy* (1992) 13 Cr. App. R. (S.) 619 (CA), 621 (Laws J).

134 Sentencing Act 2020, Schedule 10, paras 23(2) and 25(2).

135 ibid.

Key point

It is essential to emphasise that the exercise of the court's powers is entirely discretionary. The court is permitted to take no action in respect of such convictions. This is unlike breach of the requirements of a community order, or breaches of suspended sentence orders, where the court is obligated to take some action.

The "circumstances which have arisen since the order was made" include the extent to which the offender has complied with the requirements of the community order.[136] The individual circumstances of the offender, will also be relevant including the reasons for the breach taking place. Furthermore, a common argument raised relates to an apparent shortfall in the quality of supervision by the Probation Service which may have contributed to the likelihood of a breach.

As discussed in Chapter 7, the similarity and seriousness of the new offence compared to the offence subject to the community order should be considered. In the context of suspended sentence orders, the mere fact that the new offence is dissimilar to the offence subject to the order is not a reason for re-sentencing the offender.[137] There is no reason why the same cannot apply to community orders. In a similar vein, the fact that the new offence/ further conviction does not warrant imprisonment does not prevent the court from re-sentencing the offender for the offence subject to the community order.[138]

A full discussion on the law relevant to revocation and re-sentence, including the interests of justice test, and the circumstances to be considered by the court, is had in Chapter 10. For an example of revoking

---

136 ibid, Schedule 10, paras 23(5) and 25(5).

137 See, for example, *R v Fleming* (1989) 11 Cr. App. R. (S.) 137 (CA).

138 *Nobbs v DPP* [2008] EWHC 1653 (Admin).

and re-sentencing an offender, see *R v Palmer*[139] (discussed in Chapter 10).

> **Key point**
>
> Advocates must be astute to the powers of the Crown Court when re-sentencing offenders. When re-sentencing an offender for breach of a magistrates' court community order, the Crown Court is restricted to the powers available to the magistrates' court. (section 402(2) SA 2020).[140]

Dealing with the new offence

Where an offender is convicted of a further offence during the currency of a community order, the court will need to deal with the new offence first before turning its attention to the original offence.

Structuring sentence

As discussed above, there is no obligation for the court to take any action whatsoever where an offender has been convicted of a further offence during the currency of a community order. Despite that, it is advised that the court deals with the two matters separately. In Chapter 7, the case of *R v Ithell*[141] is discussed in respect of the "proper approach" to sentencing where a fresh offence has been committed during the period of suspension of an earlier sentence. Whilst this case relates to suspended sentence orders, it is advised that the same approach be taken in respect of community orders. Lord Justice Edmund Davies would explain:

139 [2019] EWCA Crim 2231; [2020] 1 Cr. App. R. (S.) 54. See also *R v Murray* [2021] EWCA Crim 1441.

140 *R v Murray* [2021] EWCA Crim 1441.

141 (1969) 53 Cr. App. R. 210 (CA).

> the court should first sentence him in respect of the fresh offence by punishment appropriate to that offence, and thereafter address itself to the question of the suspended sentence.[142]

The court is advised to adopt the same approach: determine the appropriate penalty for the new offence, and then consider whether to exercise the court's powers to revoke or revoke and re-sentence for the original offence.

Taking no action

The court must deal with the new offence in the ordinary way. However, as noted above, the court is not obliged to take any action in respect of the offence subject to a community order. The court need only deal with the offence where it is in the interests of justice to do so. This means, if the court is not so satisfied that it is in the interests of justice, the court may take no action and allow the community order to continue.[143]

Aggravating the new offence

Naturally, the fact that the offender committed the offence whilst subject to a community order is an aggravating feature of the new offence.[144]

---

142 ibid, 212 (Edmund Davies LJ).

143 If the court does allow the order to continue, the court should give the offender a warning that the order is to continue, and the offender must continue to comply with it.

144 *R v Clarke* [1997] 2 Cr. App. R. (S.) 163 (CA), 166 (Toulson J). This is also evident in the Definitive Sentencing Council Guidelines.

Restrictions

The court should have regard to the following restrictions.

Powers of the court

For the restriction on the maximum powers of the court when re-sentencing, see above.

Presence of offender

Unless the offender is before it, neither the magistrates' court nor the Crown Court is empowered to revoke and resentence unless it has summonsed the offender to appear before it.[145] If the offender fails to appear in answer to a summons, the court may issue a warrant for the offender's arrest.[146] The Court is technically permitted to re-sentence the offender in their absence (so long as they have been summonsed), but are unlikely in practice to do so.

Legal representation when re-sentencing to custody

Where an offender has been sentenced to a community order, and the court is considering revoking that order, and re-sentencing the offender, it must consider whether legal representation is required. Where the court does not intend to impose a custodial sentence, there is no restriction in place preventing the court from dealing with an unrepresented offender.

However, where the court considers that the offender should be re-sentenced to a term of imprisonment, the court must consider the restriction imposed by s.226 of the Sentencing Act 2020. Section 226(3)

---

[145] Sentencing Act 2020, Schedule 10, para 23(3); Schedule 16, para 25(3).

[146] ibid, Schedule 10, para 23(4); Schedule 16, para 25(4).

states that the court may not pass a sentence of imprisonment unless the offender:

- is legally represented in that court, or
- has failed, or is ineligible on financial grounds, to benefit from relevant representation, or
- has previously been sentenced to imprisonment by a court in any part of the United Kingdom.

Suppose an offender has a large body of previous convictions, but has never served a period of imprisonment, the court *cannot* revoke and re-sentence them to custody[147] unless they are legally represented or unless they have failed to obtain, or are ineligible for, legal representation.[148] A previous term of imprisonment that has been suspended but never activated does not count as a previous sentence of imprisonment.[149] Therefore, the court may be required to adjourn any proceedings where they are presented with an unrepresented offender and the court is considering re-sentencing to a term of imprisonment.

Appeals

Where an offender has been re-sentenced by a magistrates' court, they may appeal against that sentence to the Crown Court.[150] This provision is simply designed to preserve the automatic right to appeal that an

---

147 To "re-sentence" an offender to a term of imprisonment is the same as "passing" a sentence of imprisonment for the purposes of s.226(3).

148 The position is different for breach of suspended sentence orders on account that the imposition of a suspended sentence order is *itself* a sentence of imprisonment; activation of that order does not feature the same restriction (see Chapter 7).

149 Sentencing Act 2020, s.266(4).

150 ibid, Schedule 10, para 14(8).

individual convicted by a magistrates' court has to the Crown Court.[151] Of course, should an offender wish to appeal against a re-sentence in the Crown Court, they will require leave to appeal in the ordinary way.[152]

Cases involving both a breach and a further conviction

There may be circumstances where the court is faced with an offender who, not only is in breach of the requirements of a community order, but has also been convicted of a further offence during the currency of the order.

In this circumstance, the court cannot take action on the community order twice. It cannot, for example, take action and impose a penalty for failing to comply, and then also impose a penalty for having been convicted of an offence during the currency of the order. The court must only take action once.[153] In the case of a community order, taking action on the breach, as opposed to the further conviction, is more appropriate given that the court has a wider array of powers available to it.

Expired community orders

What is the situation if the end date of the community order has passed (i.e. the community order has expired)? As we know from the above discussion, a court can only deal with an offender for further convictions during the community order where the community order remains in force.[154]

---

[151] See Magistrates' Courts Act 1980, s.108.

[152] See Criminal Appeal Act 1968, s.9(1).

[153] See *R v Maunder* [2015] EWCA Crim 778, [2015] 2 Cr. App. R. (S.) 26 in the context of suspended sentence orders (see Chapter 7).

[154] Sentencing Act 2020, Schedule 10, paras 22(1) and 25(1) (see above). See also the Sentencing Council Guideline, *Totality* (1 July 2023).

What is the situation, however, where the offender failed to comply with a community order requirement during the currency of that order, but that order has now expired?

Timeframe for breaches

In Chapter 4, we discussed the case of *West Yorkshire Probation Board v Cruickshanks.*[155] Lord Justice Leveson was clear that whilst the information must be laid within the operational period of the suspended sentence order, the breach proceedings do not need to be heard within that period. Whilst that case was concerned with suspended sentence orders, there appears to be no reason for not extending it to community orders. Furthermore, the Sentencing Act 2020 appears to envisage the situation where breach proceedings are heard following the expiration of a community order. Paragraphs 10(10)[156] and 11(7)[157] of Schedule 10 to the Sentencing Act 2020 both provide that where a court is re-sentencing an offender for an offence, the court must revoke the community order "if it is still in force". "If it is still in force" would seem to suggest that the court may re-sentence where the order is *no longer* in force.

Therefore, it does appear permissible for the court to deal with breaches following the expiration of the community order.

Powers of the court

Whilst it is seemingly the case that breach proceedings may be heard following the end date of a community order, the more important questions become: What are the powers of the court when dealing with an expired community order? Is the court restricted by the fact that the end date of the community order has passed?

---

155 [2010] EWHC 615 (Admin); [2011] 1 W.L.R. 2154.

156 Which deals with the powers of a magistrates' court following breach.

157 Which deals with the powers of the Crown Court following breach.

One could make the argument that the court is subject to no such restrictions. There is no statement in the Sentencing Act 2020 that the court is restricted in its powers to deal with the offender; rather, it simply provides that the court "must deal with the offender in respect of the breach in any one of the following ways".[158]

On the other hand, it could be argued that the court is restricted to two options:

- Re-sentence the offender, or
- Order that the offender pay a fine (maximum £2,500).

With the exception of community orders that qualify for special procedures, the only remaining option for the court would be to amend the terms of the community order so as to impose more onerous requirements. As discussed above, the effect of this power is to allow the order to continue. However, as s.220(1)(a) makes clear, a community order ceases to be in force "at the end of the end date". To that extent, if the community order has ceased in law following the end date, the court cannot possibly be able to impose more onerous requirements, and, in doing so, extend the community order itself. In essence, if there is no longer an order in force, how can that order be made more onerous?

Indeed, if an offender is re-sentenced for the original offence, the court should generally revoke the community order.[159] However, should the order have expired, there is no order to revoke. The view favoured, therefore, is that the court's only options where the order has expired is to re-sentence the offender, or impose a fine.

---

[158] Sentencing Act 2020, Schedule 10, paras 10(5) and 11(2).

[159] ibid, Schedule 10, Paras 10(10) and 11(7).

Summary

This Chapter has covered the law and practice relating to breach of community orders and the conviction of further offences during the currency of a community order. When considering the legal principles applicable to this area of law, consider:

- The court is empowered to deal with an offender for the offence subject to a community order where the offender fails to comply with the community order requirements, or where the offender has been convicted of an offence during the currency of a community order.

- In respect of breach of community order requirements, the court must take action on the breach. Such action includes the ability to re-sentence the offender, impose a fine (not exceeding £2,500), make the order more onerous, or commit the offender to custody (in special review cases).

- A breach of community order requirements can still be acted even after the order has expired, though the powers of the court are likely restricted.

- The court may only deal with the offence subject to the community order, following a further conviction, if the community order remains in force.

- In respect of conviction for further offences during the currency of a community order, the court is not obligated to take any action. The court may, if it is in the interests of justice to do so, revoke the community order entirely, or revoke the order and re-sentence the offender.

CHAPTER SEVEN

BREACH OF SUSPENDED SENTENCE ORDERS

Introduction

In this Chapter, we consider the circumstances where an offender is in breach of a suspended sentence order as a result of a breach of the community requirements of that order, or by way of a conviction for further offences committed during the operational period of that order.

The powers available to both a magistrates' court and the Crown Court are largely identical and shall both be considered in this chapter.

Key provisions

The relevant provisions are provided in the Sentencing Act 2020, as such:

- Breach of community requirement or conviction of further offence during suspended sentence orders: Schedule 16, Part 2.

This chapter attempts to adopt a logical sequence to breaches of a suspended sentence order, and a structure which will be the most beneficial to practitioners. In light of that, the Chapter is broken down as such:

- Consideration of the law relating to breach of community requirements of suspended sentence orders.

- Consideration of the law relating to the commission of further offences during the operational period of a suspended sentence order.

- The procedure adopted at a hearing.
- The powers of the court following an admission/ finding of breach.

It is hoped that this structure will follow the sequence of events as it plays out in the practitioner's preparation: First they will consider whether the breach is made out in law (the first two sections of this chapter), then they will prepare for the hearing itself (the third section of this chapter), and then they will consider what powers are available to the court (the final section of this chapter).

Let us consider each in turn.

Breach of community requirements

As discussed in Chapter 2, a suspended sentence order does not need to impose community requirements; the imposition of such requirements is discretionary.[1] Where, however, the sentencing court does impose such requirements, the offender is required to comply with those requirements. Any failure to comply with the requirements without reasonable excuse may result in breach action being taken.

In this section, we shall discuss the requirements in order to be breached for failing to comply with the community requirements of a suspended sentence order.

1 Unlike community orders, for which see s.200(1) of the Sentencing Act 2020, and Chapters 2 and 6.

Conditions applicable

Before we consider the powers of a magistrates' court and the Crown Court in dealing with any such breach, it is necessary to understand the pre-requisites or conditions before any such power can be exercised.

It will be of assistance to break our discussion down into three matters:

1. There must be a "breach"

2. The breach must be of a "community requirement"

3. The breach must be "without reasonable excuse".

We shall take each in turn.

There must be a breach

The court must be satisfied that the offender has "breached" a community requirement without reasonable excuse. For our purposes, a "breach" refers to "any failure of the offender to comply with a requirement imposed by the order."[2]

It is to be noted that para 1(2) of Schedule 16 refers to a "community order" as opposed to a "suspended sentence order". It is submitted that is simply a typographical error on account that Schedule 16 is concerned with suspended sentence orders, and the wording in para 1(2) is identical to that found in Schedule 10 for community orders.

Meaning of "breach"

The reference to "failure... to comply" would suggest that an offender can only breach a community requirement by omission. However, the distinction between an act and omission is not strictly necessary. On any

2 Sentencing Act 2020, Schedule 16, para 1(2).

interpretation, an offender's conduct could be interpreted as an act or a failure to act. Take for example:

- An offender is required to attend their unpaid work requirement. They fail to attend and do not provide any explanation for their non-compliance.

- An offender is required to attend a Rehabilitation Activity Requirement (RAR). They attend, but are abusive to staff and refuse to engage.

In both examples, the offender could be said to have failed to comply (omission) or deliberately made a decision not to comply (an act). It is for that reason, it is said that the distinction is not necessary; it must simply be proven that the offender has failed to comply.

Timeframe of breach

As discussed in Chapter 2, a suspended sentence order need not impose community requirements; the imposition of such requirements is entirely discretionary. Where the court does impose community requirements, it must also state a supervision period.[3] Such period must be no less than six months, and no longer than two years (or no longer than the operational period if that period is shorter than two years).[4]

The legislation is clear that the offender must comply with any such community requirements "during the supervision period" of a suspended sentence order.[5] Given that compliance is *only* required during the supervision period, any such breaches or contraventions of those requirements must be done during the supervision period. This is clear in section 286(3)(b) of the Sentencing Act 2020 which states that an

3 ibid, s.288(3).

4 ibid, s.288(4).

5 ibid, s.286(2).

activation event occurs where the offender "during the supervision period, contravenes any community requirement imposed by the order." This is equally clear in Schedule 16 to the Sentencing Act 2020, which states that an information must allege a breach "during the supervision period" of a magistrates' court order or Crown Court order.[6]

> **Key point**
>
> Generally speaking, the supervision period will be the same length as the operational period. Advocates must, however, ensure that any such breach has occurred during the supervision period and not following the expiry of such period.

The breach must be of a community requirement

In order to bring breach proceedings, an offender must have failed to comply with a community requirement of a suspended sentence order. The Sentencing Act 2020 makes clear that a breach of a community requirement includes:

- A failure to comply with any community requirement imposed as part of the suspended sentence order.
- A failure to keep in touch with the responsible officer in accordance with such instructions as the responsible officer may give the offender from time to time.[7]

---

6 ibid, Schedule 16, paras 8 and 9.

7 ibid, s.301(2). This obligation is enforceable as if it were a community requirement imposed by the suspended sentence order. (see s.301(3) Sentencing Act 2020).

- A failure to obtain permission from the responsible officer or court before changing residence.[8]

In chapter 3, we discussed whether a breach of the Probation Service contract could amount to a failure to comply for the purposes of breach proceedings. We concluded that unless one were to take a generous interpretation of the duty to keep in touch, a failure to comply with the contract alone (e.g. inappropriate behaviour) cannot amount to a breach. We provided a detailed example in Chapter 3 to demonstrate this point and readers are advised to return to that example.

The breach must be without reasonable excuse

Finally, the court must be satisfied that any such breach has been committed "without reasonable excuse". The reference to "reasonable" would suggest that the test is an objective one; asking whether the reasonable person would consider an explanation for the failure to comply to be an acceptable one.

Whether there has been a failure to comply will be entirely case-and-fact specific. Common excuses provided by offenders include:

- Work commitments
- Caring responsibilities
- Physical or mental health difficulties
- Difficulties with addiction
- Difficulties with homelessness

---

8 ibid, s.302(2). This obligation is enforceable as if it were a community requirement imposed by the suspended sentence order. (see s.303(3) Sentencing Act 2020).

- Difficulties in communication with Probation Service.

This list is not exhaustive, nor will any of these excuses be automatically regarded as "reasonable". The individual circumstances of any excuse must be considered and assessed by the court. If the offender claims to have a reasonable excuse, and that is not accepted by the Probation Service, a contested hearing will be required.[9]

Incapability to comply

What of the situation where an offender is incapable of complying with the community requirements? To answer this question, it will be helpful to consider the Divisional Court's judgment in *Humphreys v Crown Prosecution Service.*[10] Whilst *Humphreys* was concerned with the imposition of Criminal Behaviour Orders (CBO), it remains of value to cases of requirements of orders. Where a CBO is imposed, an offender will breach the CBO if they fail to comply with any of the prohibitions of the order. That is so unless they have a "reasonable excuse" for their failure to comply.

In *Humphreys,* the offender suffered from attention deficit hyperactivity disorder (ADHD) and expert evidence was received by the Court which stated that if the offender's ADHD is not treated properly, the making of a CBO will inevitably lead to the order being breached. Whilst this case dealt with whether it was correct for the court to impose a CBO, the Divisional Court took the opportunity to deal with the question of reasonable excuse. Mr Justice Stuart-Smith would explain that:

> In my judgement [sic] if a person does or fails to do something in breach of a CBO, because they are incapable

---

[9] See Chapter 8.

[10] [2019] EWHC 2794 (Admin), [2020] 1 Cr. App. R. (S.) 39.

> of complying, the proper conclusion should be that their incapacity is a reasonable excuse[11]

Whilst his Lordship was clear that he was speaking in the context of CBOs, this *obiter* comment is of value to those considering the issue of reasonable excuse as it applies to failing to comply with community requirements.

Reasonable refusals to undergo certain treatment

In Chapter 2, we discussed that the court may impose a treatment requirement as part of the suspended sentence order.[12] As with any community requirement, a failure to comply with any treatment requirement imposed may lead to breach proceedings being initiated. However, a specific provision exists in the Sentencing Act 2020 for offenders who fail to comply with a treatment requirement. Specifically, para 17(2) of Schedule 16 to the Sentencing Act states that where an offender has refused to undergo any surgical, electrical or other treatment, the offender is not to be treated as having breached that requirement if, in the opinion of the court, the refusal was reasonable having regard to all the circumstances.

It is for the court to consider whether any such refusal was reasonable in the circumstances.

---

11 ibid [26] (Stuart-Smith J).

12 A "treatment requirement" means a mental health treatment requirement (MHTR), a drug rehabilitation requirement (DRR), or an alcohol treatment requirement (ATR).

Appeals and reasonable excuses

In *West Midlands Probation Board v Sadler,*[13] the Divisional Court was faced with the question of whether an appeal lodged against conviction could amount to a "reasonable excuse" for failing to comply. By way of brief facts, the offender had been convicted of an offence of affray. The offender was sentenced to a 12-month community order with a requirement to undertake 240 hours of unpaid work. The offender failed to attend their unpaid work and justified this on the basis that they had lodged an appeal against their conviction. The district judge in the magistrates' court agreed with that argument and dismissed the breach. On appeal, the Divisional Court ruled that the district judge had erred in law. Giving the judgment of the Court, Dyson LJ would explain:

> Although the concept of "reasonable excuse" is broad, I do not consider that it can have been intended by Parliament to be stretched to include the mere fact that the defendant has lodged an appeal against the community order or the conviction on which it is based. To do that would be to undermine the general principle that community orders take effect from the date on which they are made and remain in force until and unless they are quashed on appeal or revoked or amended by order of the court. To accept non-compliance with a community order as a reasonable excuse merely because the defendant is appealing would amount to an acknowledgement that defendants may pick and choose whether and in what circumstances they will comply. That is wrong in principle.[14]

Whilst this was an authority relating to community orders, there is no reason as to why it should not apply to suspended sentence orders. Indeed, just like community orders, a suspended sentence order takes

---

13 [2008] EWHC 15 (Admin), [2008] 1 W.L.R. 918 (also cited as *West Midlands Probation Board v Sutton Coldfield Magistrates' Court*).

14 ibid [15] (Dyson LJ).

effect immediately.[15] As such, unless and until an order is revoked or varied on appeal, it remains in force and must be complied with.[16]

Conviction for further offences

An offender who is convicted of a further offence committed during the operational period of a suspended sentence order runs the risk that the suspended sentence is activated, or is permitted to continue but is made more onerous.

Conditions applicable

Before we consider the powers of a magistrates' court and the Crown Court in dealing with a further offence, it is necessary to understand the pre-requisites or conditions before any such power can be exercised. These conditions are three-fold:[17]

1. The offender must be convicted of an offence.
2. The offence must have been *committed* during the operational period of a suspended sentence order.
3. The suspended sentence must not yet have been activated.

There are a number of issues we must consider to understand these conditions in full.

---

[15] Sentencing Act 2020, s.288(2): "beginning with the day on which the order is made". See also s.384(1) of the Sentencing Act 2020.

[16] See also of *Greater Manchester Probation Committee v Bent* (1996) 160 JP 297; *R v May* [2005] EWCA Crim 367; and *R v Day* [2014] EWCA Crim 2683, [2015] 1 Cr. App. R. (S.) 53.

[17] Sentencing Act 2020, Schedule 16, paras 11(1) and 12(3).

Requirement of conviction

The first requirement is that the offender must be convicted of an offence.

Timing of commission not conviction

As is clear from the statutory wording, the court has the power to take action on the suspended sentence order where the offender has been convicted of a further offence *committed* during the operational period of a suspended sentence order. As will be discussed below, it is not necessary for a suspended sentence order to still be in force at the time of conviction/ sentence; the focus is on the date of commission not conviction.

This means that the suspended sentence order may have expired.[18] However, provided that the offence was committed during the operational period, and the suspended sentence order has not been previously activated, the court may take action on any such further conviction.[19]

Relevance of the offence

There is no requirement that the new offence is of a particular type or kind. For example, there is no requirement that the offence be punishable by imprisonment,[20] nor for the offence to be of the same kind as the offence subject to the suspended sentence order. However, the seriousness of the new offence, and its similarity to the offence subject to

---

18 See below, "Expired suspended sentence orders"..

19 *R v Sproul* [2018] EWCA Crim 2034; *R v Beirne* [2020] EWCA Crim 1433.

20 See *Nobbs v DPP* [2008] EWHC 1653 (Admin), [2009] R.T.R. 9 [18] (Keith J).

the suspended sentence, will be relevant to the question of whether it is unjust to activate the order.

Necessity of a conviction

Whilst the relevant timeframe is determined by the date of *commission* of the further offence, there is still a requirement that the offender be *convicted* of the further offence.[21] Paragraphs 11 and 12 of Schedule 16 to the Sentencing Act are clear: "Where an offender is *convicted*...". (emphasis added)

Such conviction may arise by way of guilty plea or guilty verdict following trial. Simply: action cannot be taken on a suspended sentence order without a conviction.

Failure to comply

As discussed in Chapter 1, a simple failure to comply with the requirements of an order does not amount to a criminal offence, and therefore does not amount to a criminal conviction. This means that a court cannot use a failure to comply with one court order (e.g. a community order), as a mechanism by which it can activate a suspended sentence order. By way of example:

- Suppose an offender is subject to a both community order and a suspended sentence order at the same time.
- The community order includes RAR, whilst the suspended sentence order does not.

[21] *R v Tarry* (1970) 54 Cr. App. R. 322 (CA).

- The offender appears before the court for failing to comply with the community order by failing to attend their RAR sessions.

- The offender admits the breach.

In this case, the offender can be dealt with in respect of the community order but cannot be dealt with in respect of the suspended sentence order. They have not failed to comply with the suspended sentence order itself, nor does the failure to comply with the community order amount to the commission of an offence during the operational period of a suspended sentence order. In this circumstance, unless there is a separate breach in respect of the suspended sentence order, there is no action that the court is empowered to take with the suspended sentence.

Further offences resulting in a discharge

The requirement for a conviction raises the following question: what is the situation where an offender commits an offence during the operational period of a suspended sentence order but is sentenced for the new offence by way of an absolute or conditional discharge?

Section 82(2) of the Sentencing Act 2020 provides that an offence which results in an order for an absolute discharge, or a conditional discharge, will not be deemed a "conviction" for any purpose.[22] On that basis, a conviction for a further offence which has been dealt with by way of absolute or conditional discharge cannot be used to activate the suspended sentence order.[23] This is evident from the Court of Appeal's

---

[22] Other than the purposes of the proceedings in which the order is made, and in the case of an order for conditional discharge, any subsequent proceedings which may be taken against the offender under Schedule 2 of the Sentencing Act 2020.

[23] Which must be distinguished from the situation where a further offence is committed during the period of conditional discharge (for which see Schedule 2 to the Sentencing Act 2020).

judgment in *R v Moore*,[24] where Sedley J, giving the judgment of the Court,[25] explained:

> It therefore makes sense that an offence committed during the operational period of a suspended sentence but, in the opinion of justices with a power of disposal, meriting a conditional discharge instead of a penalty ought not to be able to bring about the activation of a suspended sentence of imprisonment.[26]

Whilst the case of *Moore* was concerned with the former law relating to "probation orders" in the Criminal Justice Act 1991, there is no reason as to why it cannot apply in the same way under the Sentencing Act 2020.[27]

Commission during the operational period

A suspended sentence order is regarded as a sentence of imprisonment (or "detention" for the purposes of youths).[28] Given that a sentence of imprisonment takes effect immediately,[29] the same can be said for the purposes of a suspended sentence order.

As discussed in Chapter 2, a suspended sentence order must include an operational period and, if the order imposes any community

---

24 (1995) 16 Cr. App. R. (S.) 748 (CA).

25 Relying on the judgment of Lord Parker CJ in *R v Tarry* (1970) 54 Cr. App. R. 322 (CA).

26 *Moore* (n24), 754 (Sedley J).

27 In *Nobbs v DPP* [2008] EWHC 1653 (Admin), [2009] R.T.R. 9, the Divisional Court chose not to answer the question of whether the decision in *Moore* applied to the then law under the Criminal Justice Act 2003.

28 Sentencing Act 2020, s.289(1).

29 ibid, s.384(1).

requirement, a supervision period.[30] Both the operational period and supervision period begin on the day on which the order is made.[31] Both periods must be for at least six months but not more than two years (a supervision period cannot be longer than the operational period).[32] A suspended sentence order therefore begins immediately upon being made and ends on the last day of the operational period, whatever period that may be.

Timeframe of commission

A further offence must, therefore, be committed at any time during the operational period of the suspended sentence order. Should an offence be committed during this period, the court will be permitted to take action (even in the circumstances where the offence was committed whilst the offender is still in the dock having just had a suspended sentence imposed, or on the last day of the order).[33] However, where an offence has been committed prior to the imposition of a suspended sentence order, or following its expiry, the court has no power to take action on the suspended sentence order.[34]

An example of this can be seen in the case of *R v H*,[35] where the offender had been sentenced on 24 April 2012 to a 12-month community order. That order was eventually revoked, and the offender re-sentenced to three

30 ibid, s.288.

31 ibid, s.288(2) and (4).

32 ibid.

33 The length of time between the imposition of the suspended sentence order and the commission of the offence will of course be relevant to whether it would be "unjust" to activate the sentence.

34 Section 286(3) of the Sentencing Act 2020 is clear: An activation event occurs if the offender commits another offence in the United Kingdom during the operational period (whether or not punishable with imprisonment).

35 [2013] EWCA Crim 2115.

months' imprisonment, suspended sentence for 12 months on 19 February 2013. The offender pleaded guilty to a further offence on 22 April 2013, committed on 1 October 2012. When sentencing the offender, the sentencing judge activated the suspended sentence order in part (two months), consecutive to the new offence. On appeal, it was rightly noted that the imposition of the suspended sentence post-dated the further offence and, on that basis, the activation of the suspended sentence was unlawful.[36]

Location of commission

Importantly, section 286(3)(a) is clear that a further offence must be committed "in the United Kingdom". There does not, therefore, appear to be a provision giving the court power to deal with an offender for a further offence committed outside of the UK.

What of the situation where an offender is convicted in Scotland or Northern Ireland? The offence counts as an offence for the purposes of breach, but the courts in Scotland and Northern Ireland are not empowered to deal with the breach. The offender must therefore be dealt with in a court in England and Wales. Paragraph 18 of Schedule 16 to the Sentencing Act 2020 prescribes that where an offender is convicted in Scotland or Northern Ireland of an offence, and the court is informed that the offence was committed during the operational period of a suspended sentence passed in England or Wales, the court must give written notice of the conviction to the appropriate officer of the court by which the suspended sentence was passed.[37]

Given that the courts in Scotland or Northern Ireland cannot deal with the suspended sentence order, the next issue is: how is the offender dealt with for the breach? This was dealt with in Chapter 4 but, in summary,

---

[36] ibid, [21] and [28] (HHJ Wait).

[37] Sentencing Act 2020, Schedule 16, para 18.

the court may issue a summons requiring the offender to appear at the place and time specified in it, or a warrant for the offender's arrest.[38]

Not yet activated

Finally, the suspended sentence order must have not already taken effect (i.e. been activated). This is because a suspended sentence order can only be activated once.[39] It cannot be imposed a second time; to do so would punish the offender twice for the same offending.[40] For a full discussion on this restriction, see below.

Procedure for dealing with an offender

Having considered the specific provisions relating to breaches of the community requirements of suspended sentence orders, and the commission of further offences, it will now be helpful to set out the procedure to be adopted, applicable to both sets of breaches.

In this section, we shall discuss the correct court at which an offender should be dealt with, and the procedure once the breach is at court.

Dealing with the offender at the correct court

It is important to clarify whether a magistrates' court or the Crown Court should deal with the suspended sentence order following a breach of a community requirement or further conviction. This section should be read in conjunction with Chapter 4.

---

38 ibid, Schedule 16, paras 19(2) and 20(2).

39 *R v Rashid* [2022] EWCA Crim 328, [2022] 2 Cr. App. R. (S.) 41.

40 *R v Maunder* [2015] EWCA Crim 778, [2015] 2 Cr. App. R. (S.) 26.

In respect of commission of further offences, the law envisages four situations:

- Offender is convicted of a further offence in the magistrates' court during the operational period of a magistrates' court suspended sentence order.

- Offender is convicted of a further offence in the Crown Court during the operational period of a Crown Court suspended sentence order.

- Offender is convicted of a further offence in the Crown Court during the operational period of a magistrates' court suspended sentence order.

- Offender is convicted of a further offence in the magistrates' court during the operational period of a Crown Court suspended sentence order.

We shall deal with each in turn. Following that, we shall then consider the situation where an offender is in breach of the community requirements of a suspended sentence order.

Convicted in the magistrates' court and magistrates' court suspended sentence order

Where:

- an offender is convicted of an offence committed during the operational period of a suspended sentence order,

- the suspended sentence order was made by a magistrates' court, and

- the offender is presently before a magistrates' court,

the present court *must* generally deal with the offender in respect of the suspended sentence order.[41] However, the magistrates' court may choose to commit the offender to the Crown Court for sentence in respect of the new offence,[42] and so may choose to commit the offender to the Crown Court in respect of the suspended sentence order also.[43] Any duty or power which would fall to be discharged or exercised by the magistrates' court will no longer be exercisable by that court but, instead, will be dealt with by the Crown Court.[44]

Convicted in the Crown Court and Crown Court suspended sentence order

In a similar vein to the magistrates' court, where an offender is convicted of an offence in the Crown Court,[45] the Crown Court must deal with the suspended sentence order.[46]

Convicted in the Crown Court and magistrates' court suspended sentence order

The Crown Court is not restricted in its powers to deal with the suspended sentence order; the legislation provides that the Crown Court may deal with "an offender to whom a suspended sentence order relates".[47] Therefore, where an offender is convicted in the Crown Court for an offence committed during the operational period of a magistrates'

41 Sentencing Act 2020, Schedule 16, para 11(1).

42 Because, for example, their powers are insufficient.

43 Sentencing Act 2020, Schedule 16, para 11(3).

44 ibid, Schedule 16, para 11(4).

45 Either by way of guilty plea or following a trial by jury.

46 ibid, Schedule 16, para 12(1).

47 ibid.

court suspended sentence order, the Crown Court will deal with a suspended sentence order despite it being made by a magistrates' court.

Convicted in the magistrates' court and Crown Court suspended sentence order

The situation where a defendant is convicted of a further offence in the magistrates' court during the operational period of a Crown Court suspended sentence order is not as straightforward as the other circumstances already considered.

Paragraph 11(2) of Schedule 16 to the Sentencing Act 2020 provides that where an offender is convicted by a magistrates' court of any offence which the court is satisfied was committed during the operational period of a Crown Court suspended sentence order, the magistrates' court must either:

- commit the offender in custody or on bail to the Crown Court,[48] or

- if it does not commit the offender, must give written notice of the conviction to the appropriate officer of the Crown Court.[49]

In essence, the magistrates' court may either send ("commit") the offender to the Crown Court for the Crown Court to deal with the suspended sentence order, or deal with the suspended sentence order itself.

The decision as to what course of action the magistrates' court takes is dependent on the order made by the original sentencing judge. Section 297 of the Sentencing Act 2020 provides that where the Crown Court makes a suspended sentence order which imposes any community requirement, it may make a direction that the order is to be subject to

48 ibid, Schedule 16, para 11(2)(a). See also para 12(2)(a)(iii).

49 ibid, Schedule 16, para 11(2)(b).

magistrates' court supervision. Where the court makes such a direction, the magistrates' court is permitted in law to deal with the suspended sentence order.[50] However, where no such direction is made, the magistrates' court has no such power to deal with the suspended sentence order and *must* commit the offender to the Crown Court.

Breach of community requirements

The final circumstance to consider is where an offender is in breach of the community requirements of an order. In Chapter 4, the case of *R v H*,[51] was discussed in detail. In that case, the Court of Appeal clarified that the Crown Court has no power to deal with breaches of the community requirements of suspended sentence orders made by the magistrates' court. Equally, the magistrates' court has no power to deal with breaches of community requirements of Crown Court orders.

As *R v H* demonstrates: should the Crown Court deal with any breaches of community requirements imposed by a magistrates' court (and vice versa), any action taken will be unlawful. It is vital, therefore, to ensure that breaches of community requirements are dealt with by the court that imposed such requirements.[52]

Procedure at court

This section will discuss the procedure undertaken at court. In summary at this stage:

- First, the breach will be put to the offender,

---

[50] ibid, s.297(1). See also Sentencing Act 2020, Schedule 16, para 3(b).

[51] [2013] EWCA Crim 2115.

[52] Unless the Crown Court has made a direction that supervision of those community requirements will be held by the magistrates' court.

- if admitted, the Probation Service will then open its case providing a summary of the breach and the offender's compliance to the court,
- the defence will then seek to mitigate the breach and make submissions on the appropriate action to be taken, and
- finally, the judge will determine what action will be taken in respect of the breach.

Putting the breach/ conviction to the offender

When the case is called on, the offender will be identified in the normal way. However, the court clerk/ legal advisor should then go on to "put" the breach or further conviction to the offender. This involves asking the offender two questions:

- whether they admit or deny that they were the subject of a suspended sentence order on a specified date.
- Upon confirmation of that, the offender will then be asked whether they admit or deny that they were convicted of a further offence committed during the operational period of the suspended sentence order, or whether they admit or deny the breach(es) of the community requirement(s) on the specified dates.

Putting a conviction or breach to the offender is not merely a formality; it is a necessary process to ensure that the court is lawfully in a position to take action in respect of the suspended sentence order.

It is worth stating that there does not appear to be any legal requirement to formally "put" a breach to an offender. This is evident from *R v*

Carver[53] where HHJ Menary QC, giving the judgment of the Court, stated:

> Although [the breach] was not formally admitted by the appellant in the Crown Court, *the statute does not require the breach to be put to a defendant as is conventionally done*, and there can be no dispute but that the appellant was in breach by the commission of a further offence. The judge could then have dealt with him in the way she did.[54]

Whilst it may not be a legal requirement to put the breach to the offender, it is advised that such is best practice. It is clear from the provisions of Schedule 16 to the Sentencing Act 2020, that the court must be "satisfied" that the offender has breached a community requirement of the order without reasonable excuse,[55] or has been convicted of an offence committed during the operational period of a suspended sentence order.[56] "Putting" the breach to the offender is the easiest and clearest way of ensuring that the court is so satisfied.[57]

Importantly, where an offender has appeared before the magistrates' court in respect of a breach of a Crown Court suspended sentence order, the magistrates' court will commit the offender to the Crown Court to be dealt with. In these circumstances, the magistrates' court will first put the breach to the offender; meaning that the Crown Court need not do so. This is evident in Schedule 16 to the Sentencing Act which provides

53 [2020] EWCA Crim 1454.

54 ibid [23] (HHJ Menary QC) (emphasis added).

55 Sentencing Act 2020, Schedule 16, para 10(1)(b) (in respect of the magistrates' court) and para 12(2)(b) (in respect of the Crown Court).

56 ibid, Schedule 16, para 11(2) (in respect of the magistrates' court) and para 12(3) and 12(4).

57 To do so will also avoid the issues faced by the magistrates' court in *West Yorkshire Probation Board v Boulter* [2005] EWHC 2342 (Admin) which found that the Probation Service had failed to prove that the offender was the same individual subject to the community order allegedly in breach.

that where the magistrates' court commits an offender to the Crown Court in respect of a breach,[58] it must send the Crown Court

- a certificate signed by a justice of the peace certifying that the offender has breached the community requirements of the suspended sentence order in the respect specified in the certificate, and
- such other particulars of the case as may be desirable.[59]

Any certificate purporting to be so signed is admissible as evidence of the breach before the Crown Court, meaning that the breaches do not need to be "put" again to the offender.[60]

Key point

Whilst the breaches may not need to be put again, the court is alternatively advised to "put" the committal to the offender (i.e. ask the offender whether they admit that they were committed to the Crown Court by the magistrates' court). Once more, this is not a mere formality; this procedure will ensure that the Crown Court is satisfied that it is lawfully entitled to deal with the offender.

Should, however, the offender deny any breach (either of the community requirements or commission of further offences), the court would need to reach a finding on that fact.[61] In the magistrates' court, this would be by a lay bench or district/ deputy district judge. In the Crown Court, this would done by the judge, and not a jury. This is evident from the

[58] Sentencing Act 2020, Schedule 16, para 10(3)(b).

[59] ibid, Schedule 16, para 10(4).

[60] ibid.

[61] For a discussion on contested hearings, see Chapter 8.

wording of para 12(4) of Schedule 16 to the Sentencing Act 2020.[62] However, it is submitted that if the offender is identified by the court at the outset, and the breach is put to them in the terms described above, it will avoid the issues raised in *West Yorkshire Probation Board v Boulter*[63] where the defence successfully argued at first instance that the prosecution had failed to prove that the offender was the same individual subject to the community order.[64]

Probation opening

Following an admitted breach, the Court will turn to the advocate for the Probation Service to open the case. The level of detail provided by the advocate will ultimately depend on the tribunal whom they appear in front of. However, as a general principle, the advocate for the Probation Service may adopt the following approach:

- <u>Identify the sentence imposed in the first instance</u>. An example may be: "Your Honour, the offender was sentenced by this Court on [DATE]. He was sentenced to 12 months' imprisonment, suspended for 18 months, with two community requirements, namely 150 hours of unpaid work and up to 35 Rehabilitation Activity Requirement days."

- <u>Identify the breaches</u>. It should be remembered that the judge will have just heard what the breaches are, but the advocate can refer to the Breach Report at this stage too. An example may be: "Your Honour has just heard and will see from the Breach Report

62 "In proceedings before the Crown Court… any question whether the offender has been convicted during the operational period of the suspended sentence, is to be determined by the court and not by the verdict of a jury."

63 [2005] EWHC 2342 (Admin).

64 The appeal was allowed on account that the magistrates' court were permitted in law to draw a reasonable inference that the offender was the same person as subject to the order.

that the offender breached the requirements of this order by failing to attend his unpaid work requirement on [DATE] and [DATE]."

- Provide an up-to-date statement on the offender's compliance with the community requirements. For example: "Your Honour, as of today, the offender has completed 90 hours, and 10 minutes of the unpaid work requirement and has 59 hours, 50 minutes outstanding. The offender has not yet completed any RAR days."

- Provide an up-to-date statement of the offender's general compliance with Probation appointments. For example: "Your Honour, the offender has been offered 55 appointments since the start of the order. He has attended ten of those appointments. Of the appointments that have not been attended, the offender has 35 absences marked as acceptable, and nine appointments marked as unacceptable. There is one appointment that has not yet been recorded." If the offender is subject to Probation Reset,[65] the judge should be informed of this also.

- Identify the level of compliance: The advocate should identify what they consider the offender's level of compliance to be, for example: "The view of the Probation Service is that the offender's compliance is "Medium", though this is of course a matter for Your Honour".

- Identify the recommendation: Finally, the advocate should identify what the recommendation of the Probation Service is from the Breach Report. If this recommendation has changed since the Breach Report (e.g. due to recent re-engagement), this should be made clear. For example: "Your Honour, the recommendation of the Probation Service is that the suspended sentence is activated. The Probation Service considers the order to be unworkable, the offender to be unmotivated to engage, and

65 See Chapter 1.

does not feel in a position that they can continue to work with him."

As stated above, the level of detail required will ultimately depend on the tribunal before which the advocate appears. Many judges will only require an update on the offender's compliance, having read the Breach Report and its contents in full already. Some judges may identify that they do not need to hear submissions from the Probation Service and simply turn their attention to the defence.

Defence submissions

The court will then turn to the defence to make their submissions in respect of the breach. It must be remembered that the default position when it comes to suspended sentence orders is that the court *must* activate (in whole or in part) unless it is unjust to do so. Realistically, therefore, a defence submission will focus on either:

- Seeking to persuade the court that it would be unjust to activate at all; or
- Seeking to persuade the court that whilst it is inevitable that the suspended sentence will be activated, it should only be activated in part (to reflect the reduction for compliance).

The decision as to what approach is taken by the defence advocate will depend on a number of factors, including:

- Whether this is the offender's first breach, or whether there have been previous instances of breach.
- The offender's general compliance with the order.
- The offender's motivation in respect of the order.
- How long remains on the order.

Ultimately, the defence advocate will be required to act in accordance with the instructions of the offender and what they are hoping to achieve. A defence advocate must have the full range of powers available to the court in mind,[66] as well as the Sentencing Guidelines applicable to breach proceedings.[67]

Judgment and remarks

Having heard the submissions from both the Probation Service and the defence, the judge will consider what action they consider most appropriate in the circumstances. Importantly, if the judge does not consider they have sufficient information to act on the breach, they should adjourn.[68]

Whatever action the judge takes, they should provide their reasons in open court. Para 14(1) of Schedule 16 to the Sentencing Act 2020 states that where the court considers activation to be unjust "the court must state its reasons." Equally, the CrimPR 2020 prescribes that where the court decides not to order that a suspended sentence of imprisonment is to take effect,[69] the court must explain why it has so decided, when it explains the sentence that it has passed.[70] Readers are advised to review the example wording provided in Part II of the *Crown Court Compendium (Sentencing)*.[71]

For a full discussion on the powers of a judge following an admitted breach, see below. In addition to the powers available to the court on

---

66 See below, "Powers of court following breach or conviction".

67 See Chapter 9.

68 As was evident in *R v Reynolds* [2015] EWCA Crim 1796, [2016] 1 Cr. App. R. (S.) 33.

69 Criminal Procedure Rules 2020, r.28.1(1)(c)(i).

70 ibid, r.28.2.

71 Courts and Tribunals Judiciary, *Crown Court Compendium – Part II Sentencing* (June 2023), p 10-6.

breach, the court may also require the offender to pay a contribution towards the costs of the proceedings (generally the request is for £250).

> **Key point**
>
> Advocates remember: A judge *must* take action on any breach; they are *not* permitted in law to take no action or issue no penalty.

Powers of court following breach or conviction

Having now considered the legal principles relevant to breaches of a suspended sentence order, and the procedure to be adopted, we can now consider the powers available to the court following a breach.

Where a court is satisfied that the offender has breached a community requirement of a suspended sentence order, or has committed an offence during the operational period of a suspended sentence order, it must deal with the offender in accordance with para 13 of Schedule 16 to the Sentencing Act.

In dealing with a suspended sentence order, the court must do one of the following:[72]

- Activate the suspended sentence order in full,
- Activate the suspended sentence order in part,
- Order that the offender pay a fine not exceeding £2,500,
- In the case where the suspended sentence order imposes one or more community requirements:

[72] Sentencing Act 2020, Schedule 16, para 13(1).

  - impose more onerous community requirements, or
  - extend the supervision period, or
  - extend the operational period,

- In particular circumstances, may commit the offender to prison for a period not exceeding 28 days, or

- In the case where the suspended sentence order does not impose any community requirements, extend the operational period.

The court may utilise a combination of these powers in marking the breach (e.g. impose a fine and impose more onerous requirements).

Reference to the court imposing a criminal courts charge[73] is to be ignored on account that from 24 December 2015[74] the sum payable was reduced to £0 (effectively abolishing the criminal courts charge).

Key point

In determining the appropriate action to take/ penalty to impose for a breach, the court will have regard to Sentencing Council Guidelines for Breach of a Suspended Sentence Order. This is discussed in full in Chapter 9.

Where a court deals with an offender in any of these ways, the appropriate officer of the court must notify the appropriate officer of the court which passed the sentence of the method adopted.[75]

---

73 ibid, Schedule 16, para 13(2).

74 As a result of The Prosecution of Offences Act 1985 (Criminal Courts Charge) (Amendment) Regulations 2015.

75 Sentencing Act, Schedule 16, para 13(3).

Before we consider each of these powers in turn, it is important to note that the court is obligated to take one of the actions in para 13(1). The court is *not* permitted to take "no action" in respect of the breach.[76] Equally, and unlike community orders, the court does not have the power to revoke the suspended sentence order,[77] nor does it have the power to re-sentence the offender.[78] The court is restricted to the powers listed in para 13 of Schedule 16. For this reason, the powers of a court in dealing with a suspended sentence order are more restrictive than the powers available to it when dealing with a community order.[79]

We shall now consider each of the powers available to the court in turn.

Default position: Activate in full or part

Where the court deals with an offender following a breach of the community requirements of a suspended sentence order, or conviction for a further offence committed during the operational period of a suspended sentence order, the court *must* activate the suspended sentence (in full or in part) unless it would be unjust in all the circumstances to

---

76 *R v Anderson* [2014] EWCA Crim 797 [10] (Jeremy Baker J); *R v Ward* [2012] EWCA Crim 3139, [2013] 2 Cr. App. R. (S.) 35 [23] (Sharp J DBE); *AG's Ref No 36 of 2018 (R v Usherwood)* [2018] EWCA Crim 1156, [2018] 2 Cr. App. R. (S.) 39; *R v Mohammed* [2023] EWCA Crim 1458 [38] (Andrews J); *R v Hilliard* [2023] EWCA Crim 1155 [20] Lambert J); *R v Lister* [2023] EWCA Crim 1741 [32] (HHJ Dhir KC). See also *R v Blakemore* [2016] EWCA Crim 1396, [2017] 1 Cr. App. R. (S.) 5.

77 *R v Blakemore* [2016] EWCA Crim 1396, [2017] 1 Cr. App. R. (S.) 5; *R v Rees* [2022] EWCA Crim 1710 [13] (Sweeting J).

78 *R v Sharp* [2020] EWCA Crim 534, [2020] 2 Cr. App. R. (S.) 33 at [14] (Pepperall J). See also *R v Clarke* [2018] EWCA Crim 2201 [16] (Cheema-Grubb J) in the context of the former law under the Criminal Justice Act 2003, Schedule 12.

79 As made clear by HHJ Warwick McKinnon, providing the judgment of the Court, in *R v Phipps* [2007] EWCA Crim 2923, [2008] 2 Cr. App. R. (S.) 20 [15].

do so.[80] This can usefully be referred to as the "default" position and is referred to as a "duty" to activate in the Sentencing Act 2020.[81]

It is important to emphasise at this stage that the element of unjustness applies to activation generally (i.e. activation "in whole *or* in part"). In *R v McDonagh,*[82] the Court of Appeal explained that the sentencing judge acted under a "misapprehension" when he stated in open court that a suspended sentence must be triggered in full, unless it would be unjust not to, with any regard to the fact that it could also be activated in part.[83]

Deciding whether to activate

When faced with a breach of the suspended sentence order, the starting point appears to be the two-stage test from the Court of Appeal in *R v Sheppard.*[84] In *Sheppard*, Coulson J (as he then was) explained that:

> It seems to us that the statutory provisions envisage a two stage test. First, where there has been a breach, the court must order that the suspended sentence take effect either in whole or in part unless it would be unjust to do so. [...] Secondly, if it is not unjust to activate the suspended sentence, then the court must decide whether or not to impose the original sentence or modify the term.[85]

In essence:

---

[80] ibid, Schedule 16, para 14(1). For a recent example, see *R v Santry* [2023] EWCA Crim 1402.

[81] See the Heading to para 14 of Schedule 16 to the Sentencing Act 2020.

[82] [2017] EWCA Crim 2193.

[83] ibid, [14] (Spencer J).

[84] [2008] EWCA Crim 799, [2008] 2 Cr. App. R. (S.) 93.

[85] ibid, [14] (Coulson J).

- The court must first determine whether it would be unjust to activate the sentence at all.

- If the court does *not* consider it to be unjust, the court must then consider whether to activate the sentence in full or in part.

As a starting point it is important note that in *R v Ansley,*[86] Coulson J explained that whether a suspended sentence order is activated, and the amount of that sentence which is activated, is:

> ultimately a matter of discretion for the judge. This court will not interfere with the exercise of that discretion unless it can be shown that the judge erred in principle.[87]

The same approach was taken in *R v Prime*[88] where the Court of Appeal reasoned:

> It is not the function of this court to tinker with sentences when the judge imposes a sentence which lies within the proper range, even if it appears to this court that the judge has gone to the upper end of that range.[89]

Let us now consider each question from *Sheppard* in turn.

Question 1: Is it unjust to activate?

The first question for the judge to consider is whether it would be "unjust" in all the circumstances to activate the order in part or full. Paragraph 14(2) prescribes three circumstances that the court must consider when assessing this question:

86 [2014] EWCA Crim 1135.

87 ibid, [8] (Coulson J).

88 [2013] EWCA Crim 2525.

89 ibid, [17] (Jackson LJ).

- the extent to which the offender has complied with any community requirements of the suspended sentence order,[90]
- where the offender has been convicted of a further offence committed during the operational period of the suspended sentence order, the facts of the subsequent offence,[91] and
- in a case where the suspended sentence order qualifies for special procedures, the ability to commit the offender to custody.[92]

The relevance of the offender's compliance with the order is dealt with below.[93] At this stage, it will be briefly worth discussing the relevance of the further offence committed during the operational period. Generally speaking, defence advocates will argue that where an offence is dissimilar, or less serious (or both), to the offence subject to the suspended sentence order, the court should step away from activation. Whilst that is a common approach taken by the courts, it is important to emphasise that in no way are courts inhibited from activating the suspended sentence where the offence is dissimilar. This was made clear by the Court of Appeal in *R v Craine,*[94] where Russell J emphasised:

> it cannot be made too plain that when suspended sentences of imprisonment are imposed they mean what they say. Only in exceptional circumstances, if further offences involving imprisonment are committed, will those suspended

[90] Sentencing Act 2020, Schedule 16, para 14(2)(a). Where an offender was sentenced to a stand-alone suspended sentence order, the court will not be in a position to assess the offender's compliance.

[91] ibid, Schedule 16, para 14(2)(b). See also *R v Craine* (1981) 3 Cr. App. R. (S.) 198 (CA); *R v Fleming* (1989) 11 Cr. App. R. (S.) 137 (CA).

[92] ibid, Schedule 16, para 14(2)(c). See Chapter 2 for a discussion of such special procedures.

[93] See below, "Question 2: If it is not unjust, should it be activated in full or part?"

[94] (1981) 3 Cr. App. R. (S.) 198 (CA).

> sentences not be activated. Here it is said the sentence imposed [...] was one involving an offence, of an entirely different character from the offences committed within 10 days of that sentence being imposed. It cannot be over-emphasised that that in itself is not an exceptional circumstance, particularly here in view of the fact the appellant was committing these offences within a very short time of the suspended sentence being imposed.[95]

This approach was reaffirmed by the Court of Appeal in *R v Fleming*[96] where Lord Lane CJ explained that:

> the fact that the subsequent offence is of a different nature does not in any way inhibit the court from ordering the suspended sentence to be implemented consecutively, or from ordering a term of imprisonment to be imposed in respect of the offences for which the man was placed on probation, because at the time when he was placed on probation, it was made perfectly clear to him that if during the term of the probation order he was to get into further trouble, then he would undoubtedly run the risk of going to prison.[97]

It is important to note that the list in para 14(2) is not exhaustive; para 14(1) is clear that the court must consider all the circumstances "including" the matters listed in para 14(2). The Sentencing Council, in the definitive guideline on *Breach of a suspended sentence order*,[98] provides that, in addition to the matters listed above, the court may also consider:

---

[95] ibid, 200 (Russell J).

[96] (1989) 11 Cr. App. R. (S.) 137 (CA).

[97] ibid, 138-139 (Lord Lane CJ). See also *R v Clitheroe* (1987) 9 Cr. App. R. (S.) 159 (CA).

[98] Sentencing Council, *Breach of a suspended sentence order* (1 October 2018). See Chapter 9.

- any strong personal mitigation,
- whether there is a realistic prospect of rehabilitation, and
- whether immediate custody will result in significant impact on others.

These factors are identical to those found in the Overarching Guideline *Imposition of community and custodial sentences*.[99] In that Guideline, these factors can be used to indicate that it may be appropriate to suspend a custodial sentence. As made clear in that Guideline, those factors should be weighed against the factors indicating that it would *not* be appropriate to suspend a custodial sentence. By utilising the same factors, the court, in essence, is considering once more whether a term of imprisonment can be suspended.

Importantly, however, the court may not rely on factors or circumstances present at the time the suspended sentence order was made. This is very clear in the *Breach of a suspended sentence order* Guideline. It states: "Only new and exceptional factors/circumstances not present at the time the suspended sentence order was imposed should be taken into account."

Common factors used in practice to show that it would be unjust to activate include:

- The physical and mental health of the offender, which may have declined since the imposition of the suspended sentence order. An offender may have been impacted by any number of external factors which have exacerbated their physical or mental health (such as bereavement).
- The residence status of the offender may have changed to a negative extent for the offender. For example, the offender having

99 Sentencing Council, *Imposition of community and custodial sentences* (1 February 2017).

been made homeless, and thus finding compliance more challenging, may be a factor towards it being unjust to activate.

An interesting factor which often comes before the courts concerns the offender's addiction to alcohol or drugs. Generally speaking, such addictions should not afford the offender an excuse for non-compliance. However, it is worth remembering that the proximity of the breach to the imposition of the order must be considered.[100] The issues and challenges faced by offenders with drink or drug problems are not solved overnight; in the early stages of such an order, it may prove unjust to activate a suspended sentence where any breach is explained by the offender's addiction. A useful way to consider this is that the earlier into the suspended sentence order, the more likely the offender's addiction problems may undermine or interfere with their compliance. That may persuade the court to afford the offender another chance.

Another factor that may be of relevance concerns factors external to the offender. An offender may suggest that their lack of compliance is caused, in part, by a shortfall in the quality of supervision by the Probation Service. The most common argument raised involves the circumstance where the offender's responsible officer has changed on a number of occasions. Such a change can often be difficult for an offender given that they may have built a rapport with their responsible officer, may have struggled to first create that relationship, and often feel as though they are being "messed about" by the Probation Service. Whilst the courts should be wary of placing blame at the doorstep of the Probation Service, the court should investigate whether there is any merit to the claim that the offender has struggled to comply due to the actions of the Probation Service.

Whilst the Judge will be the ultimate arbiter as to whether it would be unjust to activate the suspended sentence order, they will be assisted by

---

[100] See the Sentencing Council Guideline on *Breach of a suspended sentence order* (Chapter 9).

any views held by the Probation Service[101] and submissions made by the advocates in the case.

Readers are encouraged to review the case law in this area, a selection of which is provided at the end of this chapter.

Question 2: If it is not unjust, should it be activated in full or part?

Should the court consider that it would not be unjust in all the circumstances to activate the suspended sentence order generally, the court must then consider whether to activate in full or in part. The primary consideration as to whether to activate in full or in part appears to be the offender's compliance with the suspended sentence order.[102]

In *Sheppard*, Coulson J would explain that:

> Part compliance is, of course, relevant again at this stage [i.e. Question 2], because if there had been substantial and prompt compliance with the order then, even if a suspended sentence is to be activated, the court may be minded to impose a lesser term than that originally specified.[103]

The authorities in this area differ significantly. Generally, the authorities show that where there is some compliance with community requirements of a more punitive nature (such as unpaid work or a curfew), a reduction will generally be applied.[104] Compliance with more rehabilitative requirements, on the other hand, do not generally afford any

[101] See *R v Aslam* [2016] EWCA Crim 845, [2016] 2 Cr. App. R. (S.) 29

[102] Once more, this cannot be done if there were no community requirements imposed with the order.

[103] *R v Sheppard* [2008] EWCA Crim 799, [2008] 2 Cr. App. R. (S.) 93 [14] (Coulson J).

[104] *R v Kavanagh* [2010] EWCA Crim 1737, [2011] 1 Cr. App. R. (S.) 63; *R v Zeca* [2009] EWCA Crim 133, [2009] 2 Cr. App. R. (S.) 65.

reduction.[105] Indeed, in *R v Wolstenholme*,[106] the Court of Appeal drew an explicit distinction between conditions "designed to be therapeutic, rather than punitive."[107]

It is essential to note from the outset, however, that mere compliance with the community requirements of a suspended sentence order does not automatically justify a reduction in activation. There are many authorities that show that if an offender fails to engage with the principal aim of a suspended sentence order, then notwithstanding some partial compliance, they are at risk of having the entirety of that suspended sentence order activated. In *R v Locke,*[108] the offender had been sentenced to a suspended sentence of eight months' imprisonment, for an offence of handling stolen goods. The community requirements included matters such as a curfew and 200 hours of unpaid work. During the suspended sentence order, the offender attended 59 of the 64 appointments; of the five missed appointments, the Probation Service only marked two of them as having been "unacceptable". The offender completed both the Thinking Skills Programme and the 200 hours of unpaid work. Finally, he was regarded as being polite and had kept in touch with his programme tutors and probation officer.

Despite his compliance with the order, the offender was convicted of 13 offences of theft committed during the operational period of the suspended sentence order (one of the offences being committed four days after the imposition of the suspended sentence). The sentencing judge imposed a term of 40 months' imprisonment in respect of each offence of theft, concurrently, and activated the suspended sentence in full.

On appeal, it was argued on behalf of the offender that the court should have applied a reduction to the sentence of imprisonment to reflect the

---

105 R v *Wolstenholme* [2016] EWCA Crim 638, [2016] 2 Cr. App. R. (S.) 19; *R v Abdille* [2009] EWCA Crim 1195, [2010] 1 Cr. App. R. (S.) 18.

106 [2016] EWCA Crim 638, [2016] 2 Cr. App. R. (S.) 19.

107 ibid, [11] (McGowan J).

108 [2016] EWCA Crim 2120.

offender's compliance with the order. The Court of Appeal concluded that, whilst in some cases it is appropriate to reduce the term of an activated suspended sentence to reflect compliance with, and completion of, the community requirements, the activation of the suspended sentence order in full in this case was "wholly justified".[109] The Court of Appeal justified this on account that offender, whilst complying with the order, continued to commit serial and serious criminal offences. The Court was still able to activate the suspended sentence in full despite the "substantial compliance" of the offender.[110] In particular, Morris J explained "Despite the assistance of the probation service, the appellant had apparently learnt nothing from his supervision and his programme."[111] Mr Justice Morris would conclude:

> This is not a case where the offender has completed all the requirements, including the unpaid work, and got practically to the end of his suspension period without offending and then offended, perhaps once, at the end of that period. In such a case a reduction might be warranted. Rather, here, the appellant simply carried on offending, and persistently offending, in relation to the same type of offences immediately following the imposition of the suspended sentence and continually thereafter. He was given a chance and he immediately rejected that chance.[112]

Locke is a helpful authority to demonstrate that compliance with the suspended sentence order does not automatically guarantee a reduction following activation.[113] Indeed, the judgment in *Locke* is reflected in the

---

[109] ibid, [12] (Morris J).

[110] ibid, [13] (Morris J).

[111] ibid.

[112] ibid, [14] (Morris J).

[113] In *R v Hussain* [2014] EWCA Crim 643, the Court of Appeal said that in dealing with cases where it can be said that a defendant has ignored his obligations under the suspended sentence, the court may activate the

Sentencing Council Guidelines on *Breach of a suspended sentence order* (1 October 2018).[114] This provides that where an offender has committed "Multiple and/or more serious new offence(s)", the appropriate penalty would be "full activation of original custodial term" without a consideration of compliance with the order.

Given the significant quantity of authorities in this area, a selection of key cases have been provided at the end of this chapter.

Length of activation

As already discussed, a court is empowered to activate a sentence in whole or in part. In activating the sentence in part, there is no minimum period by which the court must activate the sentence. For example, the court may, if it wished, activate a suspended sentence by imposing one day's imprisonment. As will be discussed below, where an offender was remanded in custody or subject to a qualifying curfew, any time spent on custody/ curfew will count towards any term of imprisonment upon activation. The court may, therefore, activate the suspended sentence in part to be commensurate with any time spent remanded in custody (i.e. the offender would be "time served").

As part of this discussion, it is important to distinguish between the passing of a sentence, and activation of that sentence. The restrictions on passing a sentence do not apply to activation of sentence. For example, s.263(2) of the Sentencing Act 2020 provides that the minimum term for an offender aged 18-20 to a sentence of detention in a Young Offender Institution is 21 days. This restriction is relevant to the *passing* of sentence, but not to its *activation*. Should a young offender appear before the court in breach of a suspended sentence order, therefore, the

---

suspended sentence, even where the offender has complied with the requirements of the order.

[114] See Chapter 9 for a full discussion.

court is empowered to activate the suspended sentence in any part (i.e. it need not activate at least 21 days).

Timing of activation (concurrent or consecutive)

As discussed in Chapter 7, the Court may order that an activated suspended sentence order takes effect immediately, or on the expiry of another custodial sentence (i.e. consecutive to another custodial sentence).[115] Indeed, in *R v Ithell*,[116] Edmund Davies LJ would explain that "unless there are some quite exceptional circumstances, the suspended sentence should be ordered to run consecutively to the sentence given for the current offence."[117] This view is replicated in the *Totality* Guideline (1 July 2023) which provides that:

> Where an offender commits an additional offence during the operational period of a suspended sentence and the court orders the suspended sentence to be activated, the additional sentence will generally be consecutive to the activated suspended sentence, as it will arise out of unrelated facts.

Importantly, however, the power to activate the suspended sentence order consecutive to another sentence of imprisonment is restricted by s.225 Sentencing Act 2020. This section provides that no consecutive sentence can be imposed where a person was released on licence and subsequently recalled.

Totality

It is important to note that where the court activates the suspended sentence order, it must have regard to the principle of totality when dealing with further offences. The leading authority on this point is *AG's*

[115] Sentencing Act 2020, Schedule 16, para 15(2).

[116] (1969) 53 Cr. App. R. 210 (CA).

[117] ibid, 212 (Edmund Davies LJ).

Reference (No 36 of 2018) (R v Usherwood).[118] In *Usherwood*, the offender, a young man of 20, was sentenced for a number of offences committed in breach of two suspended sentence orders. In light of the sentences imposed against the offender, the sentencing judge did not activate the suspended sentence order in full; choosing to activate it in part. Lord Justice Treacy would explain that the sentencing judge was correct not to activate the suspended sentence in full. His Lordship explained that:

> Normally, where a suspended sentence has been passed and an offender re-offends in a serious and similar way (as was the case here) and where that offender has largely failed to comply with requirements imposed, a full activation of the suspended term would be entirely appropriate. In this particular case, however, it seems to us that the requirements of totality come into play, given the substantial sentence appropriate for the drugs matters.[119]

The Court of Appeal did not, therefore, interfere with the sentencing judge's decision not to activate the suspended sentence order in full. The essential point from *Usherwood* is that when dealing with further offences, the principle of totality is "in play" when considering the length of any such activation.[120]

Time spent on remand and qualifying curfew

Just as a defendant is entitled to any time spent on remand, or having been subject to a qualifying curfew, to count towards a sentence of imprisonment, so too is an offender whose suspended sentence order is activated.

---

[118] [2018] EWCA Crim 1156, [2018] 2 Cr. App. R. (S.) 39.

[119] ibid, [19] (Treacy LJ).

[120] See also *R v Ballard* [2016] EWCA Crim 1173 where the Court of Appeal reduced the period of activation to reflect totality.

In respect of remands in custody, s.240(ZA)(3) of the Criminal Justice Act 2003 states that the number of days for which the offender was remanded in custody in connection with the offence or a related offence is to count as time served by the offender as part of the sentence. This provision applies equally to suspended sentence orders.[121] In essence, any time spent remanded in custody will count automatically upon the sentence being activated.[122] Equally, where an offender has been remanded on conditional bail with an electronically monitored curfew of at least nine hours, they are entitled to have half of that time spent subject qualifying curfew count towards any activated sentence of imprisonment.[123]

Practitioners know well that a deduction of time spent whilst remanded in custody does not need to be declared or stated in open court; it is an administrative matter for the prison service and not the court.[124] Despite that, judges will normally state that any time spent on remand will count. Indeed, the Part II of the *Crown Court Compendium (Sentencing)* provides example wording for judges to use when informing an offender of time spent on remand when activating a suspended sentence:

> The days which you spent on remand in custody before you were originally sentenced will automatically count towards

---

[121] Criminal Justice Act 2003, s.240(ZA)(7).

[122] *Carruthers v Hampshire Probation Service* [2010] EWHC 1961 (Admin) [38] (Wyn Williams J); *AG Ref No 40 of 2011* (*R v Williams*) [2011] EWCA Crim 2126 [22] (Pitchford LJ).

[123] Sentencing Act 2020, s.325; Criminal Justice Act 2003, s.240A.

[124] It was previously the responsibility of the court under what was the original s.240 of the Criminal Justice Act 2003. However, with the advent of s.240(ZA), the role of the court in calculating time spent of remand was removed and was transferred to the prison service.

> the [part of the] sentence which I have now brought into operation.[125]

On the other hand, section 325(2) of the Sentencing Act 2020 obliges the court to specify the period credited for time spent on qualifying curfew.[126]

A not so uncommon scenario is where a sentencing judge indicates that they have taken the time spent remanded in custody into account when deciding to suspend the sentence of imprisonment,[127] and the offender will not be entitled to any such deduction should the sentence be activated. This is justified on account that the offender has already benefited from their time remanded in custody at the point the suspended sentence was passed. This approach is both misguided and wrong; sentencers do not have the power to dictate how much time is to be deducted from an offender's sentence. As stated above, this is an administrative matter for the prison service. Furthermore, a judge should not factor in the time spent on remand to the issue of whether to suspend a sentence of imprisonment.

This was particularly evident in the case of *Archer v Governor of Low Newton Prison.*[128] In that case, the offender had been sentenced for attempted robbery to 12 months' imprisonment, suspended for 24 months. The offender had spent a total 180 days, split across having been remanded in custody and on a qualifying curfew. The sentencing judge at first instance directed that the 180 days was taken into consideration

---

125 Courts and Tribunals Judiciary, *Crown Court Compendium – Part II Sentencing* (June 2023), 5-65.

126 See also s.325(4) which requires the court to state in open court any deductions that are made as a result of the offender breaking the curfew or electronic monitoring condition.

127 Despite the authority of *R v Rushworth* [2018] EWCA Crim 2196 where Simon LJ referred to the "erroneous approach" of taking into account time spent remanded in custody when considering whether to suspend a sentence of imprisonment (at [16]).

128 [2014] EWHC 2407 (Admin).

for the purposes of imposing the suspended sentence order and, as a result, would not be deducted from the term of imprisonment if the sentence was later activated. The offender later breached the order by committing further offences and the full 12-month sentence of imprisonment was activated. Upon activating the suspended sentence, the sentencing judge said nothing about the 180 days and the prison governor argued that they were not obliged to deduct the 180 days from the offender's term of imprisonment.

The offender applied for *habeas corpus* to the Court of Appeal. The issue was simply this: If the 180 days were to be credited, then it followed that the offender would have been unlawfully held in custody. On the other hand, if that time did not fall for consideration, she would have remained lawfully in custody. Concluding that the 180 days *did* count towards the activated sentence, Treacy LJ stated that:

> Section 240ZA retains the system that time spent on remand will continue to be credited but it removes the exercise of calculation from the sentencing court. What it does is to convert what was previously a task delegated to the sentencing judge into an administrative task to be carried out by the Prison Service as a calculation.[129]

For those reasons, the Court concluded that the offender was being detained unlawfully and ordered them to be immediately discharged out of custody. The judgment of Treacy LJ accords with the earlier view of the Court of Appeal in *R v Collier* where Keith J stated:

> Under this new regime, time spent in custody on remand automatically counts towards one's sentence[...]. Section 240ZA(7) applies the new regime to the time which a defendant spends in custody on remand prior to the imposition of a suspended sentence. That time counts

[129] ibid, [8] (Treacy LJ).

towards his sentence if the suspended sentence is subsequently activated.[130]

The following principles can be derived from the above:[131]

- The appropriate time for considering time spent on remand or subject to a qualifying curfew prior to the imposition of a suspended sentence is at the activation hearing before the judge entrusted with that task.[132]

- When a judge imposes a suspended sentence, in determining the appropriate length he should not ordinarily give credit for days spent on remand.[133]

- Time spent remanded in custody will count automatically towards any suspended sentence upon activation of that sentence (in whole or in part) without a declaration of such by the court. However, time spent subject to a qualifying curfew must be declared in open court.

- There is no power to order that time served prior to the imposition of a suspended sentence will not count towards the custodial sentence if it is later activated.[134]

- The sentencing judge need not state in open court that the time spent whilst remanded in custody counts towards the sentence;

---

[130] *R v Collier* [2013] EWCA Crim 1132 [5] (Keith J).

[131] For further cases dealing with suspended sentence orders and time spent on remand, see: *R v Mohammed* [2007] EWCA Crim 2756, [2008] 2 Cr. App. R. (S.) 14; *R v Rakib* [2011] EWCA Crim 870, [2012] 1 Cr. App. R. (S.) 1; *R v Hinds* [2018] EWCA Crim 749.

[132] *R v Mari* [2010] EWCA Crim 1143.

[133] *R v Hewitt* [2011] EWCA Crim 885.

[134] *R v Aroriode-Francis* [2021] EWCA Crim 1591 [31] (Haddon-Cave LJ); *R v Rushworth* [2018] EWCA Crim 2196.

deduction is an administrative task for the prison service. However, where the offender has the benefit of time spent on qualifying curfew, this must be openly stated in court.[135]

Restrictions on Activation I: Not previously activated

What is the situation if the suspended sentence order has already been activated? Quite simply, no action can be taken by the court where the suspended sentence order has already been activated.[136] This was evident most recently in *R v Rashid*.[137] In *Rashid*, the offender had been sentenced to four months' imprisonment, suspended for 24 months, for an offence of possession of a bladed article in a public place. Subsequent to that sentence:

- On 10 April 2019, in the Crown Court at Snaresbrook, the offender was sentenced for breaching a Criminal Behaviour Order. At that time, the suspended sentence of four months' imprisonment was activated.

- On 29 November 2019, in the Crown Court at Inner London, the offender was sentenced for false imprisonment, kidnapping, and robbery. The suspended sentence was also activated in full and ordered to run consecutively.

---

135 Sentencing Act 2020, s.325(2).

136 Paragraphs 11(1)(a) (in respect of the magistrates' court) and 12(3)(b) (in respect of the Crown Court) of Schedule 16 to the Sentencing Act 2020 states that the court may only deal with an offender where the suspended sentence has not already "taken effect".

137 [2022] EWCA Crim 328, [2022] 2 Cr. App. R. (S.) 41.

On appeal, Dingemans LJ stated in no uncertain terms: "it is not possible to activate twice a suspended sentence of imprisonment."[138] His Lordship would conclude:

> In our judgment, the activation of the suspended sentence for a second time was unlawful. It is unlawful because when it was first activated, the suspended sentence came into force. It cannot be imposed a second time; to do so would punish the applicant twice for the same offending.[139]

Restrictions on activation II: Cannot activate and suspend in part

Suppose the court imposes a suspended sentence order on an offender. Should the offender breach a community requirement of that order or commit a further offence, is it possible for the court to activate the suspended sentence in part, and allow the remaining part to not be activated (and thus continue to be suspended)?

This was the issue that arose in the case of *R v Bostan*,[140] where the offender had been sentenced to a term of 18 months' detention,[141] suspended for 23 months. Importantly for our purposes, the 18 months' sentence comprised of three sentences (nine months, six months and three months' detention), to be served consecutively. The offender breached the order by committing further offences during the operational period of the order. The sentencing judge activated the suspended sentence in part to the extent of three months' detention. It appeared, however, from the sentencing remarks of the learned judge that they may

138 ibid, [6] (Dingemans LJ).

139 ibid, [9] (Dingemans LJ).

140 [2018] EWCA Crim 494.

141 The offender was under the age of 21, and thus the correct terminology is "detention" as opposed to "imprisonment".

have intended to activate only the three months' detention for one of the offences imposed and not the "other" suspended terms also imposed.

On appeal, it was argued (inter alia), that although the suspended sentence order was built on separate consecutive custodial sentences, the sentence was nevertheless in law "a single, indivisible custodial term of 18 months, suspended for 24 months."[142] The Court of Appeal agreed; Andrew Baker J ruled that by activating the suspended sentence order in part, the entire order had been "substituted… by an immediate custodial sentence with a reduced term".[143]

In summary, therefore, the effect of activation (whether in part or in full) is that the suspended sentence order no longer exists; it is not possible, therefore, to both activate and suspend at the same time.[144]

Restrictions on Activation III: Length of custody cannot be increased

Importantly, the power to activate the sentence does not entail a power to increase the length of the custodial term;[145] Maddison J usefully phrased it as such: "If 34 weeks' imprisonment was the correct sentence… on 13 August [the date of the imposition of the suspended sentence], it was the correct sentence on 13 September [the date of sentence of the breach]."[146] In short, the court may activate the suspended sentence in full, or in part (i.e. reducing the length), but may

142 *Bostan* (n140) [11] (Andrew Baker J).

143 ibid, [12] (Andrew Baker J).

144 *Bostan* was approved in *R v Whitham* [2019] EWCA Crim 1933.

145 *R v Cassidy* [2010] EWCA Crim 3146.

146 ibid [16] (Maddison J).

not extend the length of the sentence.[147] The court must consider all the circumstances, including the facts/ nature of the new offence.[148]

Unrepresented offenders and activation

A common feature in probation cases is that an offender will often be unrepresented. In some cases, such as applications to amend the requirements, this can be unproblematic. In cases involving breach proceedings, however, the court may be reluctant to proceed to deal with the breach where an offender is unrepresented. A question that may arise is whether the court is *technically* permitted to deal with an offender who is unrepresented.

Readers will know that s.226 of the Sentencing Act 2020 provides a general restriction on courts when imposing custodial sentences. Specifically, a court may not impose a sentence of imprisonment for an adult (i.e. aged 21 and over) unless the offender:[149]

- is legally represented in that court, or
- has failed, or is ineligible on financial grounds, to benefit from relevant representation, or
- has previously been sentenced to imprisonment by a court in any part of the United Kingdom. [150]

---

[147] See also *R v Phipps* [2007] EWCA Crim 2923, [2008] 2 Cr. App. R. (S.) 20.

[148] Sentencing Act 2020, Schedule 16, para 14(2)(b). The suspended sentence may still be activated even where the new offence/ further conviction does not warrant imprisonment: *Nobbs v DPP* [2008] EWHC 1653 (Admin).

[149] Sentencing Act 2020, s.226(3).

[150] A suspended sentence which has not been activated does not amount to a previous sentence of imprisonment (see s.226(4) Sentencing Act 2020).

A suspended sentence order is treated in law as a sentence of imprisonment.[151] Therefore, an offender must be represented before the court may pass a suspended sentence order, unless any of the exceptions above apply. However, what is the position where the court is considering activating the suspended sentence order?

Technically speaking, the provisions of s.226 do not apply to the position where the court activates a suspended sentence. This is so on account that the sentence of imprisonment has already been passed (at the time that the suspended sentence order was made); "activation" does not amount to "imposing" that sentence.[152] The court is therefore able, if it so wishes, to activate the term of imprisonment where the offender is unrepresented without having to concern itself with s.226.[153] However, in practice, such is an unlikely course of action to be taken by the courts; it is more likely that the court will adjourn the proceedings to allow the offender to obtain legal representation. Whilst not strictly necessary in law, it does present the fairest approach for all parties involved in breach proceedings.

Key point

Where an offender is unrepresented, the court will expect submissions from the advocate from the Probation Service as to whether the offender requires, or will benefit from, legal representation.

---

151 Sentencing Act 2020, s.289(1).

152 *R v Chamberlain* (1992) 13 Cr. App. R. (S.) 525 (CA). *NB The Court in Chamberlain was not concerned with legally represented offenders and activation, but the principles relating to the meaning of activation for the purpose of a sentence of imprisonment remain relevant.*

153 The position is, of course, different for breach of community orders for which the restrictions in s.226 will apply in the normal way where an offender is re-sentenced to imprisonment (see Chapter 6).

The recommendation of the Probation Service on any breach proceedings will assist the court (and the advocate for the Probation Service) in determining this question. For example, where the Probation Service recommends that the suspended sentence order continues, but the breach is marked by the imposition of a fine or some other penalty, the court may feel able to continue with the proceedings in the absence of legal representation. Where, on the other hand, the recommendation is to activate the suspended sentence order, the advocate may advise the court that legal representation is appropriate.

Fine

The first alternative to activating the suspended sentence (in whole or in part) is for the court to order the offender to pay a fine.[154] This power is available irrespective of whether the order imposes community requirements.

The fine payable by the offender cannot exceed £2,500, irrespective of the offender's financial position. Lastly, para 16(1) provides that a fine imposed under paragraph 13(1)(c) is to be treated for the purposes of any enactment as being a sum adjudged to be paid by a conviction.

Effect of power on suspended sentence

The effect of a fine is that the order will continue. It is important, therefore, that where the court imposes a fine the judge warns the offender that the order remains in effect and they are obligated to continue to comply with the order.

[154] Sentencing Act 2020, Schedule 16, para 13(1)(c).

Key point

It is common for the Breach Report from the Probation Service to recommend the court impose more onerous community requirements by replacing an unworkable requirement with a fine. This is not a permissible option. The power to impose a fine is entirely separate to the power to impose more onerous requirements.

Impose more onerous community requirements

The second alternative to activation applies where the suspended sentence order imposes community requirements.[155] In those circumstances, the court may amend the order by imposing more onerous community requirements.[156]

Restrictions

The court is restricted in its powers to impose more onerous community requirements. Specifically, the court may only impose a requirement which the original sentencing court could impose.[157] This restriction is repeated in para 16(2) of Schedule 16 to the Sentencing Act 2020 which provides that the power to impose more onerous requirements is subject to any provision that applies to the court in making a suspended sentence order as if the court were making the order.

[155] As discussed in Chapter 2, the imposition of such requirements are discretionary. Where the suspended sentence order does not impose community requirements, the court has no power to impose any community requirements on breach (see below, "What powers do the courts not have?").

[156] Sentencing Act 2020, Schedule 16, para 13(1)(d)(i).

[157] ibid.

Specifically, the court may only impose a requirement that is listed in column 1 of the community requirements table in s.287 of the Sentencing Act 2020. The list of requirements are:

- unpaid work requirement
- rehabilitation activity requirement
- programme requirement
- prohibited activity requirement
- curfew requirement
- exclusion requirement
- residence requirement
- foreign travel prohibition requirement
- mental health treatment requirement
- drug rehabilitation requirement
- drug testing requirement
- alcohol treatment requirement
- alcohol abstinence and monitoring requirement
- attendance centre requirement
- electronic compliance monitoring requirement
- electronic whereabouts monitoring requirement

In addition to only being permitted to impose a requirement listed in the community requirements table, the court must also comply with any conditions or restrictions applicable to the requirements. For example, where a judge imposes a curfew requirement as a result of breach proceedings, the judge must also impose an electronic monitoring requirement unless one of the exceptions apply.[158] By way of second example, a court cannot amend a mental health treatment requirement, a drug rehabilitation requirement, or an alcohol treatment requirement unless the offender expresses their willingness to comply with the requirement as amended.[159]

The application of these restrictions is also dependent on whether the order already imposes a particular community requirement.

For example:

- where the community requirements do not presently impose an unpaid work requirement, the court may order such requirement and will be restricted by the minimum number of hours (not less than 40)[160] and the maximum number of hours (not more than 300).[161]

- where an unpaid work requirement already exists, the court is not restricted by the minimum number of hours that can be added to the order, but is restricted according to the maximum number

[158] As required by para 10(1) of Schedule 9 to the Sentencing Act 2020. See Chapter 2 for further details.

[159] See Sentencing Act 2020, Schedule 9, paras 17, 20, and 22.

[160] The ability to impose a minimum of 20 hours for a new unpaid work requirement following breach proceedings applies only to community orders. This is evident from para 2(2) of Schedule 9 to the Sentencing Act 2020.

[161] Sentencing Act 2020, Schedule 9, para 2(1)(b).

of overall hours.[162] The same can be said for any of the community requirements.[163]

Key point

Practitioners must remember the "Probation Reset"[164] when the court is considering imposing more onerous requirements. If an offender has completed, or is close to completing, two-thirds of their community order or suspended sentence order, the Court should not impose more RAR days to mark the breach on account that the Probation Service will not offer, supervise or manage such activities. There is, however, no restriction on imposing any further requirements to mark the breach.

Effect of power on suspended sentence

The effect of imposing more onerous requirements is that the order will continue. It is important, therefore, that where the court does so, the judge warns the offender that the order remains in effect and they are obligated to continue to comply with the order.

Extending the supervision period

In the case of a suspended sentence order that imposes one or more community requirements, the court is empowered to amend the order by extending the supervision period of the order.[165] This power is, however, subject to section 288(4) of the Sentencing Act 2020 which states that

---

[162] i.e. the court cannot impose so many unpaid work hours to mark the breach such that the overall hours exceed 300.

[163] See Chapter 2 for the full list of restrictions on the imposition of community requirements.

[164] See Chapter 1.

[165] Sentencing Act 2020, Schedule 16, para 13(1)(d)(ii).

the supervision period cannot exceed two years, nor the operational period if that period is less than two years.[166]

In practice, this power is rarely exercised on account that the supervision period is often the same length as the operational period. Where, however, the operational period is extended,[167] the court is advised to also extend the supervision period.

Supervision periods and unpaid work requirements

Importantly, if the suspended sentence order imposes an unpaid work requirement, and the unpaid work requirement has not been completed on account that there are further hours still be worked, there is no necessity for the court to extend the supervision period. This is on account that the supervision period continues until the offender has completed the number of hours specified in the order.[168]

Effect of power on suspended sentence

Given that by extending the supervision period, the order will remain in force, the judge should warn the offender that the order remains in effect, and they are obligated to continue to comply with the order.

Extending the operational period

In addition to extending the supervision period, the court is empowered on breach, to amend the order by extending the operational period of the order. This power applies both where the suspended sentence order

---

166 ibid, s.288(4)(b).

167 ibid, Schedule 16, para 13(1)(d)(iii).

168 ibid, s.288(5).

imposes community requirements[169] and in cases where no community requirements are imposed.[170]

In both instances, however, the power to extend the operational period is restricted by s.288(2) of the Sentencing Act 2020 which provides that the operational period cannot exceed two years.

It is important to note that the Court of Appeal has sought to restrict the court's use of this power where the court is also dealing with a further offence. In *R v Crawley*,[171] the Court of Appeal ruled that it was wrong in principle to exercise the court's powers in extending the operational period of a suspended sentence at the same time as imposing a sentence of immediate imprisonment.

In *Crawley*, the offender had been given a suspended sentence order. He then committed a further offence during the operational period of the suspended sentence order for which he was sentenced to three months' immediate imprisonment. In respect of the suspended sentence, the sentencing judge extended the operational period to mark the breach. The offender appealed to the Court of Appeal in respect of the extension to the operational period, submitting that it was wrong in law to do so whilst also imposing an immediate term of imprisonment.

The Court of Appeal did not consider that it was wrong in law; Stocker J would explain:

> The power exists and it therefore cannot be said in acting as he did the learned judge was exceeding his powers or acting contrary to them.[172]

---

[169] ibid, Schedule 16, para 13(1)(d)(iii).

[170] ibid, Schedule 16, para 13(1)(e).

[171] (1984) 6 Cr. App. R. (S.) 327 (CA).

[172] ibid, 328 (Stocker J).

However, his Lordship did consider it to be an "improper procedure",[173] relying on two previous judgments of the Court of Appeal.[174] As a result, the Court of Appeal quashed the decision to extend the operational period and substituted it with activation of the suspended sentences to be served concurrently.[175] The essential take away from these authorities is that, when faced with a conviction for further offences committed during the operational period of a suspended sentence order, the court should not act on the suspended sentence order by extending the operational period.

Effect of power on suspended sentence

Given that by extending the operational period, the order will remain in force, the judge should warn the offender that the order remains in effect, and they are obligated to continue to comply with the order.

Commit the offender to custody

The final power available to the court is restrictive in operation and relatively new.[176] The power to commit the offender to custody is subject to the following conditions:[177]

---

[173] Relying on the Court of Appeal's judgment in *R v Sapiano* (1968) 52 Cr. App. R. 674 (CA), where it was held to be improper to pass both a term of immediate imprisonment, and a suspended sentence at the same time.

[174] *R v Goodlad* (1973) 57 Cr. App. R. 717 (CA); *R v Treays* [1981] Crim. L.R. 511 (CA).

[175] *Crawley* and *Goodlaw* were subsequently approved by the Court of Appeal in *R v Osbourne* (1993) 14 Cr. App. R. (S.) 265 (CA).

[176] The power being added by para 13(6) of Schedule 14(1)to the Police, Crime, Sentencing and Courts Act 2022.

[177] Sentencing Act 2020, Schedule 16, para 13(1)(da).

- the suspended sentence order must qualify for special procedures,[178]
- the offender must be before the court for breach of the community requirements of the suspended sentence order,[179] and
- the offender must be aged 18 or over.

Should these conditions be satisfied, the court may order the offender to be committed to prison[180] for such period as the court considers appropriate, not exceeding 28 days.[181]

The Sentencing Act 2020 directs readers to "see also paragraph 13A"; no such para 13A exists in Schedule 16. Rather, the relevant provision is contained in para 16A of Schedule 16; it is evident that this is simply a typographical error.[182] Paragraph 16A provides that no more than three orders committing an offender to custody may be made in relation to the same suspended sentence.[183]

---

[178] Reference to "special procedures" simply means that the suspended sentence order is subject to review in accordance with s.293A(1) (see Chapter 2 for further detail of suspended sentence orders subject to such review).

[179] This means that the power to commit to custody is not available where the offender is before the court for the commission of further offences during the operational period of a suspended sentence order.

[180] Or a Young Offender Institution in the case of a person under the age of 21 (Sentencing Act 2020, Schedule 16, para 16A(1)(a)).

[181] Sentencing Act 2020, Schedule 16, para 13(1)(da).

[182] Paragraph 13A is the relevant provision in Schedule 10, as discussed in Chapter 6.

[183] ibid, Schedule 16, para 16A(3).

Effect of power on suspended sentence

Committing an offender to custody is not the same as activating the suspended sentence;[184] therefore, the order continues, and the judge should warn the offender that the order remains in effect, and, upon release from custody, they are obligated to continue to comply with the order.

What powers do the courts not have?

The final discussion necessary under this section is to explain what powers the courts do not have when faced with a probation breach. This section is primarily designed to ensure that errors are not made by parties to the case when dealing with any such breach.

The following details what powers the court does not have.

- The court has no power to take "no action" following a breach.[185]
- The court has no power to revoke a suspended sentence order.[186]
- Where the original sentence court did not impose community requirements as part of the suspended sentence order, the breach court *cannot* impose community requirements. Where the sentencing court did not impose community requirements in the first instance, the only powers available to the court are to activate

[184] This is evident from para 14(2)(c) of Schedule 16 to the Sentencing Act 2020 which provides that in considering whether it would be unjust the activate a suspended sentence order, the court should consider "the possibility" of committing the offender to custody.

[185] *R v Mohammed* [2023] EWCA Crim 1458.

[186] *R v Rees* [2022] EWCA Crim 1710.

the sentence (in whole or in part),[187] impose a fine not exceeding £2,500,[188] and to extend the operational period.[189]

- Whilst the court is empowered to order the offender to pay a contribution to the prosecution costs, the court is not empowered to order that the offender pay a statutory surcharge. The offender will have been liable to pay such surcharge when first sentenced for the offence subject to the suspended sentence order; breach proceedings do not give the court a power to order a second surcharge.[190]

Expired suspended sentence orders

What is the situation if the suspended sentence order has expired? To answer that question, it will be appropriate to start with an example. Suppose the following:

- On 10 April 2022, an offender is sentenced to 18 months' imprisonment, suspended for two years.
- On 15 November 2023, the offender commits a further offence.
- On 20 June 2024, the offender is convicted of the further offence.

In this situation, the offender has committed the offence during the operational period of a suspended sentence order, but has only been convicted (and can therefore only be dealt with) after the expiry of the

[187] Sentencing Act 2020, Schedule 16, para 13(1)(a) and (b).

[188] ibid, Schedule 16, para 13(1)(c).

[189] ibid, Schedule 16, para 13(1)(e).

[190] The Criminal Justice Act 2003 (Surcharge) Order 2012 (SI 1696/2012); *R v George* [2015] EWCA Crim 1096, [2015] 2 Cr. App. R. (S.) 58 [8]-[9] (Macur LJ) (in respect of community orders); *R v Abbott* [2020] EWCA Crim 516, [2020] 2 Cr. App. R. (S.) 39 [78] (Fulford LJ).

order. In a similar situation, imagine the offender breached a community requirement of the suspended sentence order during the operational period, but breach proceedings have only been brought following the expiry of the order. Can the court take action in respect of the suspended sentence order in either case? There is no direct authority on this point. As a matter of statutory interpretation, the court cannot deal with the suspended sentence order where it has been previously activated.[191] There appears to be no apparent restriction in terms of expired orders. We shall consider this in more detail now.

Timeframe for further offences

There are a number of authorities which seem to show that there is no requirement that the suspended sentence order still be in force in order to take action, provided that it has not been previously activated.

For example, in *R v Sproul*[192] the offender:

- was sentenced to 12 months' imprisonment, suspended for 24 months, in March 2014,
- committed further offences in February 2016, and
- was convicted of the further offences in 2018.

At no point in the appeal did any party argue that the court could not act on the suspended sentence order because it had expired. Rather, the appeal turned on whether it was unjust to activate the sentence.

Likewise, in *R v Beirne*[193] the offender:

[191] See above "Restrictions on Activation I: Not previously activated".

[192] [2018] EWCA Crim 2034.

[193] [2020] EWCA Crim 1433.

- was sentenced to 16 months' imprisonment, suspended for 24 months, in July 2017,
- committed further offences in March 2019, and
- was convicted of the further offences in January 2020.

Whilst neither authority explicitly states that an order can still be acted upon even when expired, the simple fact is that the Court of Appeal did not comment or interfere with the activation for these purposes. It can, therefore, be said with certainty that there is no restriction on the suspended sentence order having expired.

Timeframe for breaches

In Chapter 4, we discussed the timeframe within which an information must be laid in respect of breach proceedings. In *West Yorkshire Probation Board v Cruickshanks*,[194] Leveson LJ was clear that whilst the information must be laid within the operational period of the suspended sentence order, the breach proceedings do not need to be heard within that period.

For those reasons, it is clear that the court does have the power to deal with an expired suspended sentence order where:

- In the case of further offences, the further offence is committed during the operational period of the suspended sentence order, irrespective of the date of conviction.
- In the case of breach of community requirements, the information alleging any such breach is laid before the expiry of the operational period.

[194] [2010] EWHC 615 (Admin), [2011] 1 W.L.R. 2154.

> **Key point**
>
> The fact that the suspended sentence order is no longer in force may, however, be relevant to the question of whether it is unjust the activate the sentence in full or in part. This will be a factor considered alongside the offender's compliance with the order.

Powers of the court

One final question must be asked at this stage: where the suspended sentence order has expired, is the court restricted as to what actions it can take in respect of the breach?

On the one hand, there is no explicit restriction on the court's powers in the Sentencing Act 2020. Specifically, para 13 of Schedule 16 does not say that the suspended sentence order must be in force, or that the operational period must not have expired. On that reasoning, there is no restriction in the court's powers.

The view of the author, however, is that in dealing with the offender following expiration of the suspended sentence order, the court only has three options available to it. The Court may only:

- Activate the suspended sentence order in full,
- Activate the suspended sentence order in part,
- Order that the offender pay a fine (maximum £2,500).

This is justified on the basis that, as a matter of common sense, the remaining powers in para 13(1) of Schedule 16 to the Sentencing Act 2020 involve the court extending the supervision or operational period of the order. However, once the operational period has passed, the order is no longer in existence (i.e. the order has expired).[195] In essence, there is no order to extend, or enforce.

Furthermore, this approach would avoid potential difficulties and legal challenges that could arise in future. Take the following example:

- An offender is subject to a suspended sentence order, which is due to expire on 11 November 2024.
- The responsible officer instigates a breach against the offender for failing to comply with the community requirements of the order on 4 November 2024 (i.e. during the operational period of the suspended sentence order).
- The offender commits an offence on 20 November 2024 (i.e. after the operational period of the suspended sentence order) and is convicted on 21 November 2024.
- The offender is brought before the court in respect of the breach proceedings on 22 November 2024 (i.e. after the operational period of the suspended sentence order).

In this example, whilst the offender has breached a community requirement during the operational period of a suspended sentence order, they have not committed an offence during that period. If the court on 22 November 2024 were to extend the operational period, it would retrospectively put the offender in breach by committing further offences during the operational period. This is unlikely to have been the intention of the legislature, and is entirely unfair on the offender. For these reasons, it would appear logical that the suspended sentence order cannot be extended following expiration of the order and, more generally, the court is restricted in its powers when dealing with an expired order.

[195] As made clear in s.288 of the Sentencing Act 2020.

Dealing with the new offence

Where an offender is convicted of a further offence committed during the operational period of a suspended sentence order, the court must deal with the new offence, as well as the decision whether to activate the suspended sentence.

Structuring sentence

Importantly, the court should sentence the offender for the new offence separately to the suspended sentence order (i.e. the court must impose a penalty in respect of the further offence *in addition* to whatever action is taken on the suspended sentence).

In *R v Ithell,*[196] Edmund Davies LJ would explain the "proper approach" to sentencing where a fresh offence has been committed during the period of suspension of an earlier sentence. His Lordship stated:

> the court should first sentence him in respect of the fresh offence by punishment appropriate to that offence, and thereafter address itself to the question of the suspended sentence.[197]

This will be achieved by the judge stating openly in court what the sentence for the new offence is, before then stating clearly and separately what action is being taken in respect of the suspended sentence order.[198]

This approach makes logical sense on account that should an offender be sentenced to an absolute discharge or a conditional discharge for the new offence, they will not have been "convicted" of an offence.[199] It is vital,

---

[196] (1969) 53 Cr. App. R. 210 (CA).

[197] ibid, 212 (Edmund Davies LJ).

[198] *R v Blakeway* (1969) 53 Cr. App. R. 498 (CA), 502 (James J).

[199] See above "Further offences resulting in a discharge" for more detail.

therefore, that the court satisfies itself first of the appropriate penalty for the new offence, before it turns its mind to the suspended sentence order.

In *Nobbs v DPP*,[200] counsel for the offender sought to argue that the activation of a suspended sentence order was unlawful on account that the sentencing judge should not have proceeded to determine whether to activate the suspended sentences until it had decided what the proper sentence for the subsequent offences should be. Counsel for the offender justified this submission on the basis that if it was decided that the sentences for the subsequent offences should be a conditional discharge, there will not have been a conviction capable of triggering the activation of the suspended sentences. This argument was not considered by the Divisional Court on account that it was not a part of the case stated by the magistrates' court. However, the Divisional Court did state in *obiter* that on the facts of that case:

> this is not a case in which a conditional discharge could conceivably have been an appropriate sentence for the offence of driving with excess alcohol, even when viewed in isolation.[201]

Nobbs is not an authority which overrules or changes the position in *Ithell*. Rather, *Nobbs* is a demonstration that where an absolute or conditional discharge is inconceivable on the facts of a given case, the fact that the judge dealt with the suspended sentence order first will not render the order unlawful.

Irrespective of *Nobbs*, it is still advised that the sentencing judge deals with the new offence first.

---

[200] [2008] EWHC 1653 (Admin), [2009] R.T.R. 9.

[201] ibid, [18] (Keith J).

The court must impose a penalty for the new offence

By structuring the sentence in the manner described in *Ithell*, it would appear that the court is not permitted to impose no separate penalty in respect of the new offence. The court must impose a penalty commensurate with the seriousness of the offence, irrespective of the suspended sentence order. This view is justified on account that if the court was dealing with an offender for a new sentence alone (i.e. there was no suspended sentence order), the court would not be empowered to order "no separate penalty" in respect of the single offence.

Restrictions on activating and the new offence

Readers will know that the magistrates' courts are restricted in their sentencing powers. Specifically, the magistrates' court may only impose a maximum of six months' imprisonment for a single offence (whether this is summary-only or either-way).[202] The court is restricted to a statutory maximum of 12 months' imprisonment where an offender has been convicted of two or more either-way offences.[203]

What is the situation where, by both activating the suspended sentence and imposing imprisonment for the new offences, the offender is imprisoned for an aggregate period in excess of 12 months? This issue was considered by the Court of Appeal in *R v Chamberlain*[204] where Tudor Evans J explained:

> In our view the implementation of a suspended sentence does not involve the imposition of a sentence of imprisonment. The sentence was imposed when the original suspended sentence was passed. When the suspended

[202] Sentencing Act 2020, s.224(1A).

[203] Magistrates' Courts Act 1980, s.133.

[204] (1992) 13 Cr. App. R. (S.) 525 (CA).

> sentences were activated in the present case the judge did not pass a sentence of imprisonment[205]

In essence, s.133 does not apply to the activation of a suspended sentence so as to confine the power of the sentencing court in such cases to the stated maxima.[206] *Chamberlain* was approved by the Court of Appeal in *R v Hester-Wox.*[207]

Aggravating the new offence with the suspended sentence

A question which arises at this stage is whether it is permissible for the court to aggravate the new offence, on account that it is committed during the operational period of a suspended sentence order. The Sentencing Council Guidelines, *General guideline: overarching principles* (1 October 2019) include as an aggravating factor that the offence was "committed on licence or while subject to court order(s)". It could certainly be argued that the court is empowered to aggravate the offence by this factor on account that a suspended sentence order is a "court order". The guidance associated with that factor refers to offenders subject to licence, post-sentence supervision and "relevant" court orders.

It does not, however, specifically reference suspended sentence orders (or community orders for that matter). Furthermore, ss.64 and 65 of the Sentencing Act 2020 expressly require the court to treat, as an aggravating feature, that the offence was committed whilst on bail and

---

205 ibid, 527-528 (Tudor Evans J).

206 This is the same as when the Crown Court is dealing with matters where it is restricted to the powers of the magistrates' court.

207 [2016] EWCA Crim 1397, [2016] 2 Cr. App. R. (S.) 43. See also: *R v Jex* [2021] EWCA Crim 1708, [2022] 1 W.L.R. 4015; *R v Palmer* [2019] EWCA Crim 2231, [2020] 1 Cr. App. R. (S.) 54; *R v Upton* [2019] EWCA Crim 2232; *R v Hancock* [2009] EWCA Crim 1629; *R v Worthing and District Justices* [1998] 1 Cr. App. R. (S.) 175 (QBD); *R v Bexley* (1993) 96 Cr. App. R. 442, (1993) 14 Cr. App. R. (S.) 462 (CA).

an offender's previous convictions. However, the Act is silent as to the relevance of the suspended sentence order as an aggravating factor.

The matter was considered by the Court of Appeal in *R v Levesconte*[208] in respect of the former law under the Criminal Justice Act 2003. In that case, the sentencing judge had activated a suspended sentence order in full following an offender's conviction for a further offence committed during the operational period of a suspended sentence order. In addition to activating the suspended sentence in full, the sentencing judge also regarded the new offence as being aggravated by the fact that it was committed during the currency of the suspended sentence order. This was successfully challenged in the Court of Appeal. Lord Justice Elias considered this approach as wrong in law. His Lordship would explain:

> it was not appropriate for the Recorder to treat the fact that the offence was committed during the operational period of the suspended sentence as a factor justifying the increase of the second sentence, not at least in circumstances where the suspended sentence was activated in full. The reason is that the Defendant had already been dealt with for that very fact by the implementation of the full original sentence. To take it into account again when the Recorder was fixing the sentence for the second offence was to increase the sentence referable to that fact beyond the maximum for which the Defendant had been at risk. Precisely the same factor was carrying weight with respect to two separate offences.[209]

In essence, a sentencing judge would be double counting in the circumstances where they treated the commission of the offence during

[208] [2011] EWCA Crim 2754, [2012] 2 Cr. App. R. (S.) 19.

[209] ibid, [15] (Elias LJ).

the operational period of a suspended sentence order as an aggravating feature, at the same time as activating the suspended sentence order.[210]

Importantly, however, *Levesconte* is not an authority for the proposition that commission of a further offence during the operational period of a suspended sentence order can never be an aggravating factor. Indeed, in *Levesconte*, Elias J stated "[w]e recognise that the same argument may not run where the suspended sentence is not fully implemented; that is an argument for another day."[211] Where a suspended sentence order is only activated in part, therefore, it is possible that the suspended sentence may be treated as an aggravating feature for the new offence.[212]

By way of two further examples:

- Where the suspended sentence is not activated at all, and the court utilises one of its other powers in para 13(1), it may be permissible for the court to treat the suspended sentence order as an aggravating factor for the new offence.

- Where the offender has previously had a suspended sentence activated, but subsequently falls to be sentenced for an offence committed during the operational period of the now activated suspended sentence order, the court can regard that fact as aggravating. This was evident in the case of *Rashid*.[213]

The final point to note is that *Levesconte* and all authorities subsequently citing it were concerned with the former guidelines of the Sentencing

---

210 Approved in *R v Edwards* [2014] EWCA Crim 1165 by Jeremy Baker J at [14] and *R v Visan* [2015] EWCA Crim 982 by Holgate J at [17].

211 *Levesconte* (n208) [15] (Elias LJ).

212 The Court of Appeal in *Levesconte* certainly left the door open for that argument. Cf *Ellis v His Majesty's Solicitor General* [2023] EWCA Civ 585.

213 [2022] EWCA Crim 328, [2022] 2 Cr. App. R. (S.) 41 at [6] (Dingemans LJ).

Guidelines Council,[214] namely the *Overarching Principles: Seriousness.* This Guideline was in effect from 2012 until 2019 when the *General guideline: overarching principles* came into effect. The relevance of this is that there is a distinctive variation in the wording between the two guidelines. The former referred to "failure to respond to previous sentences" and "offence committed whilst on licence" as aggravating factors, but did not refer to suspended sentence orders specifically, or court orders generally for that matter. This fact was touched upon by Elias J in *Levesconte* at [14].

The present Guideline, however, includes as an aggravating factor: "Offence committed on licence or while subject to court order(s)". As discussed above, there is no explicit reference to suspended sentence orders in the list of aggravating factors, but the Sentencing Council deliberately changed the wording of the aggravating factor. Might it be argued that *Levesconte* no longer reflects proper sentencing practice in light of the *General guideline: overarching principles*? The likely answer is that *Levesconte* continues to reflect proper sentencing practice on account that the guidance applicable to the aggravating factor of "offence committed on licence or while subject to court orders(s)" includes the two following restrictions:

- Where the offender is dealt with separately for a breach of a licence or order, regard should be had to totality.

- Care should be taken to avoid double counting matters taken into account when considering previous convictions.

These two factors both represent the spirit of *Levesconte* and the authorities that follow, namely that to take account of the fact the offence was committed during the operational period of a suspended sentence, at the same time as activating the suspended sentence, would be to double count. The offender would, in essence, be punished twice. In light of that, practitioners are advised of the following:

---

[214] The precursor to the now Sentencing Council.

- Where a suspended sentence order is activated in full, the sentencing judge should not treat the fact that the new offence(s) was committed during the operational period of that order as an aggravating factor.

- However, where the suspended sentence order is activated in part, or the court marks the breach in a way other than activation, it is arguable that the court is permitted to regard it as an aggravating factor. The key is to ensure that double counting does not take place.

Cases involving both a breach and a further offences

What is the position where an offender appears before the court having breached a community requirement of a suspended sentence order and having been convicted of a further offence(s) during the operational period of a suspended sentence order? Can the court deal with the offender for both?

The short answer is: No. This is evident from the case of *Maunder*,[215] where the offender, having been sentenced to six months' imprisonment, suspended for 18 months, failed to comply with the supervision requirement by failing to report to his responsible officer. The offender also committed a further offence during the operational period of the suspended sentence order. The sentencing judge took the following action:

- In respect of the new offence, the sentencing judge imposed a sentence of 12 months' imprisonment.

- In respect of the fact that the new offence was committed during the operational period of a suspended sentence order, the sentencing judge activated the suspended sentence in part by

[215] *R v Maunder* [2015] EWCA Crim 778, [2015] 2 Cr. App. R. (S.) 26.

imposing a sentence of three months' imprisonment, consecutive to the 12-month sentence for the new offence.

- In respect of the breach of the community requirements, the sentencing judge imposed a further consecutive sentence of three months' imprisonment.

In total, the sentencing judge imposed a term of imprisonment of 18 months' imprisonment. The offender appealed to the Court of Appeal. Mr Justice Haddon-Cave provided the judgment of the Court; his Lordship considered that the additional three months sentence for the breach of the community requirement was unlawful. His Lordship said:

> [I]n our judgment, having already activated the suspended sentence in passing a term of three months[...], it was not possible for the learned judge to activate the suspended sentence for a second time. Alternatively, if the judge's intention was to sentence the applicant for a substantive offence of "failing to comply with a requirement of the suspended sentence", he was not entitled to do so because there is no such offence in law. Accordingly, in our view the additional sentence of three months was unlawful and must be quashed.[216]

In essence, therefore, where the court is faced with an offender who has both committed further offences during the operational period of a suspended sentence order, and has committed breaches of the community requirements of the order, the court may only take action against the offender once. Naturally, the defendant's poor compliance (by breaching the community requirements of the order) can and will be taken into account by the court when considering the appropriate penalty to impose.[217]

---

[216] ibid, [10] (Haddon-Cave J).

[217] See Chapter 9 where this matter is discussed in full.

Case law on activation

The final part of this chapter will consider the vast array of case law concerned with the two questions from *Sheppard* considered above. These questions are:

- whether it is unjust to activate the suspended sentence order at all; and,
- if it is not unjust, whether the sentence should be activated in full or in part.[218]

At this stage, we shall consider some of the key authorities in answering those questions.

Is it unjust to activate the suspended sentence at all?

Should it be relevant, an offender's compliance with the community requirements of the order may permit the court to step back from activating the suspended sentence order.

In *Sheppard*, Coulson J explained that "if 95 per cent of the order had been complied with, a court might conclude that it was unjust to order that any part of the custodial term take effect."[219] This is a high threshold and it is questionable how far Coulson J intended a numerical calculation to play a part in the court's assessment of whether it would be unjust.

In *R v Blakemore,*[220] the offender had been convicted of further offences committed during the operational period of a suspended sentence order. The further offences committed were of a serious nature and would result in a substantial term of imprisonment. When sentencing, the learned judge identified that they were not going to activate the suspended

---

[218] See above, "Default position: Activate in full or part".

[219] *R v Sheppard* (n84) [14] (Coulson J).

[220] [2016] EWCA Crim 1396, [2017] 1 Cr. App. R. (S.) 5.

sentence because a substantial sentence was going to be passed for the further offences. The judge revoked that suspended sentence order and imposed no separate penalty in respect of the breach. The sentencing judge said it was an act of mercy which reflected the principle of totality.

The appeal was not concerned with the suspended sentence order, per se. Rather, it was concerned with the length of the sentence passed for the further offences, the principle of totality, and the age of the offender. However, as a side note to the appeal, the Court identified a difficulty with the sentencing judge's approach to the suspended sentence order. Specifically, Laing J, giving the judgment of the Court, explained that the sentencing judge was obliged to activate the sentence in full or in part as a result of the further offences, unless it would be unjust to do so. If the judge did consider it so unjust, they should have stated their reasons for this[221] and then proceeded to exercise one of their other powers in respect of the order (e.g. fine, making the order more onerous etc).

In fact, the judge was wrong to impose no separate penalty in respect of the breach; there was also no power to revoke a suspended sentence order. In terms of the question of whether it would be unjust to activate the sentence, Laing J explained that as the Judge was sentencing the offender to imprisonment for several offences, the Court could not consider that the judge could feasibly have reached the conclusion that it was unjust not to activate this suspended sentence in full.

Should the court activate in full or in part?

The following aims to distil the principles arising from the case law in this area. It will be broken down into cases where a reduction was made, and those where no such reduction was made. We shall further sub-divide these discussions into cases where the requirement was unpaid work, and those cases involving other requirements.

---

[221] As is now required by para 14(1) of Schedule 16 to the Sentencing Act 2020.

Cases where a reduction was made (unpaid work)

The leading authorities in this area are that of *R v Kavanagh*[222] *and R v Zeca.*[223] In *Kavanagh*, the offender was sentenced to 32 weeks' imprisonment, suspended for two years, with a requirement of two years' supervision by his probation officer, 200 hours of unpaid work, and a requirement to attend the Think First programme for 22 days. The offender subsequently committed further offences during the currency of the order and the suspended sentence was activated in full. The sentencing judge was not informed of the offender's compliance when they activated the suspended sentence. The Court of Appeal allowed the appeal and reduced the term of activation to reflect the offender's compliance with his unpaid work requirement. Mr Justice Tomlinson would explain the position as such:

> In our judgment it is both necessary and appropriate in most cases to mark the commission of a further offence during the currency of a suspended sentence order by the activation of some part of the suspended sentence order. After all the warning that is given to an offender when such a sentence is imposed is that he will have to serve that sentence in the event that he commits a further offence during the currency of the suspended order. Ordinarily, therefore, it is likely to be appropriate to activate some part of the suspended sentence order.[224]

In *R v Zeca*, the offender had been sentenced to 12 months' imprisonment suspended for a period of two years. The offender was required to complete 150 hours of unpaid work and there was a requirement to attend a Think First programme. The offender was subsequently convicted for an offence of robbery and was sentenced to three years' imprisonment. The suspended sentence was activated in full

---

[222] [2010] EWCA Crim 1737, [2011] 1 Cr. App. R. (S.) 63.

[223] [2009] EWCA Crim 133, [2009] 2 Cr. App. R. (S.) 65.

[224] ibid, [20] (Tomlinson J).

and imposed consecutively, making four years' imprisonment in total. On appeal, the offender argued that a reduction ought to have been made to reflect his compliance with the community requirement. Mr Justice Pitchford, giving the judgment of the court, reduced the full activation and ruled that "there should have been some recognition of the appellant's limited progress made under the order."[225]

In *R v Swallow*,[226] the offender was sentenced to 12 months' imprisonment, suspended for two years with 200 hours of unpaid work. The offender completed the unpaid work requirement in a short period of time (12 weeks) and committed no breaches of the community requirements of the order. However, the offender committed a further offence and the suspended sentence order was activated in full. On appeal, it was argued that the suspended sentence should not have been activated in full on account of the offender's compliance with the unpaid work requirement. The Court of Appeal agreed; Pitchford LJ ruled:

> The court will need to make an assessment to what degree an unpaid work requirement represented punishment for the offender intended to what extent that work requirement had been completed by the time of the liability for application of the sentence consecutively. In our judgment, the fact that the unpaid work requirement had been completed in full before the applicant [committed a further offence], that some allowance should be made in considering the proportion of the suspended prison sentence which should be ordered to take effect, our judgment is, having regard not just to the completion of the work requirement but also the totality of the sentence imposed, that one-half of the suspended sentence should take effect consecutively.[227]

[225] *Zeca* (n223) [14] (Pitchford J).

[226] [2013] EWCA Crim 719.

[227] ibid, [13] (Pitchford LJ).

By way of other examples:

- *R v Wright:*[228] Activation of the full suspended sentence was regarded as "plainly wrong"[229] when an offender had completed all 300 hours of an unpaid work requirement. Activation of 17 weeks' imprisonment, substituted for five weeks.

- *R v Knight:*[230] Making allowance for the 150 hours unpaid work successfully and fully completed, the Court of Appeal considered that the suspended sentence order should have been activated in part (to the extent of six months) rather than in full (12 months).

- *R v Brindley:*[231] Completion of all of the hours of unpaid work and consistent attendance at weekly supervision appointments resulted in a reduction of one-half to the activated suspended sentence.[232]

- *R v Bell:*[233] The offender's completion of the unpaid work requirement was sufficient to justify a reduction in activation, despite the fact the offender had failed to comply with other community requirements (namely the Building Better Relationships programme).

- *R v Ross:*[234] Given that the offender had completed the unpaid work requirement attached to the suspended sentence and that the pre-sentence report stated that his current attitude towards

---

228 [2011] EWCA Crim 665.

229 ibid, [11] (Bean J).

230 [2011] EWCA Crim 1635.

231 [2012] EWCA Crim 1767.

232 This was so despite the order being relatively recently imposed.

233 [2019] EWCA Crim 2079.

234 [2014] EWCA Crim 2701.

the order had been good, there was a strong case not to activate it in full.[235] 12-month activation reduced to seven months.

Cases where a reduction was made (requirements other than unpaid work)

There are significantly fewer authorities where the court has reduced any activation of the suspended sentence to reflect compliance with community requirements other than unpaid work.

In *R v Hicks*,[236] for example, the Court of Appeal reduced the period of activation to reflect the compliance of the offender with the curfew requirement imposed. Mrs Justice Swift justified this approach on account that "[t]he curfew requirement imposed significant restrictions on the appellant"[237] and this should have been reflected in sentence. In a similar vein, the Court of Appeal has, on a number of occasions, reduced a period of activation based on the offender's compliance with a curfew requirement and a supervision requirement.[238]

Cases where no reduction was made (unpaid work)

In *R v Ansley*,[239] the offender was sentenced to eight months' imprisonment suspended for 24 months with 300 hours unpaid work.[240] The offender breached the order on two occasions (which resulted in the imposition of a curfew requirement) and on the third breach, the sentencing judge activated the suspended sentence in full. On appeal, the

---

235 ibid, [12] (Cranston J).

236 [2009] EWCA Crim 629.

237 ibid, [17] (Swift J).

238 *R v Grand-Man S* [2009] EWCA Crim 1980; *R v Pash* [2013] EWCA Crim 576, [2014] 1 Cr. App. R. (S.) 4; *R v Ballard* [2016] EWCA Crim 1173.

239 [2014] EWCA Crim 1135.

240 Later reduced to 250 hours.

offender argued that because he had completed 55.5 hours of the unpaid requirement, and complied with the electronically monitored curfew, it was manifestly excessive to activate the entirety of the suspended sentence. The Court of Appeal disagreed; Coulson J explained that the sentencing judge was absolutely entitled to activate the suspended sentence in full. Usefully, his Lordship explained:

> It is important to stress that a suspended sentence order does not work as some sort of set-off, whereby an applicant can trade a reduction in the length of that sentence by reference to some element of partial compliance. In our view, the applicant in this case has wholly failed to engage with the order.[241]

His Lordship considered the offender's compliance to be "dilatory, spasmodic and grudging".[242] In addition, his Lordship considered that the fact that the offender had been re-assessed by the Probation Service as a high-risk of re-offending was a relevant circumstance to the judge activating the suspended sentence.[243]

In *R v Barratt*,[244] the offender was sentenced to six months' imprisonment, suspended for 18 months for dangerous driving. As part of that suspended sentence, the offender was ordered to complete 150 hours of unpaid work. The offender committed several fresh offences during the suspended sentence order; the sentencing judge activated the suspended sentence in full. On appeal, it was argued that a reduction should have been made by the sentencing judge to reflect the fact that offender had completed all of the unpaid work hours. The Court of Appeal disagreed and considered it "clearly just and right" that the order

---

[241] *R v Ansley* (n239) [9] (Coulson J).

[242] ibid, [10] (Coulson J) borrowing his own words used in *Sheppard.*

[243] ibid, [11] (Coulson J).

[244] [2017] EWCA Crim 1631.

was activated in full.[245] Mr Justice Lewis, giving the judgment of the Court, justified this course of conduct on the basis that:

> notwithstanding the fact that one element had been completed, given the number and the seriousness of the offences which the appellant committed during the operational period of the suspended sentence.[246]

Cases where no reduction was made (requirements other than unpaid work)

The Court of Appeal has typically distinguished conditions which are purely rehabilitative or therapeutic in nature from conditions that are punitive. In *R v Wolstenholme*,[247] the offender was sentenced to eight months' imprisonment, suspended for 18 months for affray. The offender was ordered to attend a Thinking Skills Programme, to undertake alcohol treatment for three months, and to continue under supervision for the total term of 18 months. The offender completed the Thinking Skills Programme, but it was evident from the pre-sentence report that it had not worked. Likewise, in respect of the alcohol treatment, the Court found that if it had ever worked, it had clearly not continued to work beyond the end of the three months. Mrs Justice McGowan, giving the judgment of the Court, concluded that:

> We note on this occasion that the conditions imposed were designed to be therapeutic, rather than punitive. Whilst it is right that the appellant appears to have complied in the sense of attending and completing courses, he certainly has not succeeded in putting what he learned into practice.[248]

---

[245] ibid, [26] (Lewis J).

[246] ibid.

[247] [2016] EWCA Crim 638, [2016] 2 Cr. App. R. (S.) 19.

[248] ibid, [11] (McGowan J).

Full activation of the suspended sentence was justified and upheld. Mrs Justice McGowan would explain that in light of the fact the offender had no punitive elements to his suspended sentence order: "The appellant cannot claim that he has been punished".[249]

The approach in *Wolstenholme* was not, however, the first of its kind to distinguish restorative elements from punitive elements. The focus of these authorities has been if the offender's attendance on a course has altered their thinking or attitude; if not, activation in full may be justified.[250]

In *R v Finn*,[251] for example, the offender was sentenced to nine months' imprisonment, suspended for two years, for one offence of affray and one offence of possession of a bladed article in a public place. The offender was also required to complete 140 hours of unpaid work. During the suspended sentence, the offender committed a further offence of theft and breached the order on several occasions. In respect of the new offence, he was sentenced to six months' imprisonment and the sentencing judge activated the suspended sentence in full. On appeal, it was argued that the completion of the 140 hours unpaid work, and the fact that the breach was only triggered towards the end of the supervision period, should have afforded the offender a reduction to the activated sentence. The Court of Appeal disagreed; the Court agreed with the sentencing judge that there was a "wholesale failure to comply".[252]

Mr Justice Coulson distinguished this case from the cases of *Zeca* and *Kavanagh* considered above. His Lordship said that in those cases "the unpaid work requirement had been complied with in full and in both of

---

249 ibid.

250 *R v Ballard* [2016] EWCA Crim 1173 [10] (Dingemans J).

251 [2012] EWCA Crim 881, [2012] 2 Cr App R (S) 96.

252 ibid, [9] (Coulson J).

those cases there had been no other breaches until those matters which led to the activation of the suspended sentence."[253]

The key element of his Lordship's judgment was summed up as such:

> We recognise that some judges might have given the appellant modest credit for the unpaid work he had carried out, but that is not the test. A suspended sentence order must be complied with in full; non-compliance risks activation of the suspended sentence in full. In those circumstances, a defendant such as the appellant in the present case, who does not comply with the terms of the suspended sentence order, only has himself to blame if non-compliance leads to activation of the suspended sentence in full.[254]

In *R v Abdille*,[255] the offender was sentenced to six months' imprisonment, suspended for 18 months. As part of the suspended sentence order, the offender was required to complete the Think First Programme. The offender did so, but also committed a further offence within the operational period of the suspended sentence order. The sentencing judge activated the suspended sentence in full. On appeal, the offender argued that, as with unpaid work, where there is compliance with a community requirement, a reduction should follow. The Court of Appeal disagreed with Clarke J explaining:

> There was not an unpaid work requirement in this case. The supervision element involved and required attendance at the Think First Programme which the appellant did, it seems, attend, but the facts show that he learned nothing from it. His conduct on this night exhibited a total failure to think first. Indeed, he committed two offences in the operational

[253] ibid, [13] (Coulson J).

[254] ibid, [12] (Coulson J).

[255] [2009] EWCA Crim 1195, [2010] 1 Cr. App. R. (S.) 18.

> period of that order. In our judgment, the judge was right to impose that in full and we shall not interfere with it.[256]

The same outcome was seen in *R v Collins-Reed*,[257] where the Court of Appeal considered that if the only supervision requirement has involved attendance on a course, and it is clear that the completion of that requirement has done nothing to alter the offender's thinking or attitude, with the result that the breach offence has been committed, it may well not be appropriate to reduce the term of the suspended sentence at all.

In that case, the offender had been sentenced to 16 weeks' imprisonment, suspended for two years with a programme requirement. 16 months into the operational period, the offender committed a further offence. The sentencing judge activated the suspended sentence in full. On appeal, the offender contended that his compliance with the programme requirement and supervision should have resulted in a reduction to the activation. The Court of Appeal disagreed; Spencer J adopted the approach of the Court in *Abdille* and concluded that:

> All that the defendant had been required to do was to attend the course. As the pre-sentence report said, this had resulted in no significant positive impact on his behaviour given his later and more serious conviction for violence arising broadly from the same background of troubled personal relationships. As [counsel for the offender] realistically conceded, the one thing which the appellant had to do, in order to comply with the suspended sentence order, was not to commit a further offence and that signally he failed to do.[258]

---

[256] ibid, [14] (Clarke J).

[257] [2012] EWCA Crim 2036, [2013] 1 Cr. App. R. (S.) 95.

[258] ibid, [10] (Spencer J).

By way of other examples:

- *R v Shariff*:[259] Partial completion with the curfew order and supervision order of a suspended sentence order did not justify any reduction to the activation.

- *R v Roscoe*:[260] Completion of a drug rehabilitation requirement did not justify a reduction from full activation. Lord Justice Elias would reason that "[t]his case was not one where there was a work requirement or anything of that kind, and although he had attended the drug rehabilitation course, that is not a demanding obligation and furthermore it had plainly not helped him."[261]

- *R v Gregory*:[262] Completion of the Thinking Skills course and attendance at 45 out of 52 appointments with the Probation Service did not justify a reduction from full activation.

Summary

This Chapter has covered the law and practice relating to breach of suspended sentence orders. When considering the legal principles applicable to this area of law, consider:

- A breach of a suspended sentence order may occur where an offender fails to comply with the community requirements of a suspended sentence order, or where the offender is convicted of an offence committed during the operational period of a suspended sentence order.

---

[259] [2009] EWCA Crim 2687.

[260] [2012] EWCA Crim 306.

[261] ibid, [8] (Elias LJ).

[262] [2013] EWCA Crim 1070.

- The default position on breach is to activate the suspended sentence in full or in part unless it would be unjust to do so in light of all the circumstances.

- Where the court does not activate the suspended sentence, the court may impose a fine (not exceeding £2,500), make the order more onerous, extend the supervision or operational period, or commit the offender to custody (in special review cases).

- A breach of a suspended sentence order can still be acted on even after the order has expired, though the powers of the court are likely restricted.

- Where an offender is dealt with for a new offence, the court must consider the principles of totality but cannot issue no separate penalty for the breach or the new offence.

CHAPTER EIGHT

CONTESTED BREACH PROCEEDINGS

Introduction

In this Chapter, we consider the process and principles involved in a contested breach hearing. We shall first consider the preparations necessary for an effective contested hearing, before then considering the contested hearing itself.

> **Key provisions**
>
> There are no legislative provisions specifically relevant to the preparation of a breach case. Advocates are directed to be familiar with the provisions in Schedules 10 and 16 to the Sentencing Act 2020 as appropriate.

This chapter shall be broken down as such:

- Preparing for a contested hearing, and
- The contested hearing.

We shall consider each in turn; readers are reminded that all chapters in this Part of the text should be read together.

Preparing for a contested hearing

As discussed in Chapters 6 and 7, at the first hearing in the proceedings, the breach will be "put" to the offender. The Court Clerk/ Legal Adviser will first ask the offender whether they admit to being sentenced to a community order or a suspended sentence order. If the answer is "Yes", they shall then be asked whether they admit to the breaches alleged by the Probation Service.

> **Key point**
>
> Importantly, when the breaches are put to the offender, they will be asked whether they admit or deny the breaches, as opposed to being asked whether they plead guilty or not guilty.

Should the breach be denied, advocates are advised to consider the following questions:

1. What is the defence/ reasonable excuse?
2. Is there any chance of a resolution?
3. If not, what evidence/ witnesses are required for the contested hearing?

We shall consider each question in turn.

<u>What is the defence / reasonable excuse?</u>

Should the breach be denied, the advocate for the Probation Service should work with the defence advocate (or the offender if they are unrepresented) to identify what the offender's defence is to the breach. Specifically, what does the offender say is their reasonable excuse to the failure to comply?

For the defence advocate, it is essential that they consider whatever excuse the offender producers *actually* amounts to a defence or reasonable excuse for their failure to comply. If it does, the defence advocate should take full instructions from the offender and seek any evidence they can to support the offender's claim.

It is uncommon for the offender to suggest that they did in fact attend/ comply. Rather, it is more common for the offender to suggest that they were permitted to not attend or had a reasonable excuse for failing to comply. For example, it is common for an offender to suggest:

- That they were told that they need not attend by their responsible officer (often citing communications with their responsible officer that they were not required to attend).

- That they had informed their responsible officer, or provider of a requirement, in advance that they could not attend and had an excuse for such non-attendance.

- That they were physically or mentally unable to complete the requirement of the order (for which evidence is now forthcoming).

- That they were not informed about a particular appointment by their responsible officer.

Whatever the defence is, all parties to the case should make a clear note as to what the defence is, and on what basis the offender seeks to rely on such a defence.

Is there any chance of a resolution?

Having formalised what the defence / reasonable excuse is, the next issue is whether the case can be resolved without the need for a contested hearing. By this, we mean that either the Probation Service considers that they shall not proceed with the breach, or the offender admits all or some of the breaches. By reaching a resolution, court time and expense can be saved, as can the necessity to call witnesses to give evidence.

A number of common examples can be used to demonstrate how a resolution may be reached:

- *The offender may present evidence to provide a reasonable excuse.* As discussed in Chapter 3, the Probation Service will expect the offender to provide evidence of any failure to comply within a specified period of time (usually five days following the alleged failure). It is common for that evidence to materialise at the first hearing when the breach is to be put. If the advocate for the Probation Service views the evidence and does consider it would provide a reasonable excuse for the failure to comply, they may consider it appropriate to withdraw the breach.

- *The offender may offer to admit some breaches, but not others.* For example, the offender may deny that they failed to attend a scheduled rehabilitation activity requirement (RAR) appointment on a certain date, but may admit to failing to attend a keep in touch appointment. In this circumstance, the advocate for the Probation Service must consider the acceptability of such admissions. To avoid the necessity for a contested breach, the advocate may consider it acceptable to withdraw the first breach and proceed on the second.

- *The offender may admit the breaches on a limited basis:* Suppose an offender was required to attend several keep in touch appointments and failed to attend. The offender informs their responsible officer that they could not attend due to childcare issues. The responsible officer requests evidence of this within five working days of the non-compliance. The offender fails to provide that evidence and is breached for the failure. At the first hearing, the offender provides evidence to prove the reason for their non-attendance. In this circumstance, the offender may admit the breach on a limited basis (i.e. they deny that they failed to attend without reasonable excuse, but they admit that they failed to provide evidence as required within five working days).

Where an offender wishes to enter a basis of plea, this should be in writing and signed by the offender.[1]

- *The Probation Service may amend the terms of the alleged breach to reflect conduct an offender is willing to admit to.* For example, suppose an offender claims that they were physically unable to complete the unpaid work requirement (having obtained a sick note), but also failed to attend a keep in touch appointment. If the offender has been breached for failing to attend the unpaid work requirement and denies that breach, the offender may be willing to admit to failing to attend the keep in touch appointment instead.

Where a resolution can be sought, the advocate for the Probation Service should make a clear note of this and inform the Probation Service of it.

Key point

From experience, it is generally unnecessary to obtain the consent of the Probation Service before a resolution can be obtained, unless it would have the effect of withdrawing the breach in its entirety. In those circumstances, the advocate for the Probation Service should first seek the views of a probation practitioner before proceeding.

What evidence/ witnesses are required for the contested hearing?

Should the case be incapable of resolution, the matter must progress to a contested hearing. Advocates will be required, as with any trial, to identify how long will be required for any contested hearing (no doubt an hour or two would generally suffice).

1 Criminal Procedure Rules (CrimPR) 2020, Rule 24.11(5).

Evidence required

In order to effectively prepare for the contested hearing, the parties will need to consider what evidence will need to be called. For example, the defence may agree with the evidence of the Probation Service and may simply wish to call the offender to give evidence. In this case, very little action is required from the advocate for the Probation Service.

However, in many cases the evidence of the Probation Service is not agreed. As such, it is common for the offender's responsible officer to be called to give evidence. The advocate for the Probation Service should refer to the Breach Report, specifically Section 7, which details the availability of the responsible officer.

Where the evidence of a responsible officer is required for the contested hearing, a section 9-compliant witness statement should be obtained from them.[2] The responsible officer should be informed in good time of the necessity for them to give evidence and the need to provide a witness statement.

Importantly, the Criminal Procedure and Investigation Act 1996 (CPIA 1996) does not apply to breach proceedings. This is evident from s.1 of the CPIA 1996 which restricts the application of the disclosure regime in Part 1 of the CPIA 1996 to the prosecution of criminal offences. As discussed in Chapter 1, breach of a community order or suspended sentence order is not a criminal offence. For this reason, neither the CPIA 1996 nor the Attorney General's Guidelines on Disclosure apply to probation breaches.

Will the contested hearing be on the same day?

It is uncommon, though not unknown, for the contested hearing to be dealt with there and then. Should the court have the time and capacity, the judge may feel able to deal with the contested hearing on the same

---

2 Criminal Justice Act 1967, s.9

day (e.g. by hearing evidence from the offender). This option would only be plausible if the evidence of the Probation Service is not disputed, and the only evidence to be called is from the offender. However, there may be many reasons as to why the case cannot be dealt with at the first hearing and in fact the majority of contested breaches will be adjourned. Evidence may need to be obtained from either party to the proceedings, or the court may simply not have the capacity to deal with the matter.

Matter of bail pending contested hearing

Where breach proceedings cannot be finalised at the first hearing, the issue of bail will fall to be determined. Whilst it is technically permissible for the court to simply adjourn proceedings without the need for a remand, such is unlikely in breach proceedings. This is largely due to the fact that the offender has already been convicted of an offence and is presently alleged to have breached a court order. As such, the court will have to determine whether the offender ought to be remanded in custody or on bail pending the contested hearing. Generally, the court shall maintain the status quo and grant the offender bail. However, where the court has concerns regarding the offender, they may conclude that the offender should be remanded in custody. The ordinary principles of bail apply to breach proceedings, and readers are advised to return to Chapter 4.

The contested hearing

In this section of the chapter, we shall turn our attention to the hearing itself. We shall discuss the applicable principles relating to such hearings and the procedure adopted.

Preliminary matters

Tribunal

In the magistrates' court, the issue of whether an offender has breached the requirements of an order are to be determined by a lay bench or district judge, as appropriate. In proceedings before the Crown Court, any question whether the offender has breached a requirement of an order, or has been convicted of a further offence during the operational period of a suspended sentence, is to be determined by the court and not by the verdict of a jury.[3] Reference to "the court" of course means the judge.

Burden and standard of proof

In breach proceedings, the burden of proof is on the Probation Service to prove that the offender breached a requirement of an order, without reasonable excuse. This requires the Probation Service both prove the breach, and disprove any suggestion of reasonable excuse. Naturally, an evidential burden lies with the offender to provide evidence of reasonable excuse to make the issue live.

In respect of the standard of proof, this is not particularly clear from the legislation. The Sentencing Act 2020 states that a breach must be "proved to the satisfaction of the court".[4] In *West Yorkshire Probation Board v Boulter*,[5] however, the Divisional Court clarified that the standard of proof is the criminal standard; i.e. the tribunal must be *sure* that the offender breached a requirement of the order without reasonable excuse. In the context of the former law, Keene LJ would explain:

---

3 Sentencing Act 2020, Schedule 16, para 12(4).

4 ibid, Schedule 10, paras 10(1)(b) and 11(1)(b); Schedule 16, paras 10(1)(b) and 12(2)(b).

5 [2005] EWHC 2342 (Admin).

> It is true that neither that case nor Schedule 3 of paragraph 4 of the 2000 Act expressly refers to proof "beyond a reasonable doubt" or some such similar phrase. In my view that was because the draftsman assumed that in criminal proceedings before a magistrates' court it was enough to require the bench "to be satisfied" as to the alleged breach and that such satisfaction would have to be to the normal criminal standard.[6]

Rules of evidence

The rules of evidence apply in the ordinary way as they would in criminal cases. In *West Yorkshire Probation Board v Boulter*, Keene LJ explained that:

> the fact that a person accused of breaching a [community order] is facing the prospect of being resentenced does not take the proceedings, in my judgment, outside the normal criminal process.[7]

In light of that, evidence is required to be given on oath or following an affirmation. The restrictions on evidence relating to hearsay, character, and the like equally apply.

An example of the strict rules of evidence and procedure being applied can be seen in *R v Gainsborough Justices, ex parte Green*.[8] This was a case concerning judicial review of a magistrates' court decision to allow the prosecution to re-open its case as opposed to acceding to a submission of no case to answer. In allowing the appeal, Griffiths LJ explained that:

> The general principle is that when the prosecution closes their case they must stand or fall on the evidence they have

6 ibid, [16] (Keene LJ).

7 ibid, [15] (Keene LJ).

8 (1983) 78 Cr. App. R. 9(QBD).

> produced. It is only in exceptional circumstances that there is a discretion in the court to allow the prosecution to call further evidence. [...] The general rule is that the prosecution cannot re-open the case and have, as it were, a second bite of the cherry, having heard a submission of no case to answer, and realising they have failed to call the evidence they should have called.[9]

The key message here is that the ordinary rules as to the presentation of evidence apply; a prosecutor must be alive to the necessity to present all of their evidence before closing their case.[10]

The course of the hearing

The hearing will follow the same structure as a trial in the magistrates' court or Crown Court (save that in the Crown Court, there shall be no jury). Rule 32.4(1) of the Criminal Procedure Rules (CrimPR) 2020 provides that the rules in Part 24 of the CrimPR 2020 apply equally to breach proceedings. Part 24 concerns "Trial and sentence in the magistrates' court" and sets out the procedure to be adopted at trial, including the presentation of evidence. In short, therefore, a contested breach will adopt the same approach as a trial.

The following shall briefly summarise the process of a contested hearing.

---

9 ibid, 12 (Griffiths LJ).

10 Readers are advised to consider *R v Pilcher* (1974) 60 Cr. App. R. 1 (CA) for the general principles on the presentation of evidence and re-opening the prosecution case.

Opening speech

The advocate for the Probation Service shall provide a brief summary of what they allege the breach to be and what evidence they will call. Ideally, the advocate for the Probation Service will inform the court as part of their opening of:

- The key details relevant to the offender's sentence (i.e. the sentence imposed, length of sentence, nature of the order, requirements imposed etc),
- The alleged breaches,
- The evidence to be relied upon,
- The issues in the case (i.e. a summary of what the defence is),
- A reminder of the burden and standard of proof.

Key point

In the Crown Court, the opening speech is often dispensed with on account that the judge will have read the papers in full and will understand the allegation made against the offender. The advocate for the Probation Service should enquire whether the judge wishes for them to open the case. If such an opening is required, it will be brief.

Case for the Probation Service

Having opened the case, the advocate for the Probation Service will then call its evidence. This will generally be live evidence from the offender's responsible officer, and/or any other relevant witness to the proceedings.

It is important to remember that the ordinary rules of evidence apply, meaning that the advocate for the Probation Service must ensure that only non-leading questions are asked, and that the witness restricts their answers to matters forming part of their own knowledge, perception or recollection. However, all advocates should recall that the hearing will be restricted to the contested issue between the parties (e.g. that the offender had a reasonable excuse). For that reason, it is good practice for the advocate for the Probation Service to lead on any evidence that is not contentious and simply assists the court with understanding the matter.

In examining the responsible officer in chief, it is important to ensure that the advocate proves each element of the breach. As discussed in Chapters 6 and 7, it must be proven that:

- This offender[11]
- Breached a requirement of a community order, or community requirement of a suspended sentence order,
- Without reasonable excuse.

This will require questions asked relating to the imposition of the original order, details of the initial appointment/ induction with the offender where the rules of the order were explained to them, the details of the alleged breaches, including what communication was made with, and received from, the offender (and the medium(s) by which the communications were made and received).

[11] See *West Yorkshire Probation Board v Boulter* [2005] EWHC 2342 (Admin) for the importance of proving that this particular offender was the person subject to the court order, and is the same person now before the court in breach.

Key point

It is not for the responsible officer to give evidence that the defendant acted without reasonable excuse; that is not an opinion that the responsible officer can give. Rather, the responsible officer is to give evidence as to what steps they took to ensure the compliance of the offender, and how the offender failed to comply. Whether such failure was reasonable is for the offender to raise, and the Probation Service to disprove through cross-examination of the offender.

The witness for the Probation Service will no doubt be called to exhibit real evidence as part of the contested hearing. This may be emails, text messages, or other forms of communication sent to the offender. Other forms of evidence commonly exhibited include the records or logs from the *N-Delius* system.

Naturally, following any examination-in-chief, the defence will be permitted to cross-examine the witness. The questions to be put to the witness will ultimately depend on the issue in question. For example, where the offender's defence is that they had a reasonable excuse on account of poor mental health, the defence advocate may focus on any communications between the witness and the offender relating to their mental health. By way of another example, where the offender claims that the Probation Service did not notify them of their appointments (or a defence of a similar nature), the questions in cross-examination will focus on potential mistakes or faults on part of the witness in communicating/ engaging with the offender. In practice, the defence will often present evidence of text messages, emails or call logs showing the offender attempting to contact the Probation Service to show that any such fault was that of the Probation Service and not the offender.

Following any cross-examination, the advocate for the Probation Service is permitted to conduct any necessary re-examination and should also offer any final questions to the judge. As in the normal course of events, re-examination must be restricted to matters arising from cross-examination; advocates must not introduce new evidence at this stage.

This procedure shall be repeated for as many witnesses as are to be called by the Probation Service. Having called all of its evidence, the Probation Service will then close its case.

Half-time Submissions

As with any criminal trial, the defence are free to make a submission of no case to answer following the close of the prosecution's case. The ordinary principles from *R v Galbraith*[12] apply.

Defence case

As with any other trial, the offender is not obligated to give evidence. Simply, they have a right not to give evidence.[13] However, given that the court must be satisfied that the offender did not have a "reasonable excuse", it is highly likely that the offender will need to give evidence.

In a similar vein to the case for the Probation Service, the offender will be subject to examination-in-chief and cross-examination in the normal way.

Should there be any witness other than the offender, they too may be called to give evidence and will be subject to cross-examination.

Closing speeches

Finally, both parties may present any closing submissions to the court. Such closing submissions should focus on the issues in the hearing.

The defence may always make a closing speech. However, the advocate for the Probation Service may only make a closing speech where the

---

[12] (1981) 73 Cr. App. R. 124 (CA). Readers should consider specialist criminal texts for a discussion of the test in *Galbraith.*

[13] Criminal Evidence Act 1898, s.1(1).

offender is represented, or where the offender has called evidence other than themselves. Therefore, if the offender is unrepresented and has only given evidence themselves, the Probation Service is not permitted to make a closing speech. In practice, however, and unless the matter is particularly complex or complicated, it is common for the Probation Service to not make any such closing speech.

Verdict

Having heard all the evidence in the case, the tribunal must then consider whether they are satisfied, so that they are sure, that the offender breached a requirement of an order without reasonable excuse. The court must provide sufficient reasons for its decision, if it finds the case to be proven (i.e. that the offender did breach without reasonable excuse). The court *may* do so if it does not find the breach to be proven (though in practice the court often will).

Procedure following verdict

If the breach is proven, the court will likely proceed to "sentence" (i.e. dealing with the breach). The Court will invite the parties to identify the offender's compliance with the order using the relevant Sentencing Council Guidelines.[14] The powers of the courts in respect of breaches are dealt with in Chapter 6 (community orders) and Chapter 7 (suspended sentence orders). The advocate for the Probation Service should also consider applying for a contribution to costs of bringing the proceedings; this figure will rightly exceed the amount sought following an admission at the first hearing.[15]

If the breach is not so proven, the court will explain the effect of that finding to the offender. The offender will be advised that they remain subject to the order (if they indeed are) and the requirement to continue

---

14 See Chapter 9.

15 See Chapter 5.

to comply with the requirements of the order. If known, the offender should be informed of his next appointment in open court and the Probation Service should be encouraged to re-engage the offender following proceedings as soon as practicable. It is common for defence advocates to also seek a defence costs order.

Summary

This Chapter has covered the process and procedure of a contested breach hearing. In this Chapter, we have discussed:

- The steps necessary to prepare for a contested breach,
- The burden and standard of proof applicable to contested breach proceedings,
- The structure of a contested breach, including the calling of evidence,
- The verdict and subsequent action following a finalised contested hearing.

CHAPTER NINE

SENTENCING COUNCIL GUIDELINES ON BREACH OF ORDERS

Introduction

In this Chapter, we consider the Definitive Guidelines published by the Sentencing Council for breach of probation orders. A separate guideline exists in respect of breach of community orders and breach of suspended sentence orders. Both guidelines must be read in conjunction with appropriate case law from the appellate courts and the relevant provisions from the Sentencing Act 2020. This Chapter should also be read in conjunction with Chapters 6 and 7.

> **Key provisions**
>
> There are no legislative provisions specifically relevant to the preparation of a breach case. Advocates are directed to be familiar with the provisions in Schedules 10 and 16 to the Sentencing Act 2020 as appropriate.

Applicability of sentencing guidelines

With effect from 1 October 2018, the Sentencing Council published the definitive guidelines on *Breach of a community order* and *Breach of a suspended sentence order*. The guidelines apply to all offenders aged 18 and above,[1] who are sentenced on or after 1 October 2018. The guidelines are applicable from the date of sentence of the offender, and not date of the breach.

As with any guideline published by the Sentencing Council, a court must follow these guidelines when sentencing an offender "unless the court is satisfied that it would be contrary to the interests of justice to do so."[2]

Structure of guidelines

From the outset, it can be noted that the two breach guidelines deviate from the traditional "stepped approach"[3] adopted by the Sentencing Council in Definitive Sentencing Guidelines. In developing the breach guidelines, the Sentencing Council were quick to note that such a stepped approach would not be appropriate as the factors which affect the seriousness assessment do not lend themselves to this model. For example, the lack of presence of aggravating and mitigating factors in the guidelines is justified on account that many of the appropriate factors used to consider the seriousness of the breach would also be used as aggravating and mitigating factors resulting in double counting.

A primary focus of the guidelines is on the offender's level of compliance. This focus is well-founded given that compliance with court orders, and enforcement of such compliance, is an important aspect of securing public confidence in the justice system. Enforcing compliance, or lack thereof, is also vital in the protection of the public from harm, in the

1 Offenders under the age of 18 ("children and young people") are to be sentenced in accordance with the Sentencing Council's definitive guideline on *Sentencing Children and Young People* (1 June 2017).

2 Sentencing Act 2020, s.59(1).

3 The stepped approach requires the sentencing court to first categorise the offence according to culpability and harm factors, allowing them to identify an initial starting point and category range. The sentencing court can then consider aggravating and mitigating factors, and any other factors considered necessary to reach the overall sentence.

form of further offending or continuing criminal behaviour. These guidelines are designed to ensure that the purpose of the court order is not undermined by an offender's non-compliance.

The categories of compliance in the guidelines were designed by the Sentencing Council to strike the balance between appropriately punitive penalties to deal with the breach and providing sufficient options to enable the penalty to be suitably tailored to the circumstances. In addition, it seeks to balance the overall objective of achieving compliance, while still ensuring breaches are dealt with effectively and consistently.

Sentencing Guidelines for Breach of a Community Order

The guideline is divided into:

- Breach of community order by failing to comply with requirements, and
- Powers of the court following a subsequent conviction.

We shall deal with each in turn. Please refer to Chapter 6 for a full discussion on sentencing offenders in breach of the requirements of a community order, or those who are convicted of further offences.

<u>Breach by failing to comply with requirements</u>

As detailed in Chapter 6, both a magistrates' court and the Crown Court has extensive powers when dealing with an offender for breach of a requirement of a community order. These powers are discussed in full in Chapter 6 and shall only be referenced here as appropriate.

Assessing compliance

The sentencing guideline is clear that when considering what penalty to impose to mark the breach, the court "must take into account the extent to which the offender has complied with the requirements of the community order".[4]

There are four levels of compliance according to the sentencing guideline. These are:

- Wilful and persistent non-compliance,
- Low level of compliance,
- Medium level of compliance, and
- High level of compliance.

The advocates at any hearing will make submissions as to the offender's compliance with the order before the sentencing judge makes a determination on that compliance. The court will be assisted by the Probation Service by a statement in the Breach Report as to what level of compliance they consider the offender to be at. The opinion of the Probation Service as to whether the order remains workable and the offender's motivation to complete the order, will be important to the court's assessment.[5]

---

4 This reflects the requirement in paras 10(7) and 11(4) of Schedule 10 to the Sentencing Act 2020 (see Chapter 6).

5 See *R v Aslam* [2016] EWCA Crim 845, [2016] 2 Cr. App. R. (S.) 29.

Key point

It is of vital importance that all parties to breach proceedings (advocates, the judge, and the Probation Service) consider the consequences of a particular categorisation of the offender's compliance. For example, as will be discussed below, should an offender be regarded as demonstrating "wilful and persistent non-compliance", the court is entitled to re-sentence the offender to a term of imprisonment, even if the custodial threshold for the offence has not been passed. Advocates must, therefore, be astute to the powers of the court and the impact of a particular finding or categorisation of an offender's compliance.

The Sentencing Guidelines do not define each level of compliance; this is because compliance is not a static or broad-brush question. The individual circumstances of each offender must be considered when assessing compliance; no two breaches will ever be the same in terms of compliance.

It would no doubt be inappropriate for the court to use mathematical or percentage-based calculations to determine compliance. For example, "low compliance" is less than 50% attendance and engagement whilst "medium compliance" is over 50% attendance and engagement. Such would not reflect the individuality of each breach. However, what can be gleaned from the Sentencing Guidelines is that the lowest level of compliance ("wilful and persistent non-compliance") evidently requires the court to find *both* a "wilful" and "persistent" non-compliance. Should such non-compliance be wilful but not persistent, the court appears somewhat mandated to find the level of compliance to be "low".[6]

6 For a full discussion on the meaning of "wilful and persistent non-compliance", see Chapter 6.

Whilst there are no definitions of the various levels of compliance, the Sentencing Guideline does identify the factors that the court should consider when assessing the level of compliance:

1. *The offender's overall attitude and engagement with the order as well as the proportion of elements completed.*

   This evidence will be obtained from the Breach Report[7] of the Probation Service. In that report, they will detail the offender's engagement with the Probation Service generally, and with particular aspects of their order. The offender's general attitude and demeanour is likely to also be contained in that Breach Report. For example, the Breach Report may identify that the offender is open, honest, and polite in their dealings with the Probation Service. Alternatively, they may identify the offender to be obstructive, rude, or that their engagement is superficial.

   In addition, the offender's compliance with the order, including any requirements of the order, will be relevant. For example, an offender may have had an unpaid work requirement imposed, and had complied with part of that requirement. Importantly, the court will be interested in both the offender's compliance with requirements, and their attitude in complying. For example, in *R v Ballard*[8] Dingemans J would explain that "Compliance with an unpaid work requirement will normally justify a reduction, but dilatory and grudging compliance will not yield the same result."[9]

---

7 See Chapter 4.

8 [2016] EWCA Crim 1173.

9 ibid, [11] (Dingemans J).

Key point

As part of the community order, an offender will have regular one-to-one appointments with their responsible officer. It will be important for you to seek information from the Probation Service about any logs made of conversations had between the offender and their responsible officer to discern the offender's general attitude to the order. Such logs will be available on the *N-Delius* system, usually logged in the form of CRISSA (Check-in, Review, Implement, Summarise, Set tasks, Set next Appointment). CRISSA provides the greatest insight into attitudes and possible barriers to compliance on an order.

2. *The impact of any completed or partially completed requirements on the offender's behaviour.*

An offender may have completed, or be working towards completion of, a particular requirement that has had a positive impact on the offender and their life. For example, an offender who has been breached for failing to attend their unpaid work requirement may demonstrate that they have complied well with a drug rehabilitation requirement (DRR) to such an extent that they have reduced their intake of alcohol and have avoided social spaces where alcohol may be present. Whilst the court will be dissatisfied with the breach, it will be pleased to note that at least one aspect of the order has had a positive impact. Likewise, the building better relationships (BBR) programme is designed to assist offenders with their consequential thinking skills, their interaction with others, and to help them understand the impact of their behaviour on others. A good report from the provider of such BBR can demonstrate to the court the positive impact the BBR has had on the offender's behaviour. However, where requirements of a more rehabilitative nature may have been completed, but a change in an offender's behaviour or attitude is not demonstrated, the court would be free to regard the offender's compliance as low.[10]

3. *The proximity of breach to imposition of order.*

This factor is a follow-on from the first. The court will naturally consider an offender to have a poor attitude to the order the closer the offender's breach is to the date the order was imposed.[11] Likewise, where an offender has breached an order during its infant stages, they will have completed few (if any) requirements of the order. The court may thus be disinclined to allow the offender a second chance at the order. This is in comparison to an offender who has complied well with the order for the majority of its currency.[12] On the other hand, defence advocates will be well placed in arguing that the order has not had the opportunity to get properly underway, and the offender has not had the benefit of any impact of the requirements of the order. For example, offenders with drug or alcohol addictions, or mental health issues, may find it more difficult to comply with an order where they have only just begun relevant treatment and their problems remain somewhat unresolved. For that reason, an

---

[10] *R v Ballard* [2016] EWCA Crim 1173: "if attendance on a course has not altered the defendant's thinking attitude, activation in full may be justified." (at [11] (Dingemans J)).

[11] In *R v Brindley* [2012] EWCA Crim 1767, the Court of Appeal considered it to be appropriate to activate a suspended sentence order in part where most of the operational period of the suspended sentence was still to run when the offender committed a further offence.

[12] See, for example, *R v Carmody* [2015] EWCA Crim 1029 where the offender had complied fully with the community requirements of an 18-month suspended sentence order, and the order itself only had six weeks remaining. In this case, the Court of Appeal considered a four-month period of activation to be appropriate (compared with the eight-month activation ordered by the Crown Court).

early breach may persuade the court to give an offender a second chance.

4. *Evidence of circumstances or offender characteristics, such as disability, mental health issues or learning difficulties which have impeded offender's compliance with the order.*

   This final requirement is exceptionally important to the court's determination of any penalty to be imposed. Where the defendant has a particular circumstance or characteristic, which may be of a physical or mental nature, the court can take that into account for breach proceedings. However, the relevance of those circumstances or characteristics is limited to those that have "impeded the offender's compliance with the order". This factor commonly comes into play where an offender alleges that they could not attend at their unpaid work requirement because of ill health. Alternatively, an offender may suggest that they could not attend certain group sessions (such as may be found in RAR days) due to stress and anxiety involved in being in a group setting. The suitability of any requirement imposed should have been known to the court and Probation Service at the date of sentence through the pre-sentence report. The court may be unsympathetic to the idea, therefore, that the offender did not disclose a particular circumstance or characteristic at the time of sentence.[13]

Where the court has reached a determination on the nature of an offender's compliance with the order, the court can then consider the associated penalty with that compliance. We shall consider the suitability of these penalties now.

[13] See Chapter 2 on pre-sentence reports and suitability of requirements.

Compliance and suitable penalty

The penalties available to the court can be found in paras 10(5) and 11(2) of Schedule 10 to the Sentencing Act 2020 and have been discussed in full in Chapter 6.

The guidelines prescribe the following penalties according to the offender's compliance:

- *Wilful and persistent non-compliance*:

  Revoke the order and re-sentence imposing custodial sentence (even where the offence seriousness did not originally merit custody).[14]

- *Low level of compliance* :

  Revoke the order and re-sentence original offence; OR add curfew requirement of 20 – 30 days; OR add 30 – 50 hours additional unpaid work/add additional requirement(s); OR impose a Band C fine

- *Medium level of compliance:*

  Revoke the order and resentence original offence; OR add curfew requirement of 10 – 20 days; OR add 20 – 30 hours additional unpaid work/add additional requirement(s); OR impose a Band B fine.

[14] This reflects and repeats paras 10(9) and 11(6) of Schedule 10 to the Sentencing Act 2020.

- *High level of compliance:*

  Add curfew requirement of 6 – 10 days; OR add 10 – 20 hours additional unpaid work/add additional requirement(s); OR impose a Band A fine.

Much like other sentencing guidelines produced by the Sentencing Council, the guideline provides the court with a range of penalties available. Unlike breaches of suspended sentence orders, for which the default position is to activate the sentence unless it is unjust to do so, there is no such default position in respect of community orders. The court is therefore free to consider what penalty is the most appropriate in the circumstances before them.

In addition to stating the offender's level of compliance, the Probation Service may also make a recommendation as to the penalty they consider suitable in the circumstances. In *R v Aslam*,[15] HHJ Cooke QC, giving the judgment of the Court of Appeal stated that the views of the Probation Service should be given "very considerable weight in deciding the manner of disposal."[16] His Honour would explain:

> What is important at a breach hearing is: has there been any re-offending? Has risk been reduced? Does the Probation Service feel its work with the offender may usefully continue?[17]

Whilst it is right to say that a decision on penalty is one for the judge, the views of the Probation Service are nevertheless important. Quite simply: Does the Probation Service think that it can still work with the offender? If the Probation Service does not consider such is possible, this will weigh heavily on the court's decision as to the appropriate penalty.

---

15 [2016] EWCA Crim 845, [2016] 2 Cr. App. R. (S.) 29.

16 ibid, [13] (HHJ Cooke QC).

17 ibid.

Technical guidance

The guideline then proceeds to provide "technical guidance" to the court when considering what penalty to impose to mark a breach. It is worth repeating that guidance here and expanding on it further.

Firstly, where the court marks the breach by imposing more onerous requirements, the guideline invites the court to consider whether the length of the community order needs to be extended. Extension of community orders is discussed in full in Chapter 11 in the context of applications to amend. The law is identical when it concerns breach, in that the court may extend the length of the community order by six months (even if that has the effect of extending the order beyond three years).[18] The power to extend can be exercised only once, however.[19]

Second, the guidance reminds the court that if an unpaid work requirement is imposed, and there had been no previous imposition of such a requirement, the court must impose a minimum of 20 hours.[20] This number is 20-less than the minimum number that would have to be imposed where the unpaid work requirement is imposed at the first instance of sentence.[21]

It is important to note, however, that where the court imposes more onerous requirements by adding *further* unpaid work hours, to an order that already featured an unpaid work requirement, there is no minimum number of hours that the court must impose.[22]

---

18 This reflects and repeats para 13(2) of Schedule 10 to the Sentencing Act 2020.

19 See para 13(3) of Schedule 10 to the Sentencing Act 2020.

20 This reflects and repeats para 13(4) of Schedule 10 to the Sentencing Act 2020.

21 See para 2(1)(b)(i) of Schedule 9 to the Sentencing Act 2020 where the minimum number is set at 40 hours.

22 Though, the court remains restricted to the statutory maximum of 300 hours (see para 2(1)(b)(ii) of Schedule 9 to the Sentencing Act 2020).

Third, the guidance reminds courts that the maximum financial penalty that can be imposed for a breach is £2,500. This is irrespective of the financial position of an offender. By way of example, for a low level of compliance, the guideline proposes a Band C fine as an option for the court. A Band C fine has a starting point of 150% of the offender's relevant weekly income, with a range of 125–175% of the relevant weekly income. Whilst a Band C fine for a wealthy offender may ordinarily exceed £2,500 (reflecting their weekly income), the maximum fine available to the court on breach proceedings remains £2,500.

Fourth, the guidance reminds the court that it "MUST NOT"[23] impose a suspended sentence order as a "more sever alternative to a community order". This does not prohibit the court from re-sentencing an offender to a suspended sentence order. However, the court must be satisfied that the custodial threshold has been crossed in the normal way.[24]As discussed in Chapter 6, the court does have the power to impose a custodial sentence even if it is not of the opinion that the custodial threshold has been passed for the offence where the offender has wilfully and persistently breached the requirements of the community order.[25] This power is *only* available where the court considers the offender's non-compliance to be "wilful and persistent"; demonstrating the limited and somewhat rare circumstances in which that power may be utilised.

The final matter of technical guidance clarifies a restriction that is imposed on a magistrates' court when dealing with breach proceedings. It reminds magistrates' courts that where it is dealing with a breach of a Crown Court community order, a magistrates' court is restricted to imposing a fine or making the order more onerous. A magistrates' court *cannot* revoke, or revoke and re-sentence a Crown Court community

---

23 Original emphasis.

24 See s.230 Sentencing Act 2020 and the Sentencing Council's Guideline on the *Imposition of community and custodial sentences* (1 February 2017).

25 Sentencing Act 2020, Schedule 10, paras 10(9) and 10(6).

order.[26] If a magistrates' court considers that this is a breach that is too serious to be dealt with otherwise than by revocation and re-sentence, the magistrates' court must commit the offender to custody, or release the offender on bail, until they can be brought or appear before the Crown Court.[27]

Subsequent conviction of further offences

As has been discussed in Chapter 6, a conviction for a further offence(s) does not constitute a breach of a community order. Schedule 10 to the Sentencing Act 2020 deliberately distinguishes the procedure and relevant court's powers when faced with a breach of community order requirements, and conviction for further offences.[28]

Indeed, the Sentencing Act 2020 provides that on a subsequent conviction during the currency of a community order, the court *may* revoke the order or both revoke the order and re-sentence the offender for the original offence. As the legislation does not compel the court to exercise either of those options, it is possible that no action may be taken. For those reasons, conviction of a further offence is not regarded as a breach of the order. This is unlike convictions for further offences committed during the operational period of a suspended sentence order which are regarded as breaches of the suspended sentence order.[29]

---

26 This is clear in para 10(5)(c) of Schedule 10 to the Sentencing Act 2020 which states that a magistrates' court may re-sentence an offender "if the community order was made by a magistrates' court".

27 Sentencing Act 2020, Schedule 10, para 10(3).

28 The former in Part 2 and the latter in Part 5 of Schedule 10.

29 Because they are regarded as "activation events" as are breaches of any community requirements of suspended sentence orders, see s.286(3) Sentencing Act 2020.

The guideline repeats guidance from the *Totality* guideline.[30] The *Totality* guideline reminds courts of the following:

- The court is concerned with *conviction* during the currency of the community order and not *commission*.[31]
- The community order must be in force at the date of conviction; where the community order has ceased at the date of conviction, the court has no power to act.[32]
- It is irrelevant whether the subsequent offence was *committed* during the currency of the order if the order is no longer in force at the date of conviction (though that will be regarded as an aggravating factor when sentencing for the subsequent offence).

The *Totality* guideline goes on to provide guidance according to two factual scenarios. We shall consider those in turn here.

Community order imposed by magistrates' court

The guidance states that a magistrates' court should "ordinarily" revoke the previous community order and sentence afresh for both the original and the additional offence. It is important to emphasise that whilst the guideline suggests that a court should "ordinarily" re-sentence, the court must still be satisfied that it is in the "interests of justice to do so, having regard to circumstances which have arisen since the order was made".[33]

---

30 Sentencing Council, *Totality* (1 July 2023).

31 See also *R v Kakakhan* [2020] EWCA Crim 1236, [12] (Williams Davis J). This is discussed fully in Chapter 6.

32 ibid.

33 Sentencing Act 2020, Schedule 10, para 23(2).

Community order imposed by the Crown Court

The guidance states that where an offender is convicted of a new offence in the magistrates' court (either by way of guilty plea or following trial), the relevant magistrates' court "may, and ordinarily should, commit the offender to the Crown Court, in order to allow the Crown Court to re-sentence for the original offence."[34]

There is no provision in the Sentencing Act 2020, or guidance from the Sentencing Council as to the circumstances where a magistrates' court would not commit an offender for sentence. As detailed above, however, where a magistrates' court considers the matter capable of resolution by a financial penalty or the imposition of more onerous requirements, they are legally able to deal with the breach.

In addition to the original offence, the magistrates' court may also commit the new offence to the Crown Court for sentence. Importantly, the Crown Court has no power to deal with the new offence *unless* it has been committed by the magistrates' court for sentence.[35] The power to do so is found in ss.14-20 of the Sentencing Act 2020. The main provisions of relevance are ss.14 and 20:

- Section 14 is to be used where the new offence is so serious that the magistrates' court considers its sentencing powers to be inadequate in respect of it.[36]

---

[34] The power to commit for re-sentence is contained in para 24(2) of Schedule 10 to the Sentencing Act 2020.

[35] *R v De Brito* [2013] EWCA Crim 1134, [2014] 1 Cr. App. R. (S.) 38 [10] (Keith J).

[36] For which, the Crown Court is not restricted to the powers of the magistrates' court and may deal with the offender in any way in which it could deal with the offender if the offender had been convicted of the offence on indictment before the court. (Sentencing Act 2020, s.21(2)).

- Section 20 is to be used where the new offence is not so serious that the magistrates' court considers it sentencing powers to be adequate in respect of it.[37]

Advocates should consult a specialist sentencing text for a full discussion on the provisions of ss.14–20. For our purposes, the magistrates' court will either commit the new offence under s.14, or under s.20(1)(c) of the Sentencing Act 2020.

Assistance with sentencing

Finally, the guidance provides the court with assistance as to the approach to take when sentencing both the original offence and the new offence. In summary, the guidance states that the sentencing court should consider the overall seriousness of the offending behaviour taking into account both the new offence(s) and the original offence.[38] The similarity of the new offence (in the type of offence or facts/circumstances) to the original offence will no doubt be relevant to the court's consideration.

It goes on to say that the court should consider whether the combination of associated offences is sufficiently serious to justify a custodial sentence.

Importantly, however, where the Crown Court is re-sentencing an offender for a summary-only offence and the new offence is summary-only also, the Crown Court is restricted to the powers of the magistrates' court.[39] Any sentence of imprisonment may not, therefore, exceed an

---

[37] For which, the Crown Court is restricted to the powers of the magistrates' court and may deal with the offender for the offence in any way in which the magistrates' court could have dealt with the offender (Sentencing Act 2020, s.23(2)).

[38] See Chapter 6 for guidance as to the approach to be adopted by the court when re-sentencing the original offence. See also *R v Clarke* [1997] 2 Cr. App. R. (S.) 163 (CA) and *R v Veloz-Parra* [2012] EWCA Crim 1065.

[39] See s.133 Magistrates' Courts Act 1980.

aggregate of six months' imprisonment.[40] If the court does not consider that custody is necessary, it should impose a single community order (thus revoking the present community order) that reflects the overall totality of criminality.

Finally, the guidance reminds the court that it must take into account the extent to which the offender complied with the requirements of the previous order.

Sentencing Guidelines for Breach of a Suspended Sentence Order

The guideline is divided into:

- Conviction for further offence committed during operational period of order, and
- Failure to comply with a community requirement during the supervision period of the order.

We shall deal with each in turn. Please refer to Chapter 7 for a full discussion on sentencing offenders in breach of a suspended sentence order.

Conviction for further offence

The starting point in all cases is that the court *must* activate the custodial sentence.[41] This is so unless the court is of the opinion that it would be unjust to do so in view of all the circumstances.[42] The Sentencing Guideline makes clear that the predominant factor in determining

40 See *R v Palmer* [2019] EWCA Crim 2231 [25] (Jeremy Baker J).

41 Sentencing Act 2020, Schedule 16, para 14(1).

42 ibid.

whether activation is unjust "relates to the level of compliance with the suspended sentence order and the facts/nature of any new offence".[43]

Considering breach and compliance

The Guideline makes clear that the facts/nature of the new offence is the "primary consideration" in assessing the action to be taken on the breach, whereas the prior level of compliance is relevant as a secondary factor.

An offender's compliance is assessed by considering the same factors as identified (above) (i.e. the overall attitude and engagement with the order etc).[44]

Breach, compliance and appropriate penalty

As above with community orders, a court should consider the views of the Probation Service as to the offender's level of compliance, and invite submissions from the advocates as to such compliance.

Where the Court has reached a determination on the nature of the breach, the court can then consider the associated penalty with that breach. The penalties available to the Court can be found in para 13(1) of Schedule 16 to the Sentencing Act 2020 and have been discussed in full in Chapter 7.

The Guideline prescribes a variety of penalties according to the breach. The nature of the breach is broken down according to the circumstances of the new offence(s) and the offender's level of compliance.

---

[43] This reflects and repeats para 14(2) of Schedule 16 to the Sentencing Act 2020.

[44] See above "Assessing compliance".

Key point

In addition to fully considering the nature of the offender's compliance with the order, an advocate must be fully abreast with the nature of the new offence committed. They must consider:

- the nature of the new offence (i.e. is it an offence of the same description or same category as the original offence),
- the seriousness (or "gravity") of the new offence in comparison to the original offence, and
- whether the new offence justifies a custodial sentence.

In respect of the final factor listed above, the court should be sensitive to the fact that the lack of custodial sentence for the new offence may make activation unjust. For example, where a suspended sentence order was imposed for an offence of dwelling burglary, it may be unjust to activate that sentence for an offence of drink driving. The guideline is therefore drafted broadly to give the sentencing court the widest discretion when identifying the appropriate penalty.

In total, there are six various categories of breach according to the Guideline which are afforded suitable penalties to mark the breach:

- *Multiple and/or more serious new offence(s) committed*:

  Full activation of original custodial term.

- *New offence similar in type and gravity to offence for which suspended sentence order imposed AND No/low level of compliance with suspended sentence order:*

  Full activation of original custodial term.

- *New offence similar in type and gravity to offence for which suspended sentence order imposed AND Medium or high level of compliance with suspended sentence order:*

  Activate sentence but apply appropriate reduction to original custodial term taking into consideration any unpaid work or curfew requirements completed.

- *New offence less serious than original offence but requires a custodial sentence AND No/low level of compliance with suspended sentence order:*

  Full activation of original custodial term.

- *New offence less serious than original offence but requires a custodial sentence AND Medium or high level of compliance with suspended sentence order:*

  Activate sentence but apply appropriate reduction to original custodial term taking into consideration any unpaid work or curfew requirements completed.

- *New offence does not require custodial sentence:*

  Activate sentence[45] but apply reduction to original custodial term taking into consideration any unpaid work or curfew requirements completed; OR impose more onerous requirement(s) and/or extend supervision period and/or extend operational period; OR impose fine.

---

45 See *Nobbs v DPP* [2008] EWHC 1653 (Admin) where the Divisional Court considered that it may be appropriate to activate a suspended sentence order even in circumstances where the new offence does not cross the custodial threshold.

Key point

What is evident from the categories of breach is that where an offender is convicted of multiple offences, the Guideline recommends full activation of the original custodial term. This appears to be so regardless of the seriousness or similarity of the new offences. The remaining categories of breach refer to "offence" in the singular; it is important that an advocate is alive to this wording in the Guideline. Furthermore, the most serious breach also does not consider the offender's compliance with the order. This is a deliberate omission and demonstrates the limited discretion available to courts when dealing with multiple new offences (or offences of a serious nature).

As you will see above, the Guideline refers to applying an appropriate reduction to the original custodial term. It is for the court to identify the appropriate proportionate reduction depending on the extent of any compliance with the requirements specified.[46]

Assessing whether it would be unjust

As discussed at multiple points in this text, following a breach of a suspended sentence order, the court *must* activate the suspended sentence order unless it would be unjust to do so. The issue becomes, when would it be "unjust" to do so, or what factors are relevant to the determination of whether it would be unjust?

An overall consideration for the court is to remember that the sentencing court which imposed the original sentence concluded that the custodial threshold had been passed, and that a custodial sentence was appropriate in the original case.

46 See *R v Kavanagh* [2010] EWCA Crim 1737, [2011] 1 Cr. App. R. (S.) 63; *R v Mcdonagh* [2017] EWCA Crim 2193. Both authorities are discussed in full in Chapter 7.

The Sentencing Guideline identifies that the court must consider "all factors" in a given case, and suggests that the court may consider the following:

- any strong personal mitigation,
- whether there is a realistic prospect of rehabilitation, and
- whether immediate custody will result in significant impact on others.

Importantly, however, the court may not rely on factors or circumstances present at the time the suspended sentence order was made. This is very clear in the *Breach of a suspended sentence order* Guideline. It states: "Only new and exceptional factors/circumstances not present at the time the suspended sentence order was imposed should be taken into account."

As a final point, the powers available to the court where it considers it unjust to activate the suspended sentence have been discussed in Chapter 7 and are provided for in para 13(1) of Schedule 16 to the Sentencing Act 2020.[47]

Failure to comply with community requirements

As with the commission of further offences, where an offender has failed to comply with the community requirements of a suspended sentence order, the starting point is that the court *must* activate the custodial sentence unless it would be unjust to do so.

In respect of failure to comply with the community requirements, the Sentencing Guideline makes clear that the predominant factor in

---

47 Readers are advised generally to return to Chapter 7 for a full discussion of the law in this area.

determining whether activation is unjust relates to the "level of compliance with the suspended sentence order."

Assessing compliance

An offender's compliance is assessed by considering the same factors as identified (above).[48]

Compliance and suitable penalty

Where the Court has reached a determination on the nature of an offender's compliance with the order, the court can then consider the associated penalty with that compliance. As with commission of further offences, the penalties available to the Court can be found in para 13(1) of Schedule 16 to the Sentencing Act 2020 and have been discussed in full in Chapter 7.

The guidelines prescribe the following penalties according to the offender's compliance:

- *No/low level of compliance:*

  Full activation of original custodial term.[49]

- *Medium level of compliance:*

---

48 See above "Assessing compliance"..

49 The singular option demonstrates the fact that a low level of compliance is regarded as the most serious of breaches.

Activate sentence but apply reduction to original custodial term taking into consideration any unpaid work or curfew requirements completed.[50]

- *High level of compliance:*

  Activate sentence but apply reduction to original custodial term taking into consideration any unpaid work or curfew requirements completed; OR impose more onerous requirement(s) and/or extend supervision period and/or extend operational period; OR impose fine.[51]

As with commission of further offences, it is for the court to apply the appropriate reduction to reflect compliance, and the court is assisted in doing so by the Probation Service.

Assessing whether it would be unjust

The same factors as discussed above are relevant to the issue of whether it would be unjust to activate the suspended sentence. The penalties to be imposed in alternative to activation are identical to those for breach of the community requirements.

---

50 Given the presence of two sentencing options, the Guideline affords a greater discretion to courts in identifying the appropriate penalty according the numerous variables that may be present in any given case.

51 A high level of compliance demonstrates the lowest level of breach. The sentencing options are the most fluid in this category to account for the fact that that there is a greater likelihood of re-engaging an offender subject to an order. In such circumstances, activation may be disproportionate and potentially disruptive to the rehabilitation of the offender.

Summary

This Chapter has covered the sentencing guidelines applicable to breaches of community orders and suspended sentence orders. In this Chapter, we have discussed:

- The factors relevant to assessing an offender's compliance with the requirements of an order.
- The appropriate penalties commensurate with the offender's overall compliance with an order.
- The default position that a suspended sentence order should be activated following breach of such an order.
- The factors relevant to considering whether activation would be unjust.

PART THREE

PROBATION APPLICATIONS

CHAPTER TEN

REVOCATION OF ORDERS

Introduction

Part III of this book is concerned with circumstances, other than a probation breach, where a change is sought in respect of a community order or suspended sentence order. In this Chapter, we focus on the law relating to revoking community orders, whilst we consider amendments to orders in Chapter 11.

Importantly, there is no power to revoke a suspended sentence order[1] except in one limited circumstance in the Sentencing Act 2020, Schedule 16, para 25(7);[2] we shall also consider that power in Chapter 11 as the power flows from an amendment to the community requirements of a suspended sentence order. Likewise, the cancellation of a requirement under an order, as opposed to the order itself, is classed as an "amendment" and is therefore dealt with in Chapter 11.

---

1 *R v Miah* [2011] EWCA Crim 1850 [6] (Cranston J); *R v Blakemore* [2016] EWCA Crim 1396, [2017] 1 Cr. App. R. (S.) 5.

2 Where an offender fails to express willingness to comply with a proposed amended treatment requirement (see Chapter 11).

Key provisions

The relevant provisions are provided in the Sentencing Act 2020, as such:

- Revocation of Community Orders: Schedule 10, Part 3.

Part 32 of the Criminal Procedure Rules (CrimPR) 2020 is also of assistance.

Our discussion shall be broken down into three topics:

- Making the application to revoke,
- At the hearing,
- Following the hearing.

Making the application to revoke

The provisions relating to the revocation of a community order are contained in Schedule 10 to the Sentencing Act 2020.

The power to revoke (with or without re-sentence) is identical between a magistrates' court[3] and the Crown Court.[4] As such, the following will discuss the powers shared generally and highlight any differences as we progress.

[3] Sentencing Act 2020, Schedule 10, para 14.

[4] ibid, Schedule 10, para 15.

Who can make the application to revoke?

Both the offender and the Probation Service may apply to the court to revoke the community order.[5] Such revocation, however, cannot be done on the court's own motion. The Sentencing Act 2020 is clear that such action may only be taken on the application of the offender or an officer of the Probation Service.

Application by Probation: Summoning the offender

Any application by the Probation Service will be in writing. The Probation Service use a template form for such applications; they contain (inter alia):

- the offence(s) subject to the community order,
- the details of the community order, including length of order and requirements,
- the reason(s) for the application to revoke, and
- the offender's compliance and engagement with the community order to date.

In the Crown Court, such applications will be uploaded to the Digital Case System (DCS) and will be accessible to all involved in the case.

As shall be discussed in further detail below,[6] both a magistrates' court and the Crown Court have the ability to either "revoke" a community order outright, or "revoke" an order and "re-sentence" an offender.

Where the relevant court intends to simply revoke the order outright, there is no requirement for the offender to be present at court (though in

5 ibid, Schedule 10, paras 14(1) and 15(1).

6 See below "Power to revoke / revoke and re-sentence the order".

practice the offender will be notified by the Probation Service informally (e.g. by letter or word of mouth) or will be nevertheless summonsed).

> **Key point**
>
> Given that any decision to re-sentence is for the judge alone, it is always advisable to summon the offender to court for any application.

However, where the relevant court intends to revoke and re-sentence an offender, the court must first summon the offender to appear before the court.[7] The court cannot proceed to revoke and re-sentence where the offender has not been previously summonsed.

Should the offender have been summonsed, however, and fail to attend as directed, the court *may* issue a warrant for their arrest.[8] As is evident from the statutory provision, the court is not obligated to issue a warrant for the offender's arrest; the court may simply adjourn to a new date.[9]

Application by the Offender

Naturally, the restriction on resentencing an offender does not apply where it was the offender who made the application to the court to revoke the community order.[10]

Rule 32.3(2) of the Criminal Procedure Rules (CrimPR) 2020 provides that where an offender wants the court to exercise the power to revoke a community order, they must:

---

7 Sentencing Act 2020, Schedule 10, paras 14(4)(a) and 15(3)(a).

8 ibid, Schedule 10, paras 14(4)(b) and 15(3)(b).

9 See Chapter 4 for details on applying for, and objecting to, a warrant.

10 Sentencing Act 2020, Schedule 10, paras 14(4) and 15(3).

- apply in writing, explaining why the order should be revoked or amended; and
- serve the application on the court officer, the responsible officer or supervisor.

Upon making the application, the offender will be provided with a date on which the hearing will take place; if they fail to attend, the application is likely to simply be refused without a hearing.

Applications made in the course of proceedings

Whilst an application to revoke will *generally* be made in writing, in advance of any hearing, there appears to be no restriction on the ability of the court to allow the Probation Service or the offender to apply orally for the community order to be revoked.

There may be occasions where an offender appears before the court in relation to the community order, but not specifically for an application to revoke. For example, an offender may appear before the court in respect of breach proceedings. As discussed in Chapter 6, the court is not empowered to revoke a community order outright following breach proceedings. The court's powers are restricted to those contained in Schedule 10 to the Sentencing Act 2020, paras 10(5) and 11(2).[11] However, there is a workaround to this situation. The court *must* take one of the actions in paras 10(5) (for the magistrates' court) or 11(2) (for the Crown Court). Should the Probation Service and court be of the view that, following the breach, the order is unworkable, the court may, for example, impose a fine to mark the breach and then, subsequently, the Probation Service may separately apply to revoke the order.

11 Unless the offender is before the court following a conviction for further offences during the currency of the community order.

Timing of application

Paragraph 14(1) of Schedule 10 to the Sentencing Act 2020 is clear: an application to revoke a community order can be made "where a community order… is in force".[12]

By s.220(1) of the Sentencing Act 2020, a community order ceases to be in force:

(a) at the end of the end date; or

(b) if later, when the offender has completed any unpaid work requirement imposed by the order.

Therefore, an application to revoke the community order must be made:

- before the end date of the order, or
- if there is an unpaid work requirement, before the offender has completed all hours of the unpaid work requirement.[13]

The consequence of s.220(1)(b) is that an application to revoke the community order can be made long after the "end date" of the community order where the unpaid work requirement has not yet been completed.

12 ibid.

13 *National Probation Service v Blackfriars Crown Court* [2019] EWHC 529 (Admin), [2019] 2 Cr. App. R. (S.) 24.

Key Point

In preparation for any hearing dealing with an application to revoke, the advocate must ensure that the community order remains "in force". The advocate needs to check, therefore:

- The end date of any order,
- If there is an unpaid work requirement, whether the offender has completed that requirement, and
- Whether the community order has been previously revoked (e.g. following a "revoke and re-sentence" as a result of a previous probation breach or the commission of a further offence).[14]

<u>To which court is an application made?</u>

The rules are different depending on whether the application concerns a magistrates' court community order, or an order of the Crown Court.

Magistrates' court community order

Where the community order was made by a magistrates' court, the Sentencing Act 2020 requires any such application to be made to "the appropriate magistrates' court".[15] The general rule is that any application to revoke the order must be made to a magistrates' court acting in the offender's home local justice area.[16] There are two exceptions to this rule:

---

[14] See Chapter 6.

[15] Sentencing Act 2020, Schedule 10, para 14(1).

[16] ibid, Schedule 10, para 14(2)(b).

- Where the community order imposes a drug rehabilitation requirement (DRR), which is subject to review and there is a particular magistrates' court listed on the order as being responsible for the order, the application must be made to *that* court.[17]

- Where the community order qualifies for special procedures for the purposes of s.217A,[18] the application must be made to the magistrates' court that made the order.[19]

Crown Court community order

Where the community order was made by the Crown Court, the application should normally be made to the Crown Court centre that imposed the order. However, the Sentencing Act 2020 does not explicitly require the application to be made to the same court centre. The legislation merely provides that the application must be made "to the Crown Court".[20]

At the hearing

At the hearing, the applicant (whether that be the Probation Service or the offender) will make submissions to the court as to why the community order should be revoked. They will rely on any evidence available to demonstrate why it is in the interests of justice to revoke such an order. The respondent to the application will then make their submissions on the application (whether they accept the application or

---

17 ibid, Schedule 10, para 14(2)(a).

18 See Chapter 2.

19 Sentencing Act 2020, Sch 10, para 14(2)(aa).

20 ibid, Schedule 10, para 15(1).

oppose it) before the court will then make a determination on the application and provide reasons for their decision.

> **Key point**
>
> As has been discussed in previous chapters, many offenders will not be represented during a hearing to revoke a community order. Given the risk of loss of liberty, the judge is likely to adjourn the hearing to allow the offender to obtain legal representation. Where the hearing is to proceed without legal representation, it may be appropriate for the advocate on behalf of the Probation Service to speak with the offender to explain the process and what the application will be (if made by the Probation Service).

Power to revoke / revoke and re-sentence the order

By paras 14 and 15 of Schedule 10 to the Sentencing Act 2020, a magistrates' court and the Crown Court has the power to:

- Revoke a community order ("revoke"),[21] or
- Deal with the offender in some other way for the offence in respect of which the order was made ("revoke and re-sentence").[22]

The court may do so where it is in the interests of justice to do so, having regard to circumstances which have arisen since the order was made.

It will be worth discussing the consequences of each in turn before considering the legal test to be applied.

[21] ibid, Schedule 10, paras 14(5)(a) and 15(4)(a).

[22] ibid, Schedule 10, paras 14(5)(b) and 15(4)(b).

Revoke

To "revoke" the order means to remove it entirely/ outright, i.e. the offender will no longer be subject to such an order. In considering whether to revoke the community order (alongside the interests of justice test considered below), the court must have regard to "circumstances which have arisen since the order was made".[23]

The statute provides two examples of such circumstances:

- Where the offender is making good progress, or
- Where the offender is responding satisfactorily to supervision or treatment.[24]

Each case must be determined on its own facts, and these are merely factors that may be relevant to the court's assessment of whether it is in the interests of justice to revoke the order; they do not stand as reasons alone for revocation.

Revoke and re-sentence

Where the court chooses to re-sentence an offender, the court may deal with them in any way in which it could have dealt with them had they been convicted of the offence before that court.[25] This may include a more serious sentence, including a term of imprisonment, but any re-sentence is limited to the powers available to the court for that offence.[26] For example, in *R v Palmer*[27] the Court of Appeal confirmed that where a community order had been imposed for a summary-only offence, and

---

23 ibid, Schedule 10, paras 14(5) and 15(4).

24 ibid, Schedule 10, paras 14(6) and 15(5).

25 ibid, s.402.

26 ibid.

27 [2019] EWCA Crim 2231, [2020] 1 Cr. App. R. (S.) 54.

the offender had been further convicted of a summary-only offence, the Crown Court was limited to the powers of the magistrates' court. For the purposes of s.133(1) of the Magistrates' Courts Act 1980, the maximum sentence for multiple summary-only offences was a total period of six months' imprisonment.[28]

Importantly, where a court re-sentences an offender, it *must* revoke the community order if it remains in force.[29]

> **Key point**
>
> Advocates should ensure that where a court re-sentences an offender, the judge/ magistrates declare in open court that the community order is revoked.

Where the relevant court intends to revoke and re-sentence the offender, the statutes expressly requires the court to "take into account the extent to which the offender has complied with the requirements of the order."[30]

This will require the advocates to have made contact with the Probation Service prior to the hearing to enquire as to the offender's compliance with their order. As discussed in Chapter 5, such compliance includes:

- Compliance with the requirements of the community order (e.g. unpaid work, rehabilitation activity requirement days (RAR)),
- Whether the offender is making good progress or responding satisfactorily to supervision or treatment as the case may be, and

[28] See also *R v Murray* [2021] EWCA Crim 1441.

[29] Sentencing Act 2020, Schedule 10, paras 10(10) and 11(7).

[30] ibid, Schedule 10, paras 14(7) and 15(6).

- Compliance with general probation appointments (e.g. planned office visits, home visits, telephone calls).

As also discussed in Chapter 5, compliance with the order is assessed by observing:

- Appointments attended,
- Appointments attended, but involving a failure to comply,
- Appointments not attended (but deemed to be an acceptable absence),
- Appointments not attended (and deemed to be an unacceptable absence).

It is good practice to have a note on such compliance updated as close as possible to the date of the hearing. Officers from the Probation Service can provide these figures with ease from the *N-Delius* system.

Key point

Where there is the possibility that the judge will wish to re-sentence an offender, both advocates should have an understanding of the facts of the original offence that was the subject of the community order. At the very least, the advocates will require sight of:

- MG5 (Police Summary),
- the offender's antecedents, and
- the relevant Sentencing Council's Guidelines for the original offence (and submissions on the categorisation of such offence).

It is good practice, therefore, to have these documents to hand prior to the hearing in anticipation of any potential re-sentencing exercise.[31]

Test for revoking a community order: interests of justice

A community order may only be revoked / revoked and re-sentenced where the court is of the opinion that it is "in the interests of justice to do so".[32] As discussed above, the court must have regard to circumstances which have arisen since the order was made.

An interests of justice test allows the court to consider a wide range of factors, including:

- Interests of the offender, including their physical and mental health, their compliance with the order thus far, including their progress and response to supervision or treatment, and any other relevant circumstance,

- Interests of the victim (if any) of the offence for which the community order was imposed,

- Interests of the wider public, and the need to ensure that revocation of such an order is in accordance with the purposes of sentence.

It is worth remembering that the use of an interests of justice test reflects the fact that this provision is concerned with an *application* to revoke/ revoke and re-sentence, as opposed to dealing with an offender for a probation breach, or commission of a further offence.[33]

---

[31] See Chapter 5 on the necessary documents required to prepare for breach proceedings.

[32] Sentencing Act 2020, Schedule 10, paras 14(5) and 15(4).

[33] For which, return to Chapter 6.

There are a number of common practical examples where the court may consider it to be in interests of justice to revoke the community order outright:

- Where the offender has engaged well with the order and has shown good progress. Where such an application is made, it is common for the Probation Service to explain that all sentencing plan objectives are now completed, and there is no further work the Probation Service feels it can do with the offender.

- Where the end date of the community order has passed,[34] but the offender has not yet completed an unpaid work requirement attached to the order.[35] In this case, the court has a number of options available to it, it may: (i) allow the order to continue and require the offender to complete the unpaid work requirement;[36] (ii) cancel the unpaid work requirement (and thus bring the community order to an end that way);[37] or (iii) simply revoke the order.

- Where an offender has been convicted of another offence and has been dealt with in respect of that offence, but the court did not take any action in respect of the community order. Should an offender be sentenced to a term of imprisonment, it is not appropriate to also have a community order in place as the offender would not be in a position to comply. Likewise, where an offender is sentenced to another community order, or a

[34] See Sentencing Act 2020, s.209.

[35] As discussed elsewhere in this text, where a community order has an unpaid work requirement attached to it, the order continues until the unpaid work is completed.

[36] The court will likely need to extend the unpaid work requirement at the same time (see Sentencing Act 2020, Schedule 10, para 21(1) and Chapter 11).

[37] Sentencing Act 2020, Schedule 10, para 18(1) (see Chapter 11).

suspended sentence order, it is often unworkable having multiple orders in place.

- Where the offender is unable to comply by reason of illness or disability.

In respect of the last circumstance listed above, there are a variety of authorities on the question of revocation as a result of illness/ disability, though it must be noted that these authorities are under an old regime and each case must be determined on its own facts. Where an offender is physically unable to complete the order, e.g. due to injury, the court may consider it inappropriate to revoke the order and re-sentence the offender.[38] Indeed, in *Fielding*, Pill J would explain:

> There is power in the court to impose a custodial sentence when there has been a breach of a community service order, but, in the judgment of this Court, it is quite inappropriate to impose a custodial sentence in the circumstances which existed in this case, when, through no fault of his own, the appellant could not complete his obligations under the order.[39]

However, such a decision must always depend on the facts of each individual case.

Where an offender made it clear from the outset that there may be difficulties in completing the order due to their mental or physical health, this should weigh heavily on the court's decision to revoke the order (and not re-sentence).[40] Equally, however, where an offender failed to disclose a medical condition to the court when the order was made, the court may

---

38 *R v Fielding* (1993) 14 Cr. App. R. (S.) 494 (CA).

39 ibid, 495 (Pill J). See also *R v Bishop* [2004] EWCA Crim 2956 where it was held to be "wrong in principle" to re-sentence an offender to custody where a community order was revoked due to the ill-health of the offender ([11] (Gibbs J)).

40 *R v Jackson* [2000] 1 Cr. App. R. (S.) 405 (CA).

be unsympathetic with the offender's non-compliance; re-sentencing the offender may be more appropriate.[41] In *Jackson*, Dyson J took the view that:

> where a defendant has been certified as unfit for work due to a medical condition which he was aware of before the community service order was imposed but which he failed to disclose to the court, such that the sentencer was misled, then the fact that the defendant is unable to carry out the community service order cannot be prayed in aid as a reason for persuading the court not to impose a custodial sentence.[42]

Key point

Thought should be given to whether it is more appropriate to seek to remove a particular requirement of a community order[43] as opposed to revoking the order entirely. As will be seen in Chapter 11, unlike revocation of orders, there is no threshold or test that has to be met in order to remove (or "cancel") requirements under an order.

Following the hearing

It is essential that a detailed note of the hearing is taken, including the action taken by the court on the application, and the reasons for any decision (i.e. on what basis the judge says that it is, or is not, in the interests of justice to revoke/ revoke and re-sentence).

41 *R v Hammon* [1998] 2 Cr. App. R. (S.) 202 (CA).

42 *Jackson* (n40), 407 (Dyson J).

43 See Chapter 11.

Provision of copies of revocation

Where the court has revoked a community order, it must provide copies of the revoking order to the offender and the responsible officer.[44]

Appeal against "revoke and re-sentence"

Where an offender has been re-sentenced by a magistrates' court, they may appeal against that sentence to the Crown Court.[45] This provision is simply designed to preserve the automatic right to appeal that an individual convicted by a magistrates' court has to the Crown Court.[46] Of course, should an offender wish to appeal against a re-sentence in the Crown Court, they will require leave to appeal in the ordinary way.[47]

Summary

This Chapter has covered the law and practice involved in applications to revoke a community order. When considering the legal principles applicable to this area of law, consider:

- An application to revoke a community order can be made either by the offender or the Probation Service. The court cannot revoke a community order on its own motion.

- Before a court revokes and re-sentences an offender, the offender must be summonsed to the court.

---

44 Sentencing Act 2020, Schedule 10, para 27(2); CrimPR 2020, r.32.4(2).

45 ibid, Schedule 10, para 14(8).

46 See Magistrates' Courts Act 1980, s.108.

47 See Criminal Appeal Act 1968, s.9(1).

- If the offender fails to attend upon a summons, the court may issue a warrant for their arrest.

- An application to revoke a community order must be made whilst the community order is in force.

- A magistrates' court or the Crown Court may revoke/ revoke and re-sentence where they consider that it is in the interests of justice to do so, having regard to circumstances which have arisen since the order was made.

- Copies of any revocation order must be served on all parties to the case.

CHAPTER ELEVEN

AMENDMENT OF ORDERS

Introduction

In this chapter, we focus our attention on the law relating to amending community orders and suspended sentence order. Such applications to amend largely concern the requirements of a community order, and community requirements of a suspended sentence order (e.g. application to amend a community order to removing an unpaid work requirement).

However, in respect of community orders, a common application made is to extend the length of the order itself. This also amounts to an "amendment" and shall be dealt with in this chapter. Importantly, there is no power to amend the length of a suspended sentence order (i.e. the supervision and operational period) except where there is a breach of the community requirements of that order, or the commission of a further offence during the operational period of that order.[1]

Key provisions

The relevant provisions are provided in the Sentencing Act 2020, as such:

- Amendment of requirements of community orders: Schedule 10, Part 4.
- Amendment of community requirements of suspended sentence orders: Schedule 16, Part 3.

[1] For which, see Chapter 7.

Who can make the application to amend?

This question ultimately depends on what the application relates to. For those reasons, it is unwise to identify at this stage who can make an application to amend. In general, however, both the offender and the Probation Service may apply to amend the order in some way. Importantly, however, amendments cannot be made on the court's own motion. The Sentencing Act 2020 is clear that such action may only be taken on the application of the offender or an officer of the Probation Service.

Who can make the amendment itself?

A separate question from the one above is who can actually make the amendment itself. Amendments to orders may be made by both the responsible officer and the court; whether an application to the court is required will depend on the nature of the amendment sought.

Meaning of "appropriate court"

Throughout this chapter, there will be references to the "appropriate court". This terminology is essential given that applications to amend can only be made and determined by the "appropriate court".

Therefore, for the purposes of Schedules 10 and 16 to the Sentencing Act 2020, and to avoid repeating this fact at multiple points in the chapter, the "appropriate court" means:

- if the order imposes a drug rehabilitation requirement which is subject to review, the court responsible for the order,
- if the order qualifies for special procedures for the purposes of s.217A, the court that made the order,
- in the case of a suspended sentence order which is subject to review, the court responsible for the order,

- if the order is a Crown Court order, the Crown Court,
- in any other case, a magistrates' court acting in the offender's home local justice area.

Amendments considered

This chapter concerns the whole variety of amendments that may be made to a community order or suspended sentence order. We start our discussion with cancellation (i.e. removal) of requirements generally, before then considering amendment of requirements generally. Following that, we shall consider specific powers of amendment, including:

- Change of residence
- Variation of curfew
- Variation of treatment requirements
- Amendment of periodic review of drug rehabilitation requirement.

The chapter will then end with the court's powers to extend requirements, including extension of community orders and extension of an unpaid work requirement. We shall then consider what procedure must follow when any such amendment or variation has taken place.

Permitting the offender to go on holiday

A question often posed in practice is whether the offender must apply to the court to go on holiday during the currency of their community order or suspended sentence order. There is nothing in law that requires an offender to obtain the permission of their responsible officer, or of the court in cases of this sort. However, in order to avoid missing an appointment (and thus being liable for breach), or breaching the requirement to keep in touch, it is highly advisable that the offender informs the responsible officer of their plans. It is then a decision for the responsible officer as to whether they should, in essence, suspend the supervision of the offender, and their requirements under the order for the period of time they are on holiday before they then return, and the requirements resume. The court, however, is not involved in this process.

This process is not so straightforward where the offender is subject to a residence requirement or a foreign travel prohibition requirement. In these circumstances, the offender may require the permission of the court to allow him to go on holiday (which would, in essence, require a cancellation of the requirements).

Cancellation of all community requirements (suspended sentence orders)

As discussed in Chapter 2, a suspended sentence order imposed by the court *may* also specify one or more available community requirements with which the offender must comply during the supervision period.[2] The imposition of community requirements are therefore discretionary; there is no obligation to impose any community requirements.

Where, however, the court does impose community requirements, Schedule 16 to the Sentencing Act 2020 provides the court with the power to cancel the community requirements imposed.[3] This power may be exercised by the court upon application by either the offender or an officer of the Probation Service.[4]

2 Sentencing Act 2020, s.286(2).

3 ibid, Schedule 16, para 22.

4 ibid, Schedule 16, para 22(1).

> **Key point**
>
> The power to cancel the community requirements of a suspended sentence order in para 22 of Schedule 16 must be distinguished from a similar power in para 25. The former is concerned with removing all community requirements from the order, whereas the latter is concerned with removing specific community requirements, but allowing others to remain. It is important to refer to the correct provision when making any such application.

There is no equivalent provision as it applies to community orders in Schedule 10. This is because, by its very definition, a community order is "an order imposing one or more community order requirements".[5] As will be discussed below, para 18(1) of Schedule 10 to the Sentencing Act 2020 provides a court with the power to cancel a requirement of a community order. However, this is aimed at specific requirements, as opposed to all requirements. To remove all requirements of a community order is to revoke the order.[6]

Test to be applied

The court may cancel all of the community requirements of the suspended sentence order, if it appears to the court to be in the interests of justice to do so, having regard to circumstances which have arisen since the order was made.[7]

The "interests of justice" test was discussed in full in respect of applications to revoke a community order.[8] It stands to reason that the

5 ibid, s.200(1). See *R v Khan* [2015] EWCA Crim 835, [2015] 2 Cr. App. R. (S.) 39.

6 For which see Chapter 11; Sentencing Act 2020, Schedule 10, Part 3.

7 Sentencing Act 2020, Schedule 16, para 22(2).

8 See Chapter 10.

same approach, principles and circumstances be adopted and considered when applying the interests of justice test to applications to amend.

References to "circumstances which have arisen since the order was made" include:

- Where the offender is making good progress, and
- Where the offender is responding satisfactorily to supervision or treatment.[9]

Restriction on cancelling community requirements

No application may be made to cancel the community requirements of a suspended sentence order while an appeal against the suspended sentence is pending.[10]

Amendment of requirements generally

Where the court imposes a community order or suspended sentence order, it will normally impose a number of requirements to be attached to that order. Given the fact that there may be a variety of circumstances for which the requirements may no longer be suitable, the Sentencing Act 2020 provides the court with the power to amend those requirements.

There are different provisions between requirements of a community order and community requirements of a suspended sentence order. We shall identify these differences as appropriate.

---

9 Sentencing Act 2020, Schedule 16, para 22(3).

10 ibid, Schedule 16, para 22(4).

There is also a specific provision relating to amending community requirements of suspended sentence orders where such orders are subject to review. We shall discuss this process separately.

The application to amend

The word "amendment" has a particular meaning in the Sentencing Act 2020 for the purposes of amending requirements of an order. Schedules 10 and 16 respectively state that both the offender and the Probation Service can apply to the court to amend the requirements of the order. Whilst the terminology is slightly different between community orders and suspended sentence orders, the provisions are identical. The court is not empowered to amend the order on its own motion.

Where such an application is made, the court may:

- Cancel any of the requirements,[11] or
- Replace any of those requirements with a requirement of the same kind which the court could include if the offender had just been convicted by or before it of the offence in respect of which the order was made and it were then making the order.[12]

We shall consider these two options in further detail.

Options available to the court

The effect of Schedules 10 and 16 is that the court has two options open to it following an application to amend any requirement. The court may:

- Cancel a requirement outright, or

11 ibid, Schedule 10, para 18(1)(a); Schedule 16, para 25(1)(a).

12 ibid, Schedule 10, para 18(1)(b); Schedule 16, para 25(1)(b).

- Replace that requirement with another requirement that would have been available to the sentencing court.

In respect of the first option available to the court, a requirement can be deleted from an order outright. This simply means that it is not replaced with another order. Such an option may be appropriate where an offender has demonstrated strong compliance with the order generally, and with other requirements of the order, such that the court does not consider it necessary to impose further or alternative requirements.

For example, suppose an offender was sentenced to a suspended sentence order with three requirements, namely unpaid work, rehabilitation activity requirement (RAR), and building better relationships (BBR). Suppose that defendant has a high level of compliance with both the unpaid work requirement, RAR, and general probation appointments, but is unable to complete the BBR due to work commitments. The court may consider that it appropriate to cancel the BBR outright, if it can be satisfied that the benefits of BBR will be available in some other form (e.g. through RAR). Alternatively, a requirement may no longer be suitable for an offender due to their physical health or another change in circumstances. In this case, the court may feel that a simple cancellation of that particular requirement causing difficulties would be sufficient, without the need for a replacement requirement.

In respect of the second option open to the court, a requirement of an order can be replaced by a requirement "of the same kind" which would have been available to the sentencing court. A requirement is "of the same kind" if it is included in the table of requirements detailed in either s.201[13] or s.287[14] of the Sentencing Act 2020.[15]

---

[13] For community orders.

[14] For suspended sentence orders.

[15] Sentencing Act 2020, Schedule 10, para 18(2)(a); Schedule 16, para 25(2)(a).

The list of requirements are:

- unpaid work requirement
- rehabilitation activity requirement
- programme requirement
- prohibited activity requirement
- curfew requirement
- exclusion requirement
- residence requirement
- foreign travel prohibition requirement
- mental health treatment requirement
- drug rehabilitation requirement
- drug testing requirement
- alcohol treatment requirement
- alcohol abstinence and monitoring requirement
- attendance centre requirement
- electronic compliance monitoring requirement
- electronic whereabouts monitoring requirement.

This list of requirements is identical between community orders and suspended sentence orders. Importantly, where an electronic compliance monitoring requirement is attached to another requirement (e.g. a curfew), the court is free to replace that requirement with another requirement that equally includes an EMT requirement (e.g. an exclusion requirement).[16]

> **Key point**
>
> A common error made is to seek to replace a requirement of an order with a financial penalty. That is not a requirement listed in the tables at ss.201 or 287. Therefore, when one applies to amend the requirements of an order, a financial penalty is *not* an available alternative.

Importantly, where the court would be restricted when imposing a requirement at the original sentencing hearing, the court replacing any such requirement with another is equally restricted. For example, should the court wish to impose an unpaid requirement, the minimum number of hours is 40 and the maximum number of hours is 300.[17] This applies to both the original sentencing court, and the court which is amending a requirement by replacing it with another.[18]

Amendment of treatment requirements specifically is discussed separately below given the distinctive provisions applicable to those requirements.[19]

Test to be applied

The statute is silent as to whether there is a test to be applied when cancelling a requirement of an order. Unlike the revocation of orders considered in Chapter 10, or the amendment of other requirements

[16] ibid, Schedule 10, para 18(2)(b); Schedule 16, para 25(2)(b).

[17] ibid, Schedule 9, para 2(b).

[18] ibid, Schedule 10, para 18(6); Schedule 16, para 25(3).

[19] See below, "Amendment of treatment requirements".

considered in this chapter, the statute simply does not include a test, threshold or requirement to be met in order to cancel a requirement of an order. This includes both community orders and suspended sentence orders. For that reason, it may be argued that it is "easier" to secure the cancellation of a particular requirement, as opposed to the revocation of an order entirely.

For example, suppose the Probation Service seeks to revoke a community order. The end date of the community order passed two years ago, but the offender is subject to an unpaid work requirement under the order that remains outstanding. As discussed in Chapter 2, the community order will continue indefinitely until the unpaid work is complete, or the order is revoked. Suppose the offender has a medical conditions which means they cannot complete the unpaid work (e.g. diabetes that cannot be properly managed by the offender). This, coupled with the nature of the work suitable for the offender, means that the order is unworkable. Given that the end date of the order has passed, there is little difference between seeking to revoke the community order, and seeking the cancel the unpaid work requirement. They both achieve the same aim: ending the order. However, the Probation Service would have to satisfy the court that it would be in the interests of justice to revoke the community order, whilst there is no such requirement for simple cancellation of the unpaid work requirement. Where a court has proven difficult in acceding to the request to revoke the order, it may be a sensible option to seek to cancel the unpaid work requirement instead.

Whilst the statute is silent and, technically, there is no standard to be met, in practice, courts will often ask whether there is a "good reason" for the cancellation, or whether it would be in the "interests of justice" to cancel a requirement of an order. The court may be more inclined to cancel a requirement where it is to be replaced with another; however, that practically cannot always be achieved.

Restriction on amending requirements

There are a number of restrictions that must be discussed at this stage. A specific restriction relating to amendment of treatment requirements is discussed below.[20]

Summoning the offender first

Before the court exercises its power to amend the requirements of an order, it must summon the offender to appear before the court.[21] Where the applicant is the offender there is no requirement to summon them.[22]

The Sentencing Act provides further exceptions to the requirement to summon an offender, and these differ according to whether the application is to amend the requirements of a community order or the community requirements of a suspended sentence order.

In respect of community order requirements, the court need not summon the offender where the court would exercise the powers only to

- cancel a requirement of the community order,
- replace any such requirement with one of a shorter duration, or
- substitute a new place for one specified in the order.[23]

In respect of suspended sentence orders, on the other hand, the court need not summon the offender where the court intends only to cancel a community requirement outright.[24] It is perhaps interesting that the

---

[20] See below, "Amendment of treatment requirements".

[21] Sentencing Act 2020, Schedule 10, para 18(4); Schedule 16, para 25(5).

[22] ibid, Schedule 10, para 18(4)(a); Schedule 16, para 25(5)(a).

[23] ibid, Schedule 10, para 18(4)(b).

[24] ibid, Schedule 16, para 25(5)(b).

court has greater powers to amend a community order without first summoning the offender, compared to suspended sentence orders. The justification for this is not clear. However, what is clear from the exceptions is that the court need not summon an offender where the amendment would not result in more stringent requirements.

Where the offender fails to appear in answer to the summons, the court *may* issue a warrant for their arrest.[25]

Appeal against sentence

No application may be made to amend the requirements of a community order, or the community requirements of a suspended sentence order while an appeal against the order is pending.[26]

The exception to this rule applies where the application to amend relates to a treatment requirement, and the application is made by the Probation Service with the offender's consent.[27] In this circumstance, the court may consider the amendment irrespective of the appeal.

Amendment of requirements subject to review (suspended sentence orders)

As discussed in Chapter 2, a suspended sentence order may be ordered by the court to be subject to a period of review.[28] Furthermore, certain courts are empowered to review both community and suspended

25 ibid, Schedule 10, para 18(5); Schedule 16, para 25(6).

26 ibid, Schedule 10, para 18(3); Schedule 16, para 25(4).

27 ibid. See below, "Amendment of treatment requirements" specifically on treatment requirements.

28 See s.293 of the Sentencing Act 2020.

sentence orders qualifying for special procedures.[29] These are discussed fully in Chapter 2 also.

Amendments following review

The progress report and subsequent amendment

By s.293(2)(d), the provision for review must include a written report by the Probation Service on the offender's progress in complying with the community requirements of the order before each review hearing.[30] Having considered this report, the court *may* at a review hearing amend:

- the community requirements of the suspended sentence order, or
- any provision of the order which relates to those requirements.[31]

This provision gives the court a very broad power to amend the suspended sentence order in a variety of ways. Rather than state the amendments that the court may make, it will be easier to identify what restrictions are in place on the court's ability to amend the order.

Restrictions on amendments to the order

By s.294(3), a court is restricted by the types of amendments it may make. The following details those restrictions:

- The court is not permitted to amend the community requirements of the order so as to impose a requirement of a

[29] See s.395A of the Sentencing Act 2020.

[30] Known as "a progress report". See also s.239A(2)(d) for an equivalent provision in respect of review of suspended sentence order qualifying for special procedures.

[31] Sentencing Act 2020, s.294(2).

different kind.[32] This is so unless the offender expresses willingness to comply with that replacement requirement.[33] For example, therefore, the court would not be permitted to amend the suspended sentence order in circumstances to include an unpaid work requirement, where no such requirement previously existed, without the offender expressing a willingness to comply with that requirement.

- The court is equally not permitted to amend a mental health treatment requirement, a drug rehabilitation requirement, or an alcohol treatment requirement, unless the offender expresses willingness to comply with the requirement as amended.[34]

- The court is permitted to amend the supervision period of a suspended sentence order.[35] It is noticeable that the statute refers to the ability to "amend" the supervision period as opposed to a power to "extend" it. This would seem to suggest that the court is within its power to reduce the period of time for the supervision period.[36] This is especially so given that in other parts of the Sentencing Act, the word "extend" is specifically used.[37] However, s.294(3)(c) is clear that this power is subject to the ordinary

---

32 ibid, s.294(3)(a).

33 A community requirement is of the same kind if it is listed within the table in s.287 Sentencing Act 2020.

34 Sentencing Act 2020, s.294(3)(b). See the separate discussion below on amendment of Treatment Requirements generally and DRRs specifically.

35 ibid, s.294(3)(c).

36 Though it would likely be rare for that power to be exercised.

37 See Sentencing Act 2020, Schedule 16, para 13(1)(d)(ii).

restrictions imposed on supervision periods in s.288(4) of the Sentencing Act 2020.[38]

- The court is not permitted to amend the operational period. Once more, the statute uses the word "amend"; as such, the court is not permitted to reduce or extend the operational period.[39]

- Finally, the court is not permitted to amend the order whilst an appeal against the order is pending.[40] This is so unless the offender has consented to the amendment.

Breach of community requirements

A rather special power exists where a suspended sentence order is subject to review and the court, at that review hearing, is of the opinion that the offender has without reasonable excuse breached a community requirement of the order. In those circumstances, the court is empowered to adjourn the review hearing and deal with the breach "forthwith" (i.e. there and then).[41]

In practice, the judge would declare that the review hearing has finished and will then proceed to deal with the breach proceedings in the normal way (i.e. asking the offender whether they admit the breach and dealing with any admitted breach/ adjourning for a contested hearing).[42]

---

38 Section 288(4) stipulates that the supervision period must be for a period of at least six months, and cannot be for more than two years, or the operational period (if that is less than two years).

39 The power to extend the operational period exists only where the court is dealing with a breach of the suspended sentence order (see Chapter 6; Sentencing Act 2020, Schedule 16, para 13(1)(d)(iii)).

40 Sentencing Act 2020, s.294(3)(c).

41 ibid, s.294(5).

42 See Chapter 6 for a full discussion on breach proceedings.

Where the Court does not deal with any breach forthwith, the court may adjourn the case to a later date, issue a summons requiring the offender to appear at the place and time specified in it, or issue a warrant for the offender's arrest.[43]

Amendment to remove the requirement of a hearing

A further power to amend exists in respect of review hearings themselves. In short, where the court has considered the review officer's report, and is of the opinion that the offender's progress under the requirement is satisfactory, it may take the following actions:

- Where the court forms the opinion about the satisfactory nature of the offender's progress, *before a review hearing is held*, it may order that no review hearing is to be held at the current review, and it may amend the suspended sentence order so as to provide for each subsequent review to be held without a review hearing (i.e. on the papers).[44]

- Where the court forms the opinion about the satisfactory nature of the offender's progress, *at a review hearing*, the court may at the hearing amend the suspended sentence order so as to provide for each subsequent review to be held without a review hearing.[45]

Any such amendment, however, is capable of being reversed (or further amended as the case may be). Where the court conducts a review without a review hearing, and, having considered the progress report, forms the opinion that the offender's progress under the order is *no longer*

[43] Sentencing Act 2020, s.294(5A); Schedule 16, para 9A(2).

[44] ibid, s.295(2).

[45] ibid, s.295(3).

satisfactory, the court may require the offender to attend a hearing of the court at a specified time and place.[46]

In addition to the above, the court is also empowered (at the review hearing) if it so chooses to amend the suspended sentence order so as to vary the intervals of said review.[47]

Change of residence

As discussed in Chapter 3, the Probation Service must be provided with a current address for any offender subject to a live court order. In accordance with s.216 (for community orders) and s.302 (for suspended sentence orders), an offender must obtain permission before changing residence.[48] In addition, a change of residence may result where the court imposes a residence requirement on an amended order.[49]

This section will consider permission to change residence and the legal procedure that follows any such change, before then considering change of residence as a result of a residence requirement.

Permission to change residence

Permission to change residence can be obtained by the offender from either the responsible officer or the court.[50] An offender cannot change

46 ibid, s.295(4).

47 ibid, s.295(5).

48 This, of course, only applies whilst the order is in force.

49 Sentencing Act 2020, Schedule 9, Part 7.

50 ibid, ss.216(2) and 302(2).

residence without such permission; any change of residence without permission amounts to a breach of the order.[51]

Permission sought from responsible officer

In the first instance, it is likely that an offender will simply seek such permission from their responsible officer.[52] This will likely occur as part of a keeping in touch appointment/ planned office visit, or the offender may formally contact the responsible officer with that request.

The test to be applied by the responsible officer is considered below.[53] However, it is worth noting at this stage that the statute expressly prohibits a responsible officer from permitting a change of residence where the offender's present residence is in England and Wales and the proposed amended residence is outside of England and Wales.[54] The statute phrases it that the responsible officer "must refuse an application".[55]

Permission sought from court

Where the responsible officer has refused permission to change residence, the offender may apply to the appropriate court for permission.

The appropriate court is not restricted by the decision of the responsible officer and may give such permission.[56] Importantly, the power of the

---

51 ibid, ss.216(3) and 302(3); the obligation to obtain permission has effect as if it were a requirement imposed by a community order or a community requirement imposed by a suspended sentence order.

52 ibid, ss.216(2)(a) and 302(2)(a).

53 See below, "Test to be applied".

54 Sentencing Act 2020, ss.216(7) and 302(7).

55 ibid.

56 ibid, ss.216(4) and 302(4).

appropriate court to give such permission can be utilised in any proceedings before it under Schedule 10 or 16 to the Sentencing Act 2020 (i.e. such permission can be granted as part of breach proceedings).[57]

Test to be applied

Sections 216(6) and 302(6) of the Sentencing Act 2020 provide for the test to be applied by both the responsible officer and the court in determining whether to grant permission to vary residence. The test is phrased in a negative manner; it prescribes the circumstances where the responsible officer/ court may *refuse* an application to change residence, as opposed to granting such an application. This is to reflect the fact that, generally speaking, a change of residence should not cause the responsible officer or court concern.

In summary, the responsible officer or the court may refuse an application for permission to change residence where, in the opinion of the responsible officer or the court, the change of residence:

- is likely to prevent the offender complying with a requirement imposed by the order,[58] or

- would hinder the offender's rehabilitation.[59]

Naturally, the responsible officer or court must have evidence to support any such grounds for opposing the change of residence.

By way of examples, such evidence may include that:

---

[57] ibid, ss.216(5) and 302(5).

[58] ibid, ss.216(5)(a) and 302(5)(a).

[59] ibid, ss.216(5)(b) and 302(5)(b).

- the residence to which the offender wishes to move is considered inappropriate due to previous instances of domestic abuse at that address,

- the residence to which the offender wishes to move is outside of an area covered by an accredited programme provider, and a similar programme does not exist in the new area.

Procedure following permission to change residence

Where permission has been granted to change residence, this must be recorded on the *N-Delius* system by the Probation Service.

In addition, where the offender is given such permission to change residence, the law imposes specific obligations where the local justice area in which the new residence is situated[60] is different from the offender's home local justice area.[61] In summary:

- If the permission is given by a court, the court must amend the order to specify the new local justice area as the offender's home local justice area.[62]

- If the permission is given by the responsible officer, the officer must give notice to the appropriate court of the permission, and the court must amend the order as above.[63]

- In either case, the court must also provide a copy of the amending order to a provider of probation services that is a public sector

60 Referred to as "the new local justice area".

61 Sentencing Act 2020, Schedule 10, paras 16 and 27(3); Schedule 16, paras 23 and 28(3).

62 ibid, Schedule 10, para 16(2); Schedule 16, para 23(2).

63 ibid, Schedule 10, para 16(3); Schedule 16, para 23(3).

provider operating in that area, and the magistrates' court acting in that area.[64]

Change of residence and residence requirements

There are two separate discussions to be had at this stage:

- Varying a residence requirement, and
- Impact of change of residence where there is a residence requirement.

Varying a residence requirement

As part of a community order or suspended sentence order, the court may impose a residence requirement.[65] A residence requirement has the same effect and consequences of any other requirement imposed by the court as part of an order. Specifically, the offender must comply with that order, and failure to comply will result in potential breach action being taken.

For the purposes of our discussion at this stage, it is worth remembering the above discussion: Change of residence is a matter for the offender to make an application in relation to. The granting of permission is a matter for the responsible officer and the court, but not the application. On the other hand, as a residence requirement is part of the order, an application can be made by the Probation Service to amend the residence requirement. The relevance of this case be seen in an example.

Suppose, for example, the offender is in breach of a community order and the court wishes to mark the breach by making the order more onerous. The offender is not suitable for a curfew or unpaid work due to

[64] ibid, Schedule 10, para 27(3); Schedule 16, para 28(3).

[65] ibid, Schedule 9, para 13(1) (see Chapter 2).

mental health difficulties. The court, therefore, imposes a residence requirement as a more onerous requirement to restrict their movements (and thus their liberty). At the court hearing, the offender requests to reside with his partner; the court hears the view of the partner and approves the address for the residence requirement. It then comes to light that the partner was the victim of the offence subject to the community order (e.g. domestic abuse), and there have been a number of police "call outs" to that address. In that instance, the Probation Service may consider it appropriate to apply to the court to amend the residence requirement so that the offender must live at an address different to that stated in the original order.

As discussed below more generally, the effect in law is that the court would be required to cancel the existing residence requirement and replace it with another residence requirement.

Impact of residence requirements

The second circumstance is where an offender is mandated by a residence requirement to live at an address away from their normal residence. This may be due to the normal residence being unsuitable. The court has that power with a residence requirement. As discussed already, a residence requirement can be imposed when the court first makes a community-based order.

However, the court may also impose a residence requirement following breach proceedings. For the purposes of steps to be taken, the law is clear: Where a magistrates' court or the Crown Court:

- amends a community order, or a suspended sentence order,
- the order as amended includes a residence requirement requiring the offender to reside at a specified place, and
- the new local justice area is different from the offender's home local justice area,

the relevant court must amend the order to specify the new local justice area as the offender's home local justice area.[66]

This provision will be of relevance in cases where the offender is directed to live away from an address (often an address where the offence took place, or an address where the victim of the offence lives in cases of domestic abuse). The court may impose a residence requirement obligating the offender to live at another address (e.g. with a parent, friend, or relative) which is outside of their home area. Where this occurs, the court must update the order to reflect the new area so that the relevant probation service can supervise and enforce the order.

The rules relating to provision of copies of the amending order discussed above[67] also apply here.

Variation of curfew

In Chapter 2, we considered the imposition of curfews in respect of community orders and suspended sentence orders.[68] In this section, we briefly consider the circumstances where a curfew may be varied.

Variation of curfew is a matter for the responsible officer. There is no power for the court to "vary" a curfew. Should the court wish to amend the terms of a curfew, the court would technically need to cancel the requirement, and replace it with another curfew requirement.[69]

---

66 ibid, Schedule 10, para 17; Schedule 16, para 24.

67 See above, "Procedure following permission to change residence".).

68 See Chapter 2.

69 See above re cancelling requirements.

Variation of curfew

Where a community order or suspended sentence order is in force and includes a curfew requirement, the responsible officer has the power to vary such curfew where they consider it appropriate to do so.[70] The consent of the offender is required to vary a curfew, and a "variation notice" must be given to the offender.

The variation condition

Paragraph 10A(2) of Schedule 9 to the Sentencing Act 2020 provides that where, having regard to a change in the offender's circumstances since the relevant order was made, the responsible officer considers it is appropriate to do so, the responsible officer may:

- vary the start time of any of the curfew periods,[71] and/or
- vary the relevant place in relation to any of those periods.[72]

This is known as the "variation condition" in Schedule 9.

Factors relevant to variation

Where the responsible officer seeks to vary the relevant place where the curfew must be observed, the responsible officer must obtain and consider information about each place proposed before they give a

---

[70] This power only exists where the offender was convicted for an offence on or after 28 June 2022 (the date on which s.151 of the Police, Crime, Sentencing and Courts Act 2022 came into force).

[71] Sentencing Act 2020, Schedule 9, para 10A(2)(a).

[72] ibid, Schedule 9, para 10A(2)(b).

variation notice.[73] This restriction is essential to ensure that the location where the curfew must be observed is appropriate in the circumstances.

For example, where there is a history of domestic abuse at a particular location, or at a location where a particular person resides, it would not be appropriate to vary the curfew to require the offender to observe their curfew at that address.

In addition, the responsible officer is obligated to obtain and consider the "attitude of persons likely to be affected by the offender's enforced presence there".[74] In a similar vein to the example above, other persons within a premises where the responsible officer is considering varying the curfew to may have particular views or feelings about the offender, or the arrangement. These views must be given appropriate weight by the responsible officer.

Requirement of consent

A curfew may only be varied with the consent of the offender. Where the offender consents, the responsible officer will provide them with a variation notice, which specifies:

- the new start time of such of the curfew periods as are specified in the notice, and/or
- the new relevant place for such of the curfew periods as are so specified.[75]

---

[73] ibid, Schedule 9, para 10A(6).

[74] ibid, Schedule 9, para 10A(7).

[75] ibid, Schedule 9, para 10A(3).

The variation notice does not require the approval of the court; the effect of the variation notice is to vary the relevant order with effect from the date specified.[76]

What can and cannot be varied

As noted above, a variation notice *can* vary:

- the start time of the curfew; and/or
- the place where such a curfew must be observed.[77]

However, the variation notice *cannot vary*:

- the length of any of the offender's curfew periods (e.g. if the curfew was ordered for a period of nine hours each day, that period must remain the same),[78] nor can it
- the relevant place where the curfew must be observed where the community order or suspended sentence order also includes a residence requirement, and the variation notice would be inconsistent with that residence requirement.[79]

In addition, a particular restriction exists in respect of electronically monitored curfews. Simply, where the curfew requirement is electronically monitored,[80] the responsible officer cannot vary any such curfew if the officer considers that the court which imposed the curfew:

---

[76] ibid, Schedule 9, para 10A(4).

[77] ibid, Schedule 9, para 10A(3).

[78] ibid, Schedule 9, para 10A(8)(a).

[79] ibid, Schedule 9, para 10A(8)(b).

[80] ibid, Schedule 9, para 10(3).

- would not have imposed the monitoring requirement, or
- would have imposed a different monitoring requirement,

had the relevant court imposed the curfew requirement on the varied terms.[81] It is technically possible for a curfew with an electronic monitoring requirement to be amended so as to remove the electronic monitoring requirement specifically, but to maintain the curfew. This would require a cancellation of that part of the order as is identified in further detail below.

Procedure following variation of curfew

The responsible officer must give the appropriate court a copy of the variation notice and evidence of the offender's consent to the notice.[82]

Where the responsible officer has given the court a copy of the variation notice, and evidence of the offender's consent to that notice, the appropriate court must amend the order to reflect the effect of the variation notice.[83] The amendment of the order is merely a formality and a matter of accurate record keeping, as opposed to an act of authorising any such variation.[84]

Amendment of treatment requirements

Where an offender is subject to a treatment requirement as part of their community order or suspended sentence order, and the treatment practitioner is of the view that the treatment requirement should be amended in a particular way, the court may cancel or replace that

81 ibid, Schedule 9, para 10A(9).

82 ibid, Schedule 9, para 10A(10).

83 ibid, Schedule 10, para 17A(2); Schedule 16, para 24A(2).

84 Evident from the wording in Schedule 9, para 10A(4).

requirement.[85] There is no power on the responsible officer to amend treatment requirements; this is a power reserved to the courts.

Meaning of treatment requirement

For the purposes of this power to amend, a "treatment requirement" means:

- a mental health treatment requirement (MHTR),
- a drug rehabilitation requirement (DRR), or
- an alcohol treatment requirement (ATR).[86]

See Chapter 2 for a fuller discussion of each of these requirements.

Report of Treatment Practitioner

In order for a treatment requirement to be amended (by cancelling it or replacing it), the treatment practitioner must first make a report in writing to the responsible officer.

Who is a treatment practitioner?

The treatment practitioner means:

- the person specified in the order as the person by whom, or under whose direction, the offender is being treated in pursuance of the requirement, or

[85] Sentencing Act 2020, Schedule 10, para 18; Schedule 16, para 25.

[86] ibid, Schedule 10, para 1(1); Schedule 16, para 26(4)(a).

- in the case of an MHTR, if no such person is specified, the person by whom, or under whose direction, the offender is being treated in pursuance of the requirement.[87]

Content of report

The treatment practitioner's report must detail the reasons as to why the treatment requirement should be cancelled or replaced. Those reasons are, where the treatment practitioner is of the opinion that:

- the treatment of the offender should be continued beyond the period specified in the order,
- the offender needs different treatment,
- the offender is not susceptible to treatment, or
- the offender does not require further treatment.[88]

Alternatively, the treatment practitioner may produce a written report to the effect that they are, for any reason, unwilling to continue to treat or direct the treatment of the offender.[89]

Amending treatment requirements

Application by responsible officer

On receipt of the written report from the treatment practitioner, the responsible officer must apply to the appropriate court for the

[87] ibid, Schedule 10, para 19(2); Schedule 16, para 26(4)(b).

[88] ibid, Schedule 10, para 19(1)(a); Schedule 16, para 26(1)(a).

[89] ibid, Schedule 10, para 19(1)(b); Schedule 16, para 26(1)(b).

requirement to be replaced or cancelled.[90] Such applications are made under the general provision relating to amending community orders and suspended sentence orders.[91]

Requirement of the offender to express willingness

The starting point is that, despite any such application, the court may not amend a treatment requirement unless the offender expresses willingness to comply with the requirement as it is proposed to be amended.[92] The court must therefore assess whether the offender consents to the amendment (in that they are willing to comply with the amended requirement).

Such willingness may be demonstrated through information provided by the Probation Service or by the treatment provider (e.g. in the application made to the court), or through a statement made by the offender orally in court or in writing.

The Court may choose to warn the offender of the potential consequences should they not show such willingness to comply. We shall consider this now.

Failure to show willingness

If the offender fails to express willingness to comply with a proposed amended treatment requirement, the court has the power to:

---

90 ibid, Schedule 10, para 19(3); Schedule 16, para 26(3).

91 ibid, Schedule 10, para 18, Schedule 16, para 25.

92 ibid, Schedule 10, para 18(7); Schedule 16, para 26(4)(a).

- revoke the community order,[93] or the suspended sentence order (and thus the suspended sentence to which it relates),[94] and
- re-sentence the offender for the offence in respect of which the community order was made,[95] or the suspended sentence order was imposed.[96]

Importantly, the legislation phrases the court's power as a "may" and not a "must". The court is not, therefore, obligated to revoke and re-sentence an offender where they demonstrate an unwillingness to comply with an amended requirement.[97] The court may simply choose to allow the treatment requirement to continue unamended, or to remove the requirement outright if they consider it appropriate to do so.

Must the court re-sentence?

Where the Court does choose to revoke an order, it is not clear from the statute whether they must re-sentence the offender. The statute reads that the court "may" (a) revoke "and" (b) re-sentence. This differs from the general power to revoke and re-sentence (in respect of breaches of community orders) in the following paragraphs of Schedule 10 to the Sentencing Act 2020:

- paras 14(5) and 15(4), which concern powers following breach of the requirements of a community order, and

---

93 ibid, Schedule 10, para 18(8)(a).

94 ibid, Schedule 16, para 25(7)(a).

95 ibid, Schedule 10, para 18(8)(b).

96 ibid, Schedule 16, para 25(7)(b).

97 For a discussion of the general power to revoke and re-sentence, see Chapter 11.

- paras 23(2) and 25(2), which concern powers following subsequent conviction for further offences during a community order.

All of these paras state that the court may (a) revoke, or (b) *both* revoke and re-sentence. That is a clear statement to the reader that the court may revoke an order in its entirety, or revoke and re-sentence an offender.

A literal interpretation of paras 18(8) and 25(7), therefore, would suggest that if the court exercises its discretion to revoke the relevant order, it *must* also re-sentence the offender. This is based on the fact that the wording adopted in the statute is not consistent with the previous paragraphs. One may find that the legislature intended to require the court to re-sentence if it chose to revoke on account that there is a clear difference in the language used.

On the other hand, the language used in the subsequent paragraphs does not assist with this interpretation. Para 18(9) of Schedule 10 states "If the court deals with the offender under sub-paragraph (8)(b)". The reference to "if" and the specific reference to "sub-paragraph (8)(b)" may suggest that the court is not so obligated to re-sentence an offender. Otherwise, it is expected that the legislature would have used words to the effect of "If the court deals with an offender under paragraph 8" (i.e. in its entirety).

Furthermore, para 25(8) reads: "In dealing with the offender under sub-paragraph (7)(b)". That provision too refers specifically to the sub-paragraph concerned with re-sentencing, as opposed to the general paragraph covering the court's powers. The reference to "in dealing" as opposed to "if the court deals" is an interesting distinction. Could Parliament have intended there to be a distinction between community orders and suspended sentence orders in this context? It is highly unlikely.

Overall, the issue appears to be whether the lack of consistent language is a case of legislative oversight, or a deliberate distinction of the court's powers.

Factors relevant to re-sentencing

Where the court chooses to re-sentence an offender, it must take into account the extent to which the offender has complied with the requirements of the order.[98]

This will require the advocates before the court to provide a clear statement as to the defendant's engagement with the order generally (i.e. probation appointments, telephone calls etc) and with the specific requirements of the order (e.g. RAR, unpaid work etc).

Naturally, these provisions do not prevent the court from taking account of any other factors it considers relevant; rather, it merely prescribes that the court *must* take account of the offender's compliance with the order. A failure to do so may open the court up to a potential appeal.

Imposing custody when re-sentencing

Where the court deals with an offender by re-sentencing them on a community order, the court is empowered to impose a custodial sentence in its place.[99] This is so even if the court is *not* of the opinion that the offence, or the combination of the offence and one or more offences associated with it, was so serious that neither a fine alone nor a community sentence can be justified for the offence (i.e. the general restrictions on imposing discretionary custodial sentences).[100] This is a discretionary power available to the court and does not oblige the court to impose a custodial sentence.

---

98 Sentencing Act 2020, Schedule 10, para 18(9)(a); Schedule 16, para 25(8).

99 ibid, Schedule 10, para 18(9)(b).

100 ibid, s.230(2).

Naturally, such a power is irrelevant in the context of a suspended sentence order given that the court had already imposed a term of imprisonment (albeit it was suspended).[101]

Procedure following amendment

Where a treatment requirement is amended, the court is obligated to provide a specified person with a copy of amended order as it relates to the requirement.[102]

The person to whom a copy must be provided depends on the nature of the treatment requirement. We shall consider each in turn.

Mental health treatment requirement

The court must provide a copy of the amended order as such:[103]

- If the MHTR is in-patient treatment, the person in charge of the care home or hospital at which it is provided.[104]
- If the MHTR is institution-based out-patient treatment, the person in charge of the institution or place at which it is provided.[105]

---

[101] See s.289 Sentencing Act 2020 which states that a suspended sentence is to be treated as a sentence of imprisonment.

[102] Sentencing Act 2020, Schedule 10, para 27(4); Schedule 16, para 28(4).

[103] ibid.

[104] See also Sentencing Act 2020, Schedule 9, para 16(3)(b)(i).

[105] See also Sentencing Act 2020, Schedule 9, para 16(3)(b)(ii).

- If the MHTR is practitioner-based treatment, the person specified as the registered medical practitioner or registered psychologist (or both) by whom or under whose direction it is provided.[106]

Drug rehabilitation requirement

The court must provide a copy of the amended order as such:[107]

- If the DRR is resident treatment, the person in charge of the institution or place where it is provided.[108]

- If the DRR is non-resident treatment, the person in charge of the institution or place where it is provided.[109]

Alcohol treatment requirement

The court must provide a copy of the amended order as such:[110]

- If the ATR is practitioner-based treatment, the treatment director.[111]

- If the ATR is resident treatment, the person in charge of the institution or place where it is provided.[112]

---

[106] See also Sentencing Act 2020, Schedule 9, para 16(3)(b)(iii).

[107] Sentencing Act 2020, Schedule 10, para 27(4); Schedule 16, para 28(4).

[108] See also Sentencing Act 2020, Schedule 9, para 19(5)(b).

[109] See also Sentencing Act 2020, Schedule 9, para 19(5)(c).

[110] Sentencing Act 2020, Schedule 10, para 27(4); Schedule 16, para 28(4).

[111] See also Sentencing Act 2020, Schedule 9, para 23(5)(a).

[112] See also Sentencing Act 2020, Schedule 9, para 23(5)(c).

- If the ATR is institution-based treatment, the person in charge of the institution or place where it is to be provided.[113]

Amendment to provisions for periodic review of drug rehabilitation requirement

As discussed in chapter 2, where a court imposes a drug rehabilitation requirement (DRR), a provision for review may also follow. If the court imposes a DRR for a period longer than 12 months,[114] it *must* include a provision for review.[115] However, if the treatment and testing period is less than 12 month, the court *may* include a provision for review.[116]

Amendments following review

The review officer's report and subsequent amendment

By para 21(2)(d) of Schedule 9, the provision for review must include a written report by the Probation Service on the offender's progress under the requirement before each review hearing.[117] Having considered this report, the court *may* at a review hearing amend any relevant order (i.e. a community order or a suspended sentence order) as it relates to the DRR.

Restrictions on amendments to the DRR

By para 22(3) of Schedule 9 to the Sentencing Act 2020, the court is prevented from amending the DRR unless the offender expresses

---

[113] See also Sentencing Act 2020, Schedule 9, para 23(5)(d).

[114] Known as the "treatment and testing period": Sentencing Act 2020, Schedule 9, para 19(1).

[115] Sentencing Act 2020, Schedule 9, para 21(1)(a).

[116] ibid, Schedule 9, para 21(1)(b).

[117] Known as "the review officer's report".

willingness to comply with the amended DRR.[118] This reflects the same position as it applies to treatment requirements discussed above.

Equally, the court is not permitted to amend any requirement or provision of the order while an appeal against the order is pending.[119] This is so unless the consent of the offender has been obtained.[120]

Failure to show willingness

Where the offender fails to express willingness to comply with a proposed amended DRR, the court has the same powers as it does in respect of treatment requirements discussed above (i.e. it may revoke an order and re-sentence an offender).[121] Just like treatment requirements, the court must, when considering whether to re-sentence, take into account the extent to which the offender has complied with the requirements of the order,[122] and may impose a custodial sentence even if it is not of the opinion that the offence (or offences) are so serious to justify a custodial sentence.[123]

Amendment to remove the requirement of a hearing

A further power to amend exists where at a review hearing the court has considered the review officer's report, and is of the opinion that the offender's progress under the requirement is satisfactory. In such a case,

[118] Sentencing Act 2020, Schedule 9, para 22(3)(a).

[119] ibid, Schedule 9, para 22(3)(b).

[120] ibid.

[121] ibid, Schedule 9, para 22(4).

[122] ibid, Schedule 9, para 22(5)(a).

[123] ibid, Schedule 9, para 22(5)(b).

the court may amend the order so that for each subsequent review, the order permits such a review to be made by the court without a hearing.[124]

Such an amendment is capable of being reversed (or further amended as the case may be), so as to require the attendance of an offender at a hearing of the court at a specific time and place (for our purposes, we shall call it the "specified hearing") if, having considered the review officer's report, the court is of the opinion that the offender's progress under the requirement is no longer satisfactory.[125] At this specified hearing, the court may exercise its powers as if the specified hearing was a review hearing,[126] and may equally amend the order to re-require the attendance of the offender at review hearings.[127]

The above discussion has concerned the court's power on its own motion to relieve the offender of having to attend, or equally to require such attendance. In addition to that, the Probation Service may also apply to the court for the order to be amended to either permit subsequent reviews to be made without a hearing, or to require the attendance of an offender at a review hearing.[128] Such applications would be made in the normal way in accordance with paras 18 of Schedule 10 and 25 of Schedule 16 to the Sentencing Act 2020.

Extension of order (community orders only)

In respect of a community order, the court has the power to extend the length of the order on application by the offender or an officer of the Probation Service.[129] This power is available to both a magistrates' court

[124] ibid, Schedule 9, para 22(6).

[125] ibid, Schedule 9, para 22(7).

[126] ibid, Schedule 9, para 22(8)(a).

[127] ibid, Schedule 9, para 22(8)(b).

[128] ibid, Schedule 9, para 22(11).

[129] Sentencing Act 2020, Schedule 10, para 20(1).

and the Crown Court; there is no power available to the responsible officer.

Importantly, there is no general power available to the court to extend the supervision or operational period of a suspended sentence order. Such a power is only exercisable when the court is considering a breach of the community requirements of the order, or a further offence committed during the operational period of the order.[130] We discussed the power to extend the supervision and operational period in breach cases in Chapter 7. As such, this section shall only consider the power to extend the length of a community order.

Making the application to extend the order

Both the offender and an officer of the Probation Service may apply to the court to amend the community order by extending the length of the order. The court cannot extend the length of the order on its own motion.

The end date of the extended order

As discussed in Chapter 2, a community order must specify a date by which all the requirements in it must have been complied with (known as the "end date" in the legislation, but for our purposes we shall call it the "original end date").[131] This original end date must not be more than three years after the date of the order.[132]

A community order is extended by substituting a later date for the original end date (for our purposes, we shall call this the "substituted end

---

[130] ibid, Schedule 16, para 13(1)(d)(ii), (iii) and (e); See Chapter 6.

[131] ibid, s.209(1).

[132] ibid, s.209(2).

date").[133] By para 20(3) of Schedule 10 to the Sentencing Act 2020, the substituted end date:

- must *not* be more than six months after the original end date, but
- may be more than three years after the date of the order.

The effect of this provision is two-fold:

First, the maximum extension permitted of the community order is six months. For example, an order due to end on 10 February can therefore be extended to a maximum of six months to 10 August. There is no minimum period that the court must extend the order.[134]

Second, an extension permits the court to allow a community order to continue beyond the statutory maximum of three years, subject to the restriction that the extension cannot be for a period longer than six months from the original end date. The original end date has a statutory maximum of 36 months from the date of the order; the substituted end date has a maximum of 42 months from the date of the order (assuming the original order was for 36 months). For example, whilst unlikely in practice, suppose the court imposed a 34-month community order; the court would be permitted to extend this beyond the statutory maximum of three years, but cannot extend it for longer than six months. The new maximum substituted end date would there be 40-months.

Timing of the application

It is unclear *when* an application to extend the end date of the community order can be made. Unlike extensions to the unpaid work requirement,[135] there is no explicit reference in the Sentencing Act 2020 that the

---

[133] ibid, Schedule 10, para 20(1).

[134] However, see para 20(4) below.

[135] See below.

community order "is in force".[136] Rather, para 20(1) of Schedule 10 simply reads that the court may, on an application, "amend a community order by substituting a later date for the end date."

There are three possible alternatives envisaged:

- *The application to extend the community order need not be made or heard before the end date of the community order, so long as it is made and heard within six months after the end date.* This approach is perhaps the most extreme. Given that a community order cannot be extended for a period longer than six months, there is some argument that the order could be extended to a maximum period of what is remaining. For example, an application made and heard two months after the end date of the order can only benefit from an effective extension of four months (six months from the end date; four months from the hearing date). This approach, however, is perhaps the most unfair on the offender who will remain in a state of uncertainty as to whether they are lawfully required to comply with the directions of the Probation Service. On what lawful basis can the Probation Service direct the offender to comply where the end date has passed, and no application to extend has even been made or even determined.

- *The application to extend the community order must be made before the end date of the community order, but need not be heard prior to the end date.* This approach would marry up with the approach taken in breach cases (i.e. so long as a breach is laid prior to the end date, the breach hearing itself can take place after the end date).[137] This approach would also reflect the often challenging circumstances courts find themselves in listing matters of this

[136] See Sentencing Act 2020, Schedule 10, para 21(1) in respect of extensions to the unpaid work requirement.

[137] *West Yorkshire Probation Board v Cruickshanks* [2010] EWHC 615 (Admin), [2011] 1 W.L.R. 2154 (See Chapter 4).

nature.[138] As will be described below, the issue becomes: What is expected of the offender in the gap between the application being made and it being heard?

- *The application to extend the community order must be both made and heard before the end date of the community order.* This approach is perhaps the most loyal approach to a literal interpretation of the Sentencing Act 2020. Section 220(1)(a) prescribes that "[a] community order ceases to be in force at the end of the end date". If the order ceases at the end of the end date, then there is, technically, no order to extend after this date.

It is the latter approach that finds most favour with the author. The first two approaches would effectively leave the offender in limbo and would be somewhat unfair too. In the first two approaches, the offender is technically free from the supervision of the Probation Service at the end of the end date. By "free from supervision", we mean that the offender is not expected to comply with any requirements of the order, or keep in touch with their responsible officer.

To allow an extension to take place following the end date would mean that there is a gap in the supervision of the offender. To explain this point further, there would be a lack of clarity as to the responsibilities of the offender and the responsible officer. The obligations of the responsible officer, and the offender, are detailed in ss.214-216 of the Sentencing Act 2020. Those provisions provide that the obligations apply "where a community order is in force".

Suppose, for example, the end date of a community order is 28 August 2024; should the Probation Service schedule an RAR session for the offender on 3 September 2024 and indicate that they will seek an extension to the community order, is the offender obliged to attend the

[138] Though, as noted in Chapter 1, it is the responsibility of the Probation Service to ensure that matters are progressed in an appropriate timeframe to ensure the court's powers are in no way restricted.

session on 3 September 2024? What are the consequences if they fail to do so?

Whilst it may seem the most restrictive approach, it is submitted that the third option is the most logical and fair approach to all involved. It ensures that the Probation Service remains vigilant in seeking extensions within good time, and ensures that the offender remains under supervision at all time.[139]

Purpose of extension and test to be applied

Interestingly, the statute is silent as to the purpose for which the community order is sought to be extended and the test to be applied/ threshold that must be met in order to extend the order.

Purpose of extension

The Probation Service may consider it necessary to extend the community order for a number of reasons:

- The responsible officer may not be satisfied that the offender is ready to be released from the order and requires further support, supervision and management from the Probation Service. For example, whilst rehabilitation activity requirement (RAR) days are phrased as an "up to" figure, not requiring completion of the full amount, the Probation Service may consider that full completion of the stated amount is necessary and appropriate in the offender's circumstances.

- Linked with the above, the offender may have not yet completed all requirements attached to the order. In order to avoid breaching

[139] See also Chapter 6 where the powers of the court on breach of an expired community order are discussed.

> the offender, it will be more appropriate to seek an extension to the order to allow the offender to complete all requirements.[140]

It is more difficult, however, to envisage a situation where the offender would wish for the community order to be extended.

> **Key point**
>
> It is important to remember that where a community order features an unpaid work requirement, the community order does not end until the unpaid work is completed. For those purposes, it should generally be unnecessary to apply to extend a community order where there is outstanding unpaid work. However, the Probation Service will need to seek an extension to the unpaid work requirement if it will not be completed within the initial 12-month period (see below).

Test to be applied

The statute is silent as to whether there is a test to be applied; unlike other provisions, the statute simply does not include a test, threshold or requirement to be met in order to extend the order. Whilst the statute is silent and, technically, there is no standard to be met, in practice, courts will often ask whether there is a "good reason" for the extension, or whether it would be in the "interests of justice" to extend the community order.

[140] As discussed below, where a community order has an unpaid work requirement, it is more appropriate to extend the unpaid work requirement as opposed to the community order generally.

Key point

Regardless of what standard the court applies, the court will require a good reason for the extension of the order. Frivolous applications to extend will not be entertained given the public resources at play in having an offender managed by the Probation Service.

Restrictions on extending the community order

There are, however, restrictions on the making of an application or dealing with the application. We shall consider these briefly here.

Summoning the offender first

Before the court exercises its power to extend the community order, it must summon the offender to appear before the court.[141] Where the offender fails to appear in answer to the summons, the court *may* issue a warrant for their arrest. A court would be unlikely to extend a community order without allowing an offender to make representations as to whether they consent to such extension or object.

One extension only

Once the power to extend the community order has been exercised, it cannot be exercised again by any court.[142] In essence, a community order has the possibility of being extended once, but only once. This includes where the community order has been extended by reason of breach of the community requirements.[143] For this reason, it is common for any

[141] Sentencing Act 2020, Schedule 10, para 20(2)(a). This requirement does not apply where the offender is the applicant.

[142] ibid, Schedule 10, para 20(4).

[143] ibid, Schedule 10, para 13(3).

extension to be made for the longest permitted period of time (six months) unless the maximum period is not necessary or required for the purpose sought by the extension.

> **Key point**
>
> Advocates must ensure that they check whether the order has been previously extended (upon application or following breach)

Appeal against sentence

No application may be made to extend the community order whilst an appeal against the community order is pending.[144]

Extension of unpaid work requirement

As discussed in Chapter 2, where a court imposes an unpaid work requirement as part of a community order or suspended sentence order, the offender must complete that unpaid work within 12 months.[145] Therefore, even if a defendant is sentenced to a community order longer than 12 months,[146] or where the operational period of a suspended sentence order is longer than 12 months, the defendant is still expected to complete the unpaid work requirement within 12 months.

The unpaid work requirement can be extended beyond this initial 12-month period on application,[147] and we shall consider that power in this section. At the end of this section, we shall consider when it is more

[144] ibid, Schedule 10, para 20(4).

[145] ibid, Schedule 9, para 1(1)(b).

[146] In cases where there is more than one requirement imposed.

[147] Sentencing Act 2020, Schedule 10, para 21; Schedule 16, para 27.

suitable to seek to extend the community order generally, or seek an extension of the unpaid work requirement.

Making the application to extend unpaid work requirement

An application to amend the unpaid work requirement of a community order or suspended sentence order can be made by either the offender subject to the relevant order, or an officer of the Probation Service.[148] The court cannot extend the unpaid work requirement on its own motion.

Timing of an application

An application to extend the unpaid work requirement can only be made during the currency of the relevant order, i.e. whilst the community order remains in force, and before the end date of the operational period of a suspended sentence order.

The requirement for the application to be made whilst the community order is still in force is expressly provided by the statute.[149] However, no such express provision exists in respect of suspended sentence orders. Rather, given that the suspended sentence order cannot exist beyond the operational period imposed,[150] it is commonsense that any application must be made and determined before the end of that operational period.

As discussed in previous chapters, a community order ceases to be in force:

- at the end of the end date, or

[148] ibid, Schedule 10, para 21(3); Schedule 16, para 27(3).

[149] ibid, Schedule 10, para 21(1).

[150] ibid, s.288(1).

- if later, when the offender has completed any unpaid work requirement imposed by the order.[151]

This means that an application to extend the unpaid work requirement could be made long after the end date of the order, so long as the offender has not yet completed the unpaid work requirement.[152] Indeed, Leggatt LJ in *National Probation Service v Blackfriars Crown Court*[153] explained that:

> where an offender has been sentenced to a community order imposing an unpaid work requirement, then unless and until the offender has completed the number of hours of work specified in the order or the order is revoked, the court has power [...] to extend the period during which the work must be performed (because the order remains in force). On a plain reading of the statutory provisions, this is the position irrespective of whether the twelve month period [...] has ended or the end date specified in the order has passed.[154]

The same rule does not apply, however, to suspended sentence orders. An unpaid work requirement imposed as part of a suspended sentence order cannot extend beyond the end of the operational period; the order ends on the end date of the operational period.[155]

---

[151] ibid, s.220(1); *National Probation Service v Blackfriars Crown Court* [2019] EWHC 529 (Admin), [2019] 2 Cr. App. R. (S.) 24.

[152] Though this causes difficulties with enforcement of the order and will go towards the court's assessment of the interests of justice test.

[153] [2019] EWHC 529 (Admin), [2019] 2 Cr. App. R. (S.) 24.

[154] ibid, [10] (Leggatt LJ).

[155] *West Yorkshire Probation Board v Cruickshanks* [2010] EWHC 615 (Admin), [2011] 1 W.L.R. 2154 [19] (Leveson LJ); *National Probation Service v Blackfriars Crown Court* [2019] EWHC 529 (Admin), [2019] 2 Cr. App. R. (S.) 24, [21] (Leggatt LJ).

The distinction between community orders and suspended sentence orders in this regard was described by Leggatt LJ in *Blackfriars Crown Court* as "clearly intentional".[156] His Lordship would go on to justify the distinction as such:

> The [suspended sentence] order imposes a sentence of imprisonment which, so to speak, hangs over the head of the offender for a defined period of time (which cannot be more than two years). During that time the sentence is liable to take effect if the offender commits another offence or if conditions of the order, which may include an unpaid work requirement, are not complied with. It is understandable that such a sentence which involves loss of liberty should be subject to a time limit which applies to the sentence as a whole.[157]

The position is therefore clear: any application to extend the unpaid work requirement must be made and determined whilst the community order remains in force, and before the end of the operational period of a suspended sentence order.

The practical effect of this is that an application to extend the unpaid work requirement does not have to be made within the initial 12-month period in which unpaid work should be completed. In fact, an application to extend the unpaid work requirement could be made long after the end of the initial 12-month period so long as it is before the end date of the relevant order.[158]

---

[156] *Blackfriars* (n153) [21] (Leggatt LJ).

[157] ibid.

[158] However, the longer the delay in making the application, the more difficult it may be to prove that it is in the "interests of justice" to extend the unpaid work requirement.

Necessity of an application

One question that arises is whether an application to extend the unpaid work requirement is strictly necessary. If a community order does not cease unless and until any unpaid work requirement is complete, what is the necessity for an application to extend an unpaid work requirement? Likewise, if a suspended sentence order with an operational period of two years imposes an unpaid work requirement, and that requirement continues until the end of the operational period, what is the necessity for an application to extend an unpaid work requirement?

Indeed, in *National Probation Service v Blackfriars Crown Court*,[159] the learned judge at first instance, HHJ Hillen, expressed concerns on this point. His Honour considered the indefinite nature of community orders with incomplete unpaid work hours rendered the requirement for an application to extend time "otiose".[160] The Divisional Court disagreed with this view; their Lordships took the view that:

> The fact that an unpaid work requirement remains in force after the twelve month period… has expired, if the work has not been completed, does not reduce the effect of the twelve month time limit. An offender who fails to complete the work within that time will be in breach of the order and at risk of being resentenced for the original offence or punished for the breach. For the same reason, the provision which allows an application to be made for an extension of time is not otiose. If granted, such an extension will avoid what would otherwise be a breach.[161]

In a similar vein, in respect of suspended sentence orders, in *National Probation Service v Forbes*,[162] the Recorder of Sheffield, HHJ Richardson

---

[159] *Blackfriars* (n153).

[160] ibid, [11] (Leggatt LJ).

[161] ibid, [23] (Leggatt LJ).

[162] Sheffield Crown Ct, 23 October 2023.

KC, expressed that "[a]t first blush this provision seems superfluous as section 288(5) makes it clear the order remains operational until the UPW is complete."[163] His Lordship did, however, conclude that such applications were necessary:

> Put shortly, section 288(5) makes the position clear that the UPW components of a SSO remains functional until it is completed (providing it is completed within 2 years); but paragraph 27 of schedule 16 provides for the *procedure* to do this – an application must be made to the court for this to be done – and it can only be done if it is in the interests of justice to do this.[164]

In summary, therefore, an application to extend the unpaid work requirement beyond the initial 12-month period *is* necessary.

Effect of refusal to extend

A question that arises at this stage is this: What are the consequences if the court refuses an application to extend the unpaid work requirement?

The first point to note is that as soon as the 12-month period has expired, and the offender has not completed the ordered hours, the offender is technically in breach of the requirement. This is clear from Leggatt LJ's judgment in *Blackfriars Crown Court* at [23]. It would then be for the Probation Service to formally breach the offender and get them to court for breach proceedings (see Chapter 3).

The second point relates to the practical impact on the Probation Service where such extension is not granted. As HHJ Richardson KC makes clear in *Forbes*, s.288 provides that the supervision period of a suspended sentence order continues until the offender has completed the number of

---

163 ibid, [22] (The Recorder of Sheffield, HHJ Richardson KC) (original emphasis).

164 ibid, [36] (The Recorder of Sheffield, HHJ Richardson KC).

hours specified in the order. However, whilst the unpaid work requirement would technically remain in force until the end of an order, the Probation Service would not be in a position to instruct, supervise, or enforce the offender's compliance without an extension to the unpaid work requirement. It is for this reason that his Lordship in *Forbes* explained that the extension provision is the "procedure" for ensuring that the unpaid work requirement remains functional as part of an order. The same can be said to be true for community requirements (given that such orders only cease once the unpaid work is completed).

Naturally, where the Probation Service has sought the extension of the unpaid work requirement, it is doubtful that their desire is to breach the offender. Rather, an extension will be sought to allow the Probation Service to continue to work with the offender. This point should be emphasised by any advocate seeking an extension of the unpaid work requirement.

Extending the requirement

Test to be applied

The court may extend the unpaid work requirement if it appears to the court that it would be in the "interests of justice" to do so, having regard to circumstances which have arisen since the order was made.[165]

Note: Paragraph 21(2) of Schedule 10 to the Sentencing Act 2020 refers to it being "in the interests to do so". The omission of the words "of justice" appears to simply be legislative oversight and should be read as "in the interests of justice to do so" as with para 27(3) of Schedule 16.

The legislation does not provide examples of what may amount to being in the interests of justice to extend the unpaid work requirement. However, it does expressly reference consideration to "circumstances

[165] Sentencing Act 2020, Schedule 10, para 21(2); Schedule 16, para 27(3).

which have arisen since the order was made". There are a number of questions that will likely prove relevant to any application:

- Why has the offender not completed the unpaid work requirement within the initial 12-month period? Is this for legitimate reasons or is the offender simply not engaged/motivated to complete the order?

- If the offender has not completed the unpaid work requirement within the initial 12-month period and their reasons are not acceptable, why has the Probation Service not breached the offender for their failure to comply?

- If the application to extend the unpaid work requirement is made after the initial 12-month period, why has the Probation Service delayed the application?

- In the case of a suspended sentence order, how much time remains before the end of the operational period? The shorter the period, the more unlikely it will be in the interests of justice to extend the unpaid work requirement unless the unpaid work hours outstanding are relatively few.

- Is the unpaid work requirement still suitable to the offender's circumstances? Has there been any change to the offender's physical or mental health that means it would not be in the interests of justice to extend the unpaid work requirement?

- What difficulties have been faced by the Probation Service in ensuring that the offender completes the unpaid work requirement within the initial 12-month period? Some points are worth remembering here that could have impacted on its handling of the unpaid work requirement in any given case: the aftermath of the Covid 19 Pandemic in relation to unpaid work and the backlog that exists in respect of non-compliance and breach; a high number of staff vacancies across the Probation Service (national shortage of qualified Probation Officers); and unification of the National Probation Service with the private Community Rehabilitation Companies.

A point that is worth emphasising separately to the above list is that the unpaid work requirement is part of a court order; such orders must be respected and attain the purposes of sentencing. An offender is expected to complete their unpaid work requirement as part of the court order as a form of punishment for their offending. An extension of the unpaid work requirement would ensure that this can happen.

On the other hand, should an offender be permitted to avoid undertaking the unpaid work requirement simply because the initial 12-month period has expired would run the risk of undermining the order. Whilst breach provisions exist to avoid such risk of undermining, one must remember that the original sentencing court considered that immediate imprisonment was not appropriate in the circumstances. As such, the offender should be given the opportunity to complete the order. Should the offender continue to fail to comply, following an extension, then breach proceedings will be appropriate and necessary.

Length of extension

Where the court has granted the application to extend the unpaid work requirement, there is no statutory minimum or maximum extension period. The court is empowered to extend the unpaid work requirement by any amount (subject to the expiry of the operational period in suspended sentence order cases).

The determining factor will be the number of hours remaining on the relevant order. Where the offender has few hours to complete, the court will not justify an extension beyond a number of months. Where, however, the offender has engaged in little unpaid work and has a large amount still to complete, the court will be more inclined to grant a longer extension.

The views of the Probation Service should be sought as to what is achievable; the Probation Service is in the best place to advise on this. Relevant factors as to decision on length of extension will include:

- The number of hours that the offender has outstanding to complete: Quite simply, the greater the hours, the longer the extension required.

- The circumstances of the offender: Where the offender works a full-time job, Monday-Friday, and can only complete their unpaid work requirement on a weekend, they may require a substantially longer extension than someone who could complete the hours any day of the week. Equally, an offender with caring responsibilities may struggle to complete hours in a shorter time frame.

- The availability of work: Whilst there should not, in theory, be any difficulty in obtaining unpaid work for an offender, there may be occasions where the unpaid work cannot be completed due to oversubscription or insufficient placements. An advocate must bear this practical difficulty in mind when making their submissions.

Key point

In practice, the Probation Service will provide the advocate with the length of extension they seek. However, the decision as to length of the extension is ultimately a matter for the court. It is always advisable to have a specific date in mind as to when the requirement should be extended to.

Date of extension

A minor but critical point is the date from which the extension begins. Suppose, for example, that the Probation Service applies to extend the unpaid work requirement as part of a community order by 24 months in a case where:

- The end date of the community order is January 2025,
- The end date of the unpaid work requirement is July 2024, and
- The date of the hearing to extend the unpaid work requirement is March 2025.

From which date is the extension to apply?

There is no authority on this point, however, it would be logical to apply such an extension from the original end date of the unpaid work requirement (July 2024 in our example). This makes logical sense given that any such application is for an extension beyond the original 12-months within which the offender must ordinarily complete the unpaid work. Practically, if any other date was chosen, there would be a gap in the enforceability of the unpaid work requirement. Indeed, this approach would adopt the same principle as extension of community orders generally; the court may extend the community order by up to six months from the original end date of the order (and not, for example, from the date of the hearing).[166]

As such, it is the original end date of the unpaid work requirement from when the extension begins.

Permitted number of extensions

The statute does not restrict the number extensions to the unpaid work requirement that may be permitted in any given court order. This is unlikely to be a legislative oversight; it appears intentional. In other parts of Schedule 10 to the Sentencing Act 2020, for example, the legislation explicitly provides a restriction on the number of applications/ extensions

---

[166] See above for a discussion on extending community orders generally.

that can be made. As discussed above in respect of applications to extend a community order, the legislation is clear: "Once the power [...] has been exercised in relation to the order, it may not be exercised again in relation to it by any court."[167] For those purposes, it stands to reason that there is no restriction on the number of permitted extensions to the unpaid work requirement.

However, in practice, the court will be wary of multiple applications and will raise a number of questions, including foremost:

- Why has the offender not completed the hours in the extended time permitted?
- Why has the offender not been breached for failing to complete the hours in the extended time permitted?

Unless there is a good reason for either of these questions, the court may be unsympathetic to any application to extend the unpaid work requirement.

Restrictions on extending the unpaid work requirement

There are, however, restrictions on the making of an application or dealing with of the application. We shall consider these briefly here.

Summoning the offender first

Before the court exercises its power to extend the unpaid work requirement in respect of a community order, it must summon the offender to appear before the court.[168] Interestingly, there is no

[167] Sentencing Act 2020, Schedule 10, para 20(4). See also para 13(3) in respect of the powers of a court to extend a community order following breach; Chapter 6.

[168] ibid, Schedule 10, para 21(4)(a).

equivalent provision in respect of suspended sentence orders. This is likely to simply an oversight in the legislation and in practice, the Probation Service will summon an offender to court in cases of both community orders and suspended sentence orders.

Naturally, the requirement for a summons does not apply where the offender is the applicant. Equally, where the offender fails to appear in answer to the summons, the court *may* issue a warrant for their arrest. Unlike cases where the court is considering revoking an order/ revoke and resentence and offender, it is common for courts to proceed to consider extending an unpaid work requirement in the absence of the offender.

Appeal against sentence

No application may be made to extend the unpaid work requirement whilst an appeal against the community order or suspended sentence order is pending.[169]

Choosing between an extension of the community order and extension of the unpaid work requirement

Given that a community order with an unpaid work requirement attached will continue until the unpaid work is completed, the power to extend the community order itself is largely unnecessary. Extension of the unpaid work requirement is necessary to ensure that the Probation Service can instruct, supervise and enforce the unpaid work requirement. Extension of the community order would not achieve this goal and would be somewhat meaningless given that the order will continue indefinitely until the unpaid work is completed.

On the other hand, a community order without an unpaid work requirement will cease on the original end date. If that date is not suitable

[169] ibid, Schedule 10, para 21(3); Schedule 16, para 27(4)

(for reasons discussed above), the appropriate application would be to extend the community order generally.

> **Key Point**
>
> - Where the community order has an unpaid work requirement which is not yet completed, the appropriate application is an extension to the unpaid work requirement.
> - Where the community order does not have an unpaid work requirement, the appropriate application is an extension to the end date of the community order.

Procedure following any amendment

We have already discussed the process to be adopted following an amendment when we considered each provision in turn above. However, this section will discuss the more general requirements on the courts and responsible parties.

First, it is essential that a detailed note of the hearing is taken, including the action taken by the court on the application, and the reasons for any decision (i.e. on what basis the judge has amended a particular aspect of the community or suspended sentence order).

Where the court has amended a community order or suspended sentence order, it must provide copies of the amending order to the offender and the responsible officer.[170]

In addition to the above discussions, the Table in paras 27(4) of Schedule 10, and 28(4) of Schedule 16 to the Sentencing Act 2020, prescribes who

[170] ibid, Schedule 10, para 27(2); Schedule 16, para 28(2); CrimPR 2020, r.32.4(2).

the court must provide copies of an amending order to. Those persons who have not already been discussed in this chapter are as such:

- Where the amended order is an exclusion requirement imposed for the purpose (or partly for the purpose) of protecting a person from being approached by the offender, the court must provide a copy of the amended order on the person intended to be protected.

- Where the amended order is a residence requirement relating to residence in an institution, the court must provide a copy of the amended order on the person in charge of the institution.

- Where the amended order is an electronic monitoring requirement, the court must provide a copy of the amended order on any person who by virtue of will be responsible for the electronic monitoring.[171] The amended order must also be provided to any person without whose consent the requirement could not be included in the order.

Summary

This Chapter has covered the law and practice involved in applications to amend community orders and suspended sentence orders. When considering the legal principles applicable to this area of law, consider:

- An application to amend the requirements of a community order, or the community requirements of a suspended sentence order, can be made either by the offender or the Probation Service. The court cannot amend an order on its own motion.

- The court has a broad range of powers available to it in respect of such amendments.

---

[171] See Sentencing Act 2020, Schedule 9, para 31.

- Amendments may include extending the length of community orders, or the length of requirements. Amendments may also include the variation or cancellation of requirements, and the replacing of requirements with others of the same kind.

- Copies of any amended order must be served on all those persons specified in law.

APPENDIX

QUICK REFERENCE AND COMMON ERRORS

The law relating to community-based court orders, and breach of those orders is not straightforward. There is a complex labyrinth of case law and legislation relating to such proceedings, and applications made in respect of such orders. This Appendix is designed simply to provide readers with a quick access reference and to assist readers in avoiding certain common errors or mistakes.

Quick reference

Maximum and minimum terms:

- *Suspended sentence orders:*

  Applies to any sentence longer than 14 days, but shorter than two years. Operational period can be no less than six months, and no more than two years. Supervision period (if relevant) can be no less than six months, and no longer than the operational period.

- *Community orders:*

  No minimum length; maximum length is three years. Community order cannot exceed the length of any requirement imposed. Where multiple requirements are imposed, the community order cannot extend beyond the last of those requirements.

- *Requirements*:
    - Unpaid work: Minimum period: 40 hours;[1] Maximum period: 300 hours.
    - RAR: No minimum or maximum period.
    - Programme requirement: No minimum or maximum period.
    - Prohibited activity requirement: No minimum or maximum period.
    - Curfew requirement: Minimum period: two hours per day; Maximum period: 20 hours per day and 112 hours in any seven-day period.[2]
    - Exclusion requirement: No minimum period. Maximum period: two years.
    - Residence requirement: No minimum or maximum period.
    - Foreign travel prohibition order: No minimum period. Maximum period: 12 months from the day the order takes effect.
    - Mental health treatment requirement: No minimum or maximum period.
    - Drug rehabilitation requirement: No minimum or maximum period.

---

1 20 hours when imposing a new unpaid work requirement following a breach of a community order.

2 A curfew may be imposed for no longer than two years.

- Drug testing requirement: No minimum or maximum period.
- Alcohol treatment requirement: No minimum or maximum period.
- Alcohol abstinence and monitoring requirement: No minimum period. Maximum period: 120 days.
- Attendance centre requirement: Minimum period: 12 hours; Maximum period: 36 hours.[3]
- Electronic monitoring requirement:[4] No minimum or maximum period.

Powers on breach

- *Suspended sentence orders (breach or further conviction):*

  The court *must* take one of the following actions:[5]

  - Activate the suspended sentence in full
  - Activate the suspended sentence in part
  - Impose a fine not exceeding £2,500
  - (In cases where the suspended sentence imposes community requirements only) Amend the order by:

---

3 Also, an offender cannot be required to attend at an attendance centre, more than once on any day, or for more than 3 hours at a time.

4 Including electronic compliance monitoring requirement and electronic whereabouts monitoring requirement.

5 Sentencing Act 2020, Schedule 16, para 13.

        - imposing more onerous community requirements
        - extending the supervision period
        - extending the operational period

    - (In special review cases only) Commit the offender to custody for up to 28 days
    - Extend the operational period.

- *Community orders (breach of requirements):*

  The court *must* take one of the following actions:[6]

    - Impose a fine not exceeding £2,500
    - Amend the order by imposing more onerous requirements
    - (In special review cases only) Commit the offender to custody for up to 28 days
    - Revoke the community order, and re-sentence the offender.[7]

- *Community orders (further conviction):*

  The court *may* take one of the following actions:[8]

    - Revoke the community order outright

---

6 ibid, Schedule 10, paras 10(5) and 11(2).

7 The court cannot revoke outright, except upon an application, separate from the breach proceedings, by the offender or the Probation Service.

8 Sentencing Act 2020, Schedule 10, paras 23(2) and 25(2).

- Revoke the community order, and re-sentence the offender.

Ten common errors

The following provides a number of examples of errors commonly made in proceedings of this nature. The list is divided into three categories: Making the order; breaching the order; and revoking/ amending the order.

Making the order

1. *Community orders and punishment*:

   In respect of community orders, the court must impose at least one requirement "for the purpose of punishment."[9] This is so unless the court imposes a fine,[10] or considers there to be exceptional circumstances relating to the offence or to the offender which would make it unjust in all the circumstances for the court to impose a requirement for the purpose of punishment in the particular case, and would make it unjust in all the circumstances for the court to impose a fine for the offence concerned.[11] Therefore, a community order which only includes a rehabilitation activity requirement (RAR) will be unlawful, unless the court also imposes a fine or declares there to be exceptional circumstances.

2. *Length of community orders*:

   A community order only lasts as long as the requirements that an offender is subject to. It is therefore impermissible to impose, for

[9] Sentencing Act 2020, s.208(10).

[10] ibid, s.208(11)(a).

[11] ibid, s.208(11)(b).

example, a two-year community order with requirement(s) to be completed within a shorter period (e.g. a six-month curfew).[12] Unpaid work must be completed within 12 months; unless the order imposes any requirement in addition to unpaid work, it must last no longer than 12 months.[13]

3. *Suspended sentence orders coupled with other orders:*

   It is unlawful to impose both a suspended sentence order and a community order at the same time.[14] Whilst not unlawful, it is bad sentencing practice to impose both a suspended sentence order and a term of imprisonment at the same time.[15] Equally, it is bad sentencing practice to impose a suspended sentence order on an offender presently serving a term of imprisonment.[16]

Breaching the order

4. *No action on breach*:

   In respect of breaches of suspended sentence orders,[17] and failure to comply with community order requirements, the court is *not* permitted to take "no action" in respect of the breach.[18] This does

---

12 *R v Khan* [2015] EWCA Crim 835, [2015] 2 Cr. App. R. (S.) 39.

13 Though, of course, it can be extended.

14 Sentencing Act 2020, s.203.

15 *R v Sapiano* (1968) 52 Cr. App. R. 674 (CA).

16 *R v Hammond* [1969] Crim. L.R. 500 (CA).

17 Which includes both breach of community requirements and commission of further offences during the operational period of the order.

18 *R v Anderson* [2014] EWCA Crim 797 [10] (Jeremy Baker J); *R v Ward* [2012] EWCA Crim 3139, [2013] 2 Cr. App. R. (S.) 35 [23] (Sharp J DBE); *AG's Ref No 36 of 2018 (R v Usherwood)* [2018] EWCA Crim 1156, [2018] 2 Cr. App. R. (S.) 39; *R v Mohammed* [2023] EWCA Crim

not apply to conviction for further offences during the currency of a community order where the court *is* permitted to take no action.[19]

5. *No separate penalty on further offence*:

In respect of convictions for further offences during community orders and suspended sentence orders, the court cannot impose "no separate penalty" on the new offence. For example, where the court takes action in respect of the original court order, the court cannot thereafter impose no separate penalty for the new offence. The court must first deal with the new offence, before then turning to the court order.[20]

6. *Revoking community orders:*

A community order cannot be revoked outright without re-sentence where an offender is before the court for breach of the requirements of a community order. The court is restricted in the actions it may take by Schedule 10 to the Sentencing Act 2020, paras 10(5) and 11(2). This restriction does not apply where the offender is before the court following a conviction for further offences during the currency of the community order.[21] However, should the offender or the Probation Service make a separate application, at the breach hearing, to revoke the community order, the court does have the power to do so.

1458 [38] (Andrews J); *R v Hilliard* [2023] EWCA Crim 1155 [20] (Lambert J); *R v Lister* [2023] EWCA Crim 1741 [32] (HHJ Dhir KC).

19 This is because such convictions do not amount to a breach of a community order.

20 *R v Ithell* (1969) 53 Cr. App. R. 210 (CA).

21 Sentencing Act 2020, Schedule 10, paras 23(2) and 25(2).

7. *Aggravating the new offence*:

   Where an offender commits a further offence during the operational period of a suspended sentence order, and the court activates the suspended sentence order in full, the court cannot aggravate the new offence by the fact the offence was committed during the order.[22] It is not clear from the authorities whether the same rule applies if the court only activates the suspended sentence in part, or takes some action other than activation.

Revoking/Amending the order

8. *Revoking suspended sentence orders:*

   A suspended sentence order cannot be revoked, except in exceptionally limited circumstances (specifically, where an offender is subject to a treatment requirement and does not express willingness to consent to an amendment to a requirement).

9. *Acting in its own motion:*

   The Court is not empowered to amend or revoke an order, or a requirement in an order, on its own motion. Such action may only be taken on the application of the offender or an officer of the Probation Service. This application can be made orally or in writing; but the court cannot take such action without an application of some form from the offender or the Probation Service.

10. *Extending suspended sentence orders:*

    A suspended sentence order cannot be extended on application by the Probation Service or on the court's own motion; an extension

[22] *R v Levesconte* [2011] EWCA Crim 2754, [2012] 2 Cr. App. R. (S.) 19.

to the supervision period or operational period can only be made following breach proceedings.

MORE BOOKS BY LAW BRIEF PUBLISHING

A selection of our other titles available now:-

'A Practical Guide to Confiscation and Restraint' by Narita Bahra QC, John Carl Townsend, David Winch
'A Practical Guide to the Law of Forests in Scotland' by Philip Buchan
'A Practical Guide to Health and Medical Cases in Immigration Law' by Rebecca Chapman & Miranda Butler
'A Practical Guide to Bad Character Evidence for Criminal Practitioners by Aparna Rao
'A Practical Guide to Extradition Law post-Brexit' by Myles Grandison et al
'A Practical Guide to Hoarding and Mental Health for Housing Lawyers' by Rachel Coyle
'A Practical Guide to Psychiatric Claims in Personal Injury – 2nd Edition' by Liam Ryan
'Stephens on Contractual Indemnities' by Richard Stephens
'A Practical Guide to the EU Succession Regulation' by Richard Frimston
'A Practical Guide to Solicitor and Client Costs – 2nd Edition' by Robin Dunne
'Constructive Dismissal – Practice Pointers and Principles' by Benjimin Burgher
'A Practical Guide to Religion and Belief Discrimination Claims in the Workplace' by Kashif Ali
'A Practical Guide to the Law of Medical Treatment Decisions' by Ben Troke
'Fundamental Dishonesty and QOCS in Personal Injury Proceedings: Law and Practice' by Jake Rowley
'A Practical Guide to the Law in Relation to School Exclusions' by Charlotte Hadfield & Alice de Coverley
'A Practical Guide to Divorce for the Silver Separators' by Karin Walker
'The Right to be Forgotten – The Law and Practical Issues' by Melissa Stock
'A Practical Guide to Planning Law and Rights of Way in National Parks, the Broads and AONBs' by James Maurici QC, James Neill et al
'A Practical Guide to Election Law' by Tom Tabori
'A Practical Guide to the Law in Relation to Surrogacy' by Andrew Powell
'A Practical Guide to Claims Arising from Fatal Accidents – 2nd Edition' by James Patience
'A Practical Guide to the Ownership of Employee Inventions – From Entitlement to Compensation' by James Tumbridge & Ashley Roughton
'A Practical Guide to Asbestos Claims' by Jonathan Owen & Gareth McAloon

'A Practical Guide to Stamp Duty Land Tax in England and Northern Ireland' by Suzanne O'Hara
'A Practical Guide to the Law of Farming Partnerships' by Philip Whitcomb
'Covid-19, Homeworking and the Law – The Essential Guide to Employment and GDPR Issues' by Forbes Solicitors
'Covid-19 and Criminal Law – The Essential Guide' by Ramya Nagesh
'Covid-19 and Family Law in England and Wales – The Essential Guide' by Safda Mahmood
'A Practical Guide to the Law of Unlawful Eviction and Harassment – 2nd Edition' by Stephanie Lovegrove
'Covid-19, Brexit and the Law of Commercial Leases – The Essential Guide' by Mark Shelton
'A Practical Guide to Costs in Personal Injury Claims – 2nd Edition' by Matthew Hoe
'A Practical Guide to the General Data Protection Regulation (GDPR) – 2nd Edition' by Keith Markham
'Ellis on Credit Hire – Sixth Edition' by Aidan Ellis & Tim Kevan
'A Practical Guide to Working with Litigants in Person and McKenzie Friends in Family Cases' by Stuart Barlow
'Protecting Unregistered Brands: A Practical Guide to the Law of Passing Off' by Lorna Brazell
'A Practical Guide to Secondary Liability and Joint Enterprise Post-Jogee' by Joanne Cecil & James Mehigan
'A Practical Guide to the Pre-Action RTA Claims Protocol for Personal Injury Lawyers' by Antonia Ford
'A Practical Guide to Neighbour Disputes and the Law' by Alexander Walsh
'A Practical Guide to Forfeiture of Leases' by Mark Shelton
'A Practical Guide to Coercive Control for Legal Practitioners and Victims' by Rachel Horman
'A Practical Guide to the Law of Driverless Cars – Second Edition' by Alex Glassbrook, Emma Northey & Scarlett Milligan
'A Practical Guide to TOLATA Claims' by Greg Williams
'A Practical Guide to Elderly Law – 2nd Edition' by Justin Patten
'A Practical Guide to Responding to Housing Disrepair and Unfitness Claims' by Iain Wightwick

'A Practical Guide to the Law of Bullying and Harassment in the Workplace' by Philip Hyland
'How to Be a Freelance Solicitor: A Practical Guide to the SRA-Regulated Freelance Solicitor Model' by Paul Bennett
'A Practical Guide to Prison Injury Claims' by Malcolm Johnson
'A Practical Guide to the Small Claims Track – 2nd Edition' by Dominic Bright
'A Practical Guide to Advising Clients at the Police Station' by Colin Stephen McKeown-Beaumont
'A Practical Guide to Antisocial Behaviour Injunctions' by Iain Wightwick
'Practical Mediation: A Guide for Mediators, Advocates, Advisers, Lawyers, and Students in Civil, Commercial, Business, Property, Workplace, and Employment Cases' by Jonathan Dingle with John Sephton
'The Mini-Pupillage Workbook' by David Boyle
'A Practical Guide to Crofting Law' by Brian Inkster
'A Practical Guide to the Law of Domain Names and Cybersquatting' by Andrew Clemson
'A Practical Guide to the Law of Gender Pay Gap Reporting' by Harini Iyengar
'NHS Whistleblowing and the Law' by Joseph England
'Employment Law and the Gig Economy' by Nigel Mackay & Annie Powell
'A Practical Guide to Noise Induced Hearing Loss (NIHL) Claims' by Andrew Mckie, Ian Skeate, Gareth McAloon
'An Introduction to Beauty Negligence Claims – A Practical Guide for the Personal Injury Practitioner' by Greg Almond
'Intercompany Agreements for Transfer Pricing Compliance' by Paul Sutton
'Zen and the Art of Mediation' by Martin Plowman
'A Practical Guide to the SRA Principles, Individual and Law Firm Codes of Conduct 2019 – What Every Law Firm Needs to Know' by Paul Bennett
'A Practical Guide to Adoption for Family Lawyers' by Graham Pegg
'A Practical Guide to Industrial Disease Claims' by Andrew Mckie & Ian Skeate
'A Practical Guide to Conducting a Sheriff Court Proof' by Andrew Stevenson
'A Practical Guide to Vicarious Liability' by Mariel Irvine
'A Practical Guide to Applications for Landlord's Consent and Variation of Leases' by Mark Shelton
'A Practical Guide to Relief from Sanctions Post-Mitchell and Denton' by Peter Causton

'A Practical Guide to Equity Release for Advisors' by Paul Sams
'A Practical Guide to Financial Services Claims' by Chris Hegarty
'The Law of Houses in Multiple Occupation: A Practical Guide to HMO Proceedings' by Julian Hunt
'Occupiers, Highways and Defective Premises Claims: A Practical Guide Post-Jackson – 2nd Edition' by Andrew Mckie
'A Practical Guide to Financial Ombudsman Service Claims' by Adam Temple & Robert Scrivenor
'A Practical Guide to Running Housing Disrepair and Cavity Wall Claims: 2nd Edition' by Andrew Mckie & Ian Skeate
'A Practical Guide to Holiday Sickness Claims – 2nd Edition' by Andrew Mckie & Ian Skeate
'Arguments and Tactics for Personal Injury and Clinical Negligence Claims' by Dorian Williams
'A Practical Guide to Drone Law' by Rufus Ballaster, Andrew Firman, Eleanor Clot
'A Practical Guide to Compliance for Personal Injury Firms Working With Claims Management Companies' by Paul Bennett
'RTA Allegations of Fraud in a Post-Jackson Era: The Handbook – 2nd Edition' by Andrew Mckie
'RTA Personal Injury Claims: A Practical Guide Post-Jackson' by Andrew Mckie
'On Experts: CPR35 for Lawyers and Experts' by David Boyle
'An Introduction to Personal Injury Law' by David Boyle

These books and more are available to order online direct from the publisher at www.lawbriefpublishing.com, where you can also read free sample chapters. For any queries, contact us on 0844 587 2383 or mail@lawbriefpublishing.com.

Our books are also usually in stock at www.amazon.co.uk with free next day delivery for Prime members, and at good legal bookshops such as Wildy & Sons.

We are regularly launching new books in our series of practical day-to-day practitioners' guides. Visit our website and join our free newsletter to be kept informed and to receive special offers, free chapters, etc.

You can also follow us on Twitter at www.twitter.com/lawbriefpub.

www.ingramcontent.com/pod-product-compliance
Lightning Source LLC
LaVergne TN
LVHW052216200926
848481LV00001B/121
* 9 7 8 1 9 1 6 6 9 8 4 6 8 *